# BEING SPIRITUAL, STAYING PRACTICAL

# BEING SPIRITUAL, STAYING PRACTICAL

SWAMI SARVAGATANANDA

Edited by
SWAMI TYAGANANDA

Copyright © 2023 by Ramakrishna Vedanta Society of Massachusetts, Inc., 58 Deerfield St., Boston, MA 02215, USA

All rights reserved.

No part of this book may be reproduced in any form or by any electronic or mechanical means, including information storage and retrieval systems, without written permission from the author, except for the use of brief quotations in a book review.

# CONTENTS

*Foreword* vii

1. 1973   1
2. 1974   4
3. 1975   20
4. 1976   80
5. 1977   137
6. 1978   210
7. 1979   261
8. 1980   289
9. 1981   309
10. 1982   332
11. 1983   354
12. 1984   375
13. 1985   393
14. 1986   395
15. 1987   399
16. 1988   405
17. 1989   408
18. 1990   410
19. 1991   412
20. 1992   414
21. 1993   415
22. 1994   416
23. 1995   417
24. 1996   419
25. 1997   420
26. 1998   421
27. 1999   423
28. 2000   425
29. 2002   429

| | |
|---|---|
| 30. 2003 | 430 |
| 31. 2004 | 431 |
| 32. 2005 | 432 |
| 33. 2006 | 433 |
| 34. 2007 | 434 |
| 35. 2008 | 435 |
| *About the Author* | 437 |
| *Also by Swami Sarvagatananda* | 445 |

# FOREWORD

Swami Sarvagatanandaji (1912–2009) joined the Ramakrishna Order in 1934. After serving in Ramakrishna Order's branches in India for two decades, he was then sent to the United States, first as an assistant, and later as the head of the Vedanta centers in Boston and Providence from 1962 to 2002. His inspiring life was a testament to the power of holiness and its flowering into "unselfish loving service"—his favorite phrase to describe the essence of spirituality. More about his life can be found in my essay at the end of this book.

Sometime in early 1970s, Sarvagatanandaji told one of his devoted students to write whatever she learned every day. She quickly discovered that what she learned was what she heard the swami tell her. He gave her the name Meera. She eventually joined the convent at the Vedanta Society of Northern California in San Francisco in 1984 and, after her novitiate, was given sannyāsa vows and the name Pravrajika Mukundaprana.

While her notes were primarily meant for her own use, over the years those around her came to know of them, and she shared parts of what she had written with close friends. Finding that these teachings had enormous value, they urged her to consider publishing them. Hesitant and unsure, she referred the matter to me. It has been an honor and privilege to make these precious teachings available to a larger circle of earnest spiritual seekers, even those who may not have met Swami Sarvagatanandaji.

To those who knew the swami, these words will look familiar. He had a unique manner of sharing the ancient wisdom in a way that was both profound and practical. People tend to think that the more spiritual someone gets, the less "practical" they become. Swami Sarvagatanandaji's teachings, to my mind, show that it is possible to be deeply spiritual while not being any less practical.

Most of the contents in this book are notes of informal conversations that occurred in the mornings or after formal programs at the Vedanta Society in Providence. The notes after 1984, when Mukundaprana joined the convent, resulted from her phone conversations with the swami, or during her visits to Boston and Providence.

These notes were written down from memory soon after the conversations. When Mukundaprana showed the notes to Swami Sarvagatanandaji, as she sometimes did, he himself confirmed their accuracy. Indeed, when I went through them while getting the book ready for publication, it didn't feel as if I was reading. It felt as if I was hearing Sarvagatanandaji speak.

Being notes from a diary, it seemed best to present the contents in the order in which the conversations occurred. Sri

Ramakrishna is often referred to in the book as "Thakur," as is commonly done in Bengal. There are frequent references to events from the lives of the direct disciples of Sri Ramakrishna and often they are referred to by their pre-monastic names. Some of the observations and teachings will become clearer when the book is read alongside the *Gospel of Sri Ramakrishna*. There has been minimal editing, allowing the voice and style of Sarvagatanandaji to come through without any filters. The power they exude is unmistakable.

May these teachings awaken the dormant spirit in our hearts to the world beyond this world, the world of peace and harmony, the realm of freedom and perfection.

Swami Tyagananda<br>
July 4, 2023

# 1973

## March 20, 1973

[A student asked whether it made any difference in what form Krishna is worshipped:] It makes no difference. Krishna himself said, "Worship me in any form you like. I come to you according to your own faith." He is a perfect divine manifestation. Krishna *is* God. No mere man—nor anyone who had just a glimpse of the Truth—could have revealed the Gita. It had to come from God himself, because the Gita is a complete and incomparable revelation. Never has anyone else said, "I am that Brahman, there is nothing beyond me." Krishna can be seen even now in any form, because he takes many forms, any form according to the faith of the devotee. Read the *Mahabharata* and see how enticing and charming Krishna is.

The incarnations of God are all the very same Light. They are not really different. One might doubt this, but Ramakrishna verified it, saw it and told us about it. It is like a tremendous iron-smelting furnace that explodes. It throws off huge chunks of burning iron of different sizes and shapes, but all coming from the same fire. Ramakrishna saw the Divine like that, an infinite burning Light, manifesting through different forms and names, which then merge again in that same Light. Or it is like shooting off a rocket. It goes up for some time and then falls down. If we shoot off a more powerful one, it may go up, orbit the earth for some time, and then eventually burn out.

Again, it is like the solar system. Though all of the same solar stuff, the planets are of different sizes and shapes. Because of their great mass, they remain in orbit around the sun, and do not burn out. Just as this is true in the physical universe, it is also true in the spiritual universe. Although emerging from the same divine sun, the incarnations with different names and forms—but carrying the same Light—remain in orbit in the spiritual universe. These forms are eternal and can be seen. They remain in the spiritual universe of cosmic consciousness. When we raise our minds to the spiritual plane, they can be seen.

To see them, the mind must be absolutely pure. Any stain on the mind can prevent us from seeing them, just as a tiny cloud can hide the sun which is billions of times bigger and more powerful. To make the mind pure, we must give up all desires, surrendering the whole mind to God. It is what we do with a physical offering. Before we ritually offer food to God, we do not give any part of it to anyone else, because this is symbolic of offering the mind to God. We must offer the whole mind, without any reservation.

In the early stages, the mind succumbs relatively easily to monotony and dullness. When this happens, the best thing to do is to sing devotional songs or say a prayer that is especially dear to the heart. Keep on doing this, try to increase the devotional feeling and the prayerful attitude. The important thing is to create a flow of the mind toward God and to maintain that flow. That leads to meditation. In meditation the prayerful attitude gets intensified. Spiritual illumination is in the purified emotions. Intellect is dead there.

# 1974

## August 16, 1974

[A student asked whether Sri Ramakrishna is more for monks than householders:] Sri Ramakrishna is for everyone and is not partial to anyone in his teachings. True, he trained some as monks to spread his message, but that message is for all, the message of maintaining God-consciousness, no matter what you are doing, and always practicing self-control in every stage of life. The message of detachment and discernment is for everyone. When his words seem to stress the life of renunciation, consider the context, and do not generalize it for everyone. Sri Ramakrishna's ideal is broad and all-inclusive.

## August 17, 1974

Ramakrishna is Truth in its totality, God in his fullness. Vivekananda presents that Truth in a philosophical and scientific way that any rational person can accept. Holy Mother is not an instructor; she is an exemplar. She followed

Ramakrishna's teachings to perfection and embodied them for all to see.

## August 23, 1974

[The swami was asked whether a personal tragedy could be said to be the will of God.] The phrase, "God's will," must be understood properly. It is not like a calculated decision of God. Nature functions, that's all. The only way to cope with tragedy is to bear it patiently. As the Gita (2.14) says, "These things come and go; they are impermanent in their nature. Bear them patiently, O Arjuna." It is simple and seemingly cruel, but it is the only way.

Arjuna's son was killed on the battlefield. Arjuna's wife, who was Krishna's sister, was stricken with grief. Krishna had not been present on the battlefield when her son was killed, so when he arrived she cried to him, "Oh brother, if you had been there it would have never happened." Krishna, with all love and compassion, said quietly, "I was there."

If a tragic event involves a baby, it cannot be karma for the child because karma only functions at the conscious level when discrimination and self-consciousness are present. It is just an accident, nature functioning. Bear it and become "fit for immortality" (Gita 2.15). The whole point of karma is what we learn from it or how we bear it. If we can bear terrible suffering with patience, we move up a lot. If we commit blunders but sincerely repent and resolve to avoid them in future, we move up a lot. All we can do with nature's mysterious play is bear it and surrender to God.

Retirement is a good example of the changing patterns of nature. People must accept age and retirement. Yes, their time is over with respect to activity and contributing to society in that sense. But that does not take away their worth. We must take it easy and live with dignity and accept the changing patterns of nature. Gradually we learn that in our real essence we are eternally different from these changing patterns.

## September 1, 1974

Life is just a big show.

## September 5, 1974

The guru, or a saint-maker, is one who has struggled tremendously against the current of the river (that is, the world). After reaching the shore, he heaves a sigh of relief. Then he looks back and sees others trying to cross. Because he knows how they feel, he reaches out to pull them in. Sometimes he even jumps back in the river to help them, because he knows how to swim back to shore.

Spiritual practice is the effort to go beyond the tossing, to fly into the calm beyond the storm. On that journey, faith is everything. Suppose someone tells you that water exists and a faucet is connected to it. Only if you believe him and turn on the faucet do you get the water. Faith is like turning on the faucet. Once there is faith, the rest is easy.

A man of realization feels the misery of others completely, because he is established at the spiritual level. There is only one spirit, not many. If one is established in that which is the Ground of every being, of every mind, then he fully identifies with all. He feels their misery just as they feel it, but he does not become miserable and does not lose his ground. Swami Vivekananda said that he would come back again a thousand times even to help a dog. That was because his identification was so strong with the one spirit in all.

Saints are never dead. They have left the psycho-physical plane long before death. Leaving the body does not change anything. They are not dead; we have only to tune our minds to them.

When we repeat the name of God, we reach a point when a part of the mind always remains on that. It purifies the mind. It feels like a moving searchlight upon us, acting as a sort of voice of conscience. This is followed gradually by an emotional and spiritual awareness. Repeating the name with faith is like turning on the faucet to the reservoir of God. The water is always present, we only need to turn on the faucet. Faith is no small thing. Unlike a mere psychological process, it cannot be de-programmed. It comes from within and is a tremendous power.

Conscience is the light of the soul. The intellect rationalizes about wrong and right, but it is the light within that illumines the picture. In a dark room, we must turn the light on to see the way to the door before the intellect can decide whether to go the right or the wrong way.

## September 10, 1974

Realization has nothing to do with not coming back to this world. One must get rid of the fear of rebirth. Our only prayer should be, "Oh Lord, I don't mind coming back any number of times as long as I don't forget you." Sri Ramakrishna said that we should keep a bit of the knowledge of God in our pocket, then we can go anywhere we like. That is an important teaching.

It is like remembering you have money in your pocket. If you forget it is there or forget that you have money in the bank, then there is a problem. But if you remember that God is always present, there can be no fear of anything. What is there to fear when you know, "He is mine"? It is the feeling of "mine" that destroys fear. The mother of an insane killer is not afraid to go up to him and say, "Don't shoot!"

When we cultivate the awareness that all are our own, fear disappears. Realization means complete freedom from anguish. Where, then, is the fear of being reborn? The Lord is mine. I am his. All are my own, because the one Self, my own Self, is in all beings.

One reaches the shore after a long struggle. A devotee made it just through faith in Sri Ramakrishna and through wholehearted service and surrender. In the beginning that kind of faith and conviction are hard to come by, but then you reach a point where you feel the momentum and you start seeing the world differently.

**September 25, 1974**

The secret to cleansing the mind is, "Hate not, hurt not." Hate and hurt bubble up in the subconscious mind and disturb the mind. If you can love and serve instead of hating and hurting, you will know peace and blessedness. Try it for a day and see.

Renunciation naturally follows devotion. You cast off everything else in devotion to the ideal.

God is like space. We are in that and all is pervaded by that. It is above, below, on all sides, and within. But that space is not inert. It is Truth. It remains even when everything else disappears. It is conscious and it is full of love. We are floating in the ocean of love and that loving Being is the inner guide in every heart.

## October 11, 1974

[A disciple questioned an article which said that only those who renounce everything can really be called children of Ramakrishna.] All are his. Holy Mother said about a drunkard, "He is my child." She made no distinction. Sri Krishna says in the Gita that he sees the same Self in all. Same-sightedness is a divine attribute. The "chosen few" are so only from the standpoint of their own evolution. Come closer to the sun and you get more warmth. The monastic distinction is institutionalized, but as far as comments like the above, about only monastics being his children, forget about it! There is no distinction and no denial, ever. All are his, and all are equal in his eyes. But those who tune their minds to him are able to feel the closeness.

[A disciple asked how an incarnation is different from any other realized soul if both are divine.] There is a difference. The essence is the same, but the difference is in manifestation. The tremendous manifestation in an incarnation is the divine mystery.

To pick one path and realize God is easy, but how Ramakrishna did it over and over by following every path is tremendous.

We have to pray as Ramakrishna prayed to Mother, "Oh Mother, I don't know what you are, I don't know anything, please give me pure devotion." Pray for devotion and the rest will come.

## October 15, 1974

This universe is a mystery. The farther we go, the deeper the mystery becomes. We struggle and struggle, and finally come up against a brick wall and realize we are absolutely helpless.

The only way is to completely surrender everything, to lay all responsibility at the feet of the Lord, to feel not only that I *know* nothing, but I *am* nothing. It is when the "I" is gone that the Light comes.

Pure awareness is when we see everything but condemn nothing. We see the sin, but love the sinner.

## October 16, 1974

God is closer to us than the vein in our neck. The divine mystery is that we do not know it.

Initiation is far beyond logic and reasoning. It has a very sacred meaning because it comes from above. One should not discuss any aspect of it with anybody but him from whom it comes. Since everyone's faith is different, others may not understand it.

We must contemplate the nature of our own Self as truth, consciousness and bliss. Meditate on your nature as consciousness, as the witness, the awareness—try to catch that awareness.

We remember the different stages of life from childhood to old age. We remember that the ego wasn't there in deep sleep. Witnessing these changing scenes is the one awareness, the principle of consciousness within.

God realization does not mean realization of a personality outside us. It means realization of the Self within. When the river runs into the ocean, when all limitations are removed, the river sees the vastness of the ocean. In that sense, God is an inference after realization of the Self within. God in its totality can never be known. Rather we attain awareness of the divine presence—actual unity with it, for we realize that we are that divine presence ourselves. At the same time, it is a realization of our nothingness, the knowledge that I, as a human being, am nothing.

## October 23, 1974

To be Sri Ramakrishna's child means to be all-inclusive. Wherever you go, you are home, even if people don't understand you. You understand them because his ideal is all-inclusive.

Don't cling to personalities and you will avoid much misery.

## October 27, 1974

The most important thing in spiritual life is the development of loving consciousness, not only vertically but also horizontally. You love the Divine Mother as your own, but she is the Mother of all and we must love her children as well. We are all her children and we cannot love her without loving all.

## October 29, 1974

Moksha is a myth. My true Self is already free, already liberated, I am already God. It is only a matter of knowing it or not knowing it.

## October 31, 1974

[A disciple asked whether Sri Ramakrishna is the same as the Divine Mother.] We do not know what she is, but he manifested her since he identified with her so completely. The point for us is that he is the greatest manifestation we know. He brings only God to our minds. We cannot approach God with devotion except through that manifestation. As Sri Krishna says in the Gita, he comes to us in whatever form we approach him. It is like cutting paper; it takes the form we cut, but it is the same paper.

The reservoir is somewhere. But we do not go in search of the reservoir. We draw the water from the nearest faucet. We are so many pipes and Ramakrishna is the main closest to our street. We turn on the faucet simply by going to him and the water from the reservoir comes. Devotion to him, to God, is within every one of us. It is a matter of cultivating it—by reading and thinking about him more and more, contemplating on him, singing, japa, prayer, action geared to him—just as his devotion to Divine Mother showed in all his activity, a continuous outpouring to her.

We become whatever we put our mind on. By putting the mind on Sri Ramakrishna and Holy Mother, we will become pure. Just think of them and the rest will automatically follow, just by virtue of what they are. Reading the *Gospel of Sri Ramakrishna* is enough. Some swamis in the Order never read anything else. For 30 years one swami never read Swami Vivekananda's works; he just kept reading the *Gospel*, thinking about it, contemplating it, meditating on it. Thinking of Sri Ramakrishna is enough.

We are not separate from God. God, revelation and man are non-separate.

Ramakrishna, Vivekananda and Holy Mother are the new trinity—the Truth, the Interpreter, and the perfect Exemplar.

Seek silence within—meaningful silence, not static, dead silence. Quiet the mind and be receptive to the teaching that comes from within. In that silence we can see the mind clearly—what we are with our positive and negative tendencies. And beyond all that is the Light, the witness. That we must try to catch. Be quiet and turn to the Light and let it unfold from within. Be quiet and patient.

Sri Ramakrishna saw God everywhere, with eyes open or closed; therefore he is God. We see that which we are. To a devil, everyone is a devil. To a pure soul, everyone is a pure soul.

Think of a moving train. From somewhere we come and get on this train. There we meet so many people who are also coming and going. We are very comfortable there, have nice things, etc., and we take good care of all and enjoy the people. But we know that all those people and all those things are not ours. Everyone and everything comes and goes. We know that soon we will be getting off the train. And so we are detached from it all.

### November 13, 1974

Never judge or label anyone in a negative way because people change. Whatever mistake a man may have committed, he may never do it again.

### November 17, 1974

All of the things M. says about Sri Ramakrishna (in the book, *M. Apostle and Evangelist*) are true. When M. says, "Hold on to Ramakrishna," it means, understand Ramakrishna and move towards him. M. occupies a unique place in the Ramakrishna Order and is a proof of the fact that labels like "householder" and "monk" mean nothing in the eyes of God. From 1881-1886, M. silently observed the divine mystery and came to understand it because Sri Ramakrishna showered his grace on him.

The uniqueness of Ramakrishna is his approach to the Divine from many different paths. Other great souls chose a path, struggled, and attained the Truth; but Sri Ramakrishna did not stop there. He found the same Truth from every direction. He is the incarnation supreme because he embodies Truth in its totality.

**November 18, 1974**

Even though Sri Ramakrishna had the same unitary experience and supreme consciousness as did Sri Krishna, he never said, "I am That," or "I and my Mother are one," because he was the revelation for this age. In this age, the devotional dualistic or qualified nondualistic approach is the best. Our body consciousness and body identification are so strong that we cannot say, "I am That." Even those who take monastic vows, though they are all nondualists, salute Sri Ramakrishna as their spiritual guide. Identify with all, but be his servant.

Sri Ramakrishna's spiritual experience is unparalleled; none can touch him. We can only humble ourselves before him and follow the path he gave us. No mystical experience is possible without devotion. Since that experience cannot be explained, those who have it can only tell others about the path. Sri Ramakrishna embodied for us the path of supreme devotion.

Sri Ramakrishna showed the dualistic approach without publicly revealing his nondual knowledge. But those who know him intimately know what he is.

Only Holy Mother knew Sri Ramakrishna. She knew him better than any of us. She is the monastic guide. When the monks wonder what to do, they refer to her teachings and her actions to find what she did or what she said.

## November 19, 1974

In modern society there is no harm in having money to meet basic needs. The only harm in having money is in the idea of possession ("it is mine") or in thinking that happiness or security really lies there. Keep money with the idea that it is there if a need arises, and it is there if you find an opportunity to share or to serve.

The attitude of a child is wonderful, for the child loves without discrimination. Before God, we are all children.

## November 22, 1974

Swami Vivekananda's teachings do not contradict the practice of self-surrender. We must depend on ourselves for preparation, for discipline and for turning our mind to the Light. But we do not create the Light, rather it reveals itself. What Sri Ramakrishna said is true: if we move one step toward God, he moves a hundred steps towards us. The more we turn to Sri Ramakrishna, the more he watches over us.

The way to overcome spiritual pride and vanity is to know that the Divine is in all. Spiritual progress is not in time and space; it is in the spiritual realm. Spiritual pride is the worst kind of egoism. It is like a cork in a bottle. We must pull out that cork of egoism, so the water can get in.

## December 4, 1974

Sri Krishna says that for those who want nothing but him, he brings what they want and protects what they have. The only causes of misery are losing what we have and not getting what we want. It is the Lord's promise that he takes care of both of those things at the highest level, the spiritual. All fulfillment is in him. Krishna says himself that he is the father, mother, goal, support, refuge, etc.

## December 7, 1974

The only thing that matters is devotion, to have purity, and a heart with no bitterness toward anyone. We need knowledge and so we must study the scriptures in order to understand and imbibe spiritual thought. As to scholarship, it only takes a few years to get a degree and that has only material value. It takes lifetimes to develop a pure and selfless heart. The most important thing is to feel, "I am at the Lord's feet."

## December 9, 1974

Even when we have faith, we may run into five obstacles in our evolution.

1. Ignorance: the first step is to acknowledge it.
2. Egoism: if you want peace of mind and joy of life and want to understand others, then keep your ego in your pocket. "Not I, but Thou in me."
3. Attraction
4. Aversion
5. Clinging

Overcome these and the Light shines.

The other huge step in evolution is when we stop blaming anything outside ourselves for our misery. Turn within and change yourself. "No one but me to blame" (quoting Swami Vivekananda's poem).

. . .

## December 14, 1974

Every approach to God is good. At times, different spiritual inclinations come. We can go to Sri Ramakrishna in any relation, because in him God manifested in a very perfect way. All moods merged in him. Mathur saw him as Kali walking in one direction and as Shiva walking in the other direction—the obverse and reverse of the same coin. Call on him in any way, because he represents the Divine in its fullness.

## December 15, 1974

If you want peace of mind, make the determined resolution: I will forgive everyone. "Blessed are the merciful."

## December 16, 1974

We do not *see* God. Rather we realize our true nature, and the fact that all are a part of the Divine.

## December 19, 1974

Offering everything to God (Gita 9.27) means renunciation of selfishness, of the idea of profit and what I can get out of it. Everything must be dedicated to God, there should be no narrowness. There is no "they." It is all *we*.

## December 21, 1974

Unlike hunger, lust does not require satisfaction. Rather, turn its course. Such ideas come because of *samskaras* (mental impressions). When the idea comes, nip it in the bud. Pray, and turn its course. Don't have any fear if such ideas come. Just catch them at the thought level and apply "the philosophy of no": "No, I shall not."

. . .

## December 22, 1974

The whole essence of Christ's teaching can be given in the words "love" and "serve." Make this the ideal: "As I have loved you, love one another. As I have served you, serve one another." As Swamiji said in his poem, "To a Friend," worship God by loving all beings. If you want peace, make the vow, "I shall not hate anybody."

## December 23, 1974

> *When lust and gold have on you no hold,*
> *Nor pleasure and pain, heat and cold;*
> *Then master of mind, you are bold,*
> *And brighter you are than stars and gold.*

## December 26, 1974

Sri Ramakrishna is not dead. Due to their tremendous spiritual caliber, incarnations continue to live with name and form. He is always present, hearing every word that is exchanged. Many devotees, lay as well as monastic, have experienced him. Do not let anything depress your mind. Be cheerful and positive and take his name. Just think, "He has illumined others, he will illumine me too."

Never react, but reflect. Reaction makes you a victim; reflection makes you a person of wisdom.

Prayerful attitude transforms passion into will. One must have will and devotion.

### December 27, 1974

"We don't *see* God" means that when we see God there is no distance, the way there is when we see any other object. It is more intimate than seeing, because there is no separation.

### December 29, 1974

By *kamini-kanchana* (literally, "woman and gold"), Sri Ramakrishna meant passion and possession. The master analyst that he was, he reduced all worldly hankering to these two things. The phrase is broader than merely a reference to woman and gold; it refers to passion and possession.

To love a thing is to understand it. It is loving consciousness that can see us through this life.

### December 31, 1974

A Divine Incarnation is a special grace that is uncaused. It is a mystery. The Divine within gradually manifests in us as we evolve. But Incarnation are fully divine, no human limitation there. And they can illumine others by their mere touch. Our struggles, our seeking and knocking, are not in vain, but illumination ultimately comes from God. It is grace. The breeze is always blowing and we must unfurl our sails.

Just as Sri Ramakrishna's grace was present on January 1, 1886 (Kalpataru Day), it is equally present now, not confined to that place or that period. We only have to lift our minds. The incarnations live on in name and form in the cosmic spiritual realm and bestow their grace now, just as they did then.

# 1975

## January 5, 1975

Holy Mother is the embodiment, the perfect exemplar, of spiritual living. "All are mine"—that is how she felt. She did not discriminate or exclude anybody. She accepted all and had endless patience and forbearance. Her purity is beyond imagination. She had all-inclusive love and unrestrained giving.

## January 10, 1975

Sri Ramakrishna is all-pervasive. That is why we call him "Guru Maharaj," the supreme teacher. All we have to do is hold on to him and he will do all the rest. If we forget him, there is misery; but if we can remember him while doing our work, he takes care of everything. It is like having a wallet in your pocket. If there is money in it but you don't know it, then it does you no good. But if you know it and remember it is there, then you can make use of it. Similarly, God is always present, but I must remember him and hold to him. It is all a matter of maintaining awareness. Actually, his hand is holding ours; we must just keep our hand in his. As Ramakrishna said, "Keep a bit of the knowledge of God in your pocket and then do anything you like." He is the fire beneath the boiling potatoes—remove that and the potatoes stop jumping. The power is all his.

A new example came to mind to explain to some MIT students why we call the diving incarnations "Gods on earth." If you have a pot of milk on the stove and someone comes in and asks what it is, you say "milk," not "a pot." Or a cup of tea—you say "this is tea," not "this is a cup." We define it by what it contains. The Godmen contain only Satchidananda, so we call them God. We know them by their love for all.

## January 19, 1975

When Jesus said, "Be ye therefore perfect...," that "perfection" is the same as Krishna's teaching about being a "yogi" and Ramakrishna's about being a "bhakta." The *bhakta* is one who feels the presence of God in his heart. The perfection of that is to see God in all and realize the unity, the oneness of all existence.

## January 24, 1975

We cannot think of God in the absolute sense. When we take Ramakrishna's name, the form automatically comes before our mental horizon. Because there is nothing in him but God, the very thought of him is purifying. Touch a red hot iron ball and, like fire, it burns. Humidity is everywhere, but if we just open the mouth and do nothing else, we remain thirsty. We need water to satisfy the thirst. The incarnation is the water to satisfy our thirst. He is God in concrete form. He is the representative, the manifestation of God. We are his children without any doubt, and as such may demand from him. The moment you repeat his name, you are his child.

## January 26, 1975

Here are four obstacles to meditation and their respective solutions: (1) laziness or inertia— the solution is mental alertness; (2) scattered mind—the solution is an object of faith according to one's own inner tendencies; (3) disinterestedness —the solution is prayerful attitude; (4) getting waylaid by fascination with visions—the solution is to go forward.

If you are caught in the current of lower tendencies, just say "Not for me," and never think that they are permanent. Look back and realize, "I was not born with this. When did it come to me? At some stage of my life. Just as it came, it will go away."

## February 11, 1975

Krishna's identification with the Supreme is beyond history or personality. He is the milk in the cup, the essence. He is not the cup containing the milk. But the devotee's emphasis on Krishna's personality is not bad, as long as the devotee realizes that the milk is the essence; the milk could be in another cup. As long as the devotee has this awareness, the adoration of the container is good; but one must lift the cup to drink the milk.

The idea of an incarnation or special manifestation of God is not talked about in the Upanishads. This phenomenon was waiting for the time of Sri Krishna, just as the atom and the power within it has always existed, but it wasn't until the 20$^{th}$ century that man developed the atom bomb. Similarly, the incarnation, special manifestation, came at the time of Sri Krishna.

**February 15, 1975**

There are two types of fasting. The first is more spiritual, when one tries to feel the closeness to the Divine while fasting. The other type of fasting is more for health and discipline.

Gita (3. 30) teaches how to spiritualize work. It is theistic karma yoga—renouncing everything for him, to work without greed, egoism, or mental fever. To work that way is to be bound by nothing; no work then will be difficult.

Swami Vivekananda's message is that serving man as God is worship of God. That is the secret. Just do it all for him. Keep the thought of Ramakrishna constantly and do it all for him.

Jealousy and envy are natural, but they are among the worst things for spiritual life. You have to say, "No, I shall not." One must identify with the joy of others in what they receive, for we are all his children. Feel oneness with the person, love that person, and jealousy will find no entrance. Feel happy for them and love them. Actually, there is no "they." It is all "we." In truth everything and everyone is Divine.

Feelings like jealousy and envy come due to past habits and thoughts. The mind which is not yet enlightened will struggle with things like this. But if the effort is made to cultivate divine and pure feelings, they will come. When bad feelings come, just pray to Sri Ramakrishna. Overcoming jealousy will enable a person to overcome many difficulties in life, and to know how to handle people. The main thing is to feel joy when others are praised. Whenever someone else is leading a good and pure life, say, "I am there," and be happy in that.

**February 16, 1975**

If you want to solve an interpersonal conflict, dive deep within yourself and feel the unity there. Then all conflicts are solved. If you want to understand someone, you cannot do it as an isolated individual. If you want to really love, love as a spirit; if you want to be free, be free as a spirit; if you want to understand and feel unity, then know you are a spirit and act as a spirit.

**February 25, 1975**

The ego is always present and it tries to assert itself in various ways—power, position, fulfillment, etc. The *samskaras* will bring up unwanted thoughts. The thing is not to be frightened, but to be aware. Awareness is most important. The higher Self must say to the lower self, "Aha, I know what you are!" It is like driving down a road and seeing all sorts of things on both sides that you simply avoid; you do not stop and cry over it. Similarly, do not dwell on an unwanted thought or tendency, because that deepens the impression. Then it becomes like a hole in the road that causes a bump every time you pass over it.

Even Ramakrishna, Buddha and Jesus faced temptation. As Ramakrishna prayed to Divine Mother, "Oh Mother, you take it all and just give me pure devotion." The only way is to take refuge in prayer, meditation, and japa when these things come. That is what is meant by, "Seek ye first the Kingdom of God." What an instrument we have got in his name!

The bad tendencies we see in others are meant for our teaching. We see good and bad, and learn either what to imitate or what to avoid. The world is nothing but a big school. Whether you see evil within or without, do not be tipped off. Just look at it, be cautious, and then do not dwell on it. "Hear no evil, see no evil, speak no evil." Always be alert and never think, "Oh, now I am safe." As when driving a car, you must always be alert and cautious because something may come up at any time.

## March 1, 1975

Vivekananda said, "First become a gentleman, then become a monk." Propriety comes even before dharma. It is a means of mutual love and understanding between people. Love is most important; that is the element of the Divine that we feel and communicate. Never hurt anyone for the sake of truth.

## March 2, 1975

One swami had a unique explanation of the symbolism of the cross. The vertical line is the "I." The horizontal line chops it into two, symbolizing the renunciation of "I." It then becomes a "t," that is "Thou." Not I, but Thou.

In the Ramakrishna Order's emblem, the swan/serpent symbol means the following: The swan is the Supreme Being, seated on the lotus of devotion on the wavy waters symbolizing action, with the background of the sun of knowledge, all encircled by the serpent symbolizing the awakened *kundalini*. It emblem symbolizes the development of the total human personality and potential, and is summed up in the motto, "For the illumination of the individual and the well-being of society."

**March 5, 1975**

In the Gita (10. 12), Arjuna addresses Sri Krishna as, "Supreme Brahman." Only a devotee can appreciate this. Such terms of address are most meaningful; they show that some light has dawned on Arjuna as a result of his struggle. Everything begins to take on a different light as soon as there is a little faith and devotion and struggle. Then we begin to knock and seek, and the life of the incarnation takes on a great meaning for us, as do the lives and words of saints in whom we have faith. It is as if they are calling us. When we get a little faith, their words go into the subconscious, and then we begin to hear those voices beckoning us toward that Light from within.

**March 7, 1975**

Even when we do not yet know God, we are still in the hands of the one whom we can trust. Faith is everything; our faith is more than seeing and knowing. So many have told us about spiritual life. There is no room for any doubt. And there is such joy in leading the life. It has its own problems, no doubt, but when the problems come, we just face them and overcome them. There is great joy in putting our life in God's hands and saying, "I don't care what happens to me." Just go on leading that pure life. Keep his name on the tongue, caring not when realization comes. Entrust everything to him like a child in the lap of its mother. Have the faith, "I have taken his name—so what's there to fear?"

**March 13, 1975**

We are never stuck with old *samskaras*. Because we are a mixture of spirit, mind, and flesh, sometimes the mind will tend to dwell at the physical, sensate level. Lust, jealousy, bitterness, hatred, pettiness—it is natural that these things come. But pray to him and they will be burnt up. He is like a fire—anything put there is burnt up. Do not dwell on the negative things that come up—just put them in the fire.

**March 18, 1975**

All talents are of only relative value. The greatest thing is devotion to God. God sees your inner heart. What matters is character and concern for others. What is most important is not to see the faults of anyone. Be peaceful within and loving without. Make everyone your own. Holy Mother could not sing or dance. She just loved and served and made everyone wholly her own.

Latu Maharaj was the incarnation of faith. He proved to the whole world what simple faith can do. He also showed what a saint-maker and miracle-maker Sri Ramakrishna was. He told Latu to just do what he was doing and he would get It—and he got It. Sri Ramakrishna is not dead. We have only to tune our minds to feel his presence.

**March 20, 1975**

Two things are needed to remove any doubt: (1) *open-mindedness*. As with any other question, you must objectify it, adopt an unbiased, impartial attitude, and think deeply within. An answer will come. At the same time, you must be prepared to accept it if someone wiser than you says something different. (2) *Prayerful attitude*. You must remove the ego—say, "I don't know"—and really open up. Sri Ramakrishna would say, "Mother, you teach me. I don't know anything." If you open up like that, Sri Ramakrishna will come in the form of a thought.

Whether we call on the Divine as Christ or Krishna or Ramakrishna, the Divine is one and the same Being. Wise ones call that Being by different names, but there is only one Being. Our devotion makes the impersonal become personal, and we can see him in any form we want, according to our faith and devotion.

## March 26, 1975

In spiritual life, never compare. Even among Sri Ramakrishna's disciples, each one was so different. One must fulfill one's own path without imitating or comparing oneself with others. No imitation, no competition.

Entertain only pleasant thoughts; life is too short to waste time with gloom.

We are so blessed to be in Sri Ramakrishna's orbit. His teachings will be the religion of the future. They have not yet started to work; the groundwork is only just being laid. That wonderful unity will be the coping stone, the roof over the walls of the house being built by the various ecumenical movements of the present.

From the ultimate standpoint, Ramakrishna and Christ are one; but at the cosmic level they have their individual names and forms. Those are only so many masks for the same One Divine Fire—same Fire, different masks.

## March 31, 1975

Every person will eventually die, but the God present in the person will never die.

## April 7, 1975

When things like gloominess, egoism, or sensate feelings come, just pray, "Oh Lord, I don't know anything. I am just your child struggling. Please guide me; please give me pure devotion." Analyze where these feelings come from and know, "I wasn't born this way!" As Sri Krishna told Arjuna, "These things come and go, they are impermanent in their nature." When gloominess comes, picture that wonderful, blissful face of Sri Ramakrishna in samadhi and say, "How can I feel any gloom when he is with me?"

Sri Ramakrishna is the all-inclusive personality. What a wonderful touch, as Swami Vivekananda experienced (as recorded in *Sri Ramakrishna the Great Master*). He is so powerful, even after his passing away. Swamiji's wonderful approach to Sri Ramakrishna was universality and impersonality, combined with worship of the person; renunciation combined with devotion.

If you have a private bank account, just be a trustee and carry on all responsibilities with the thought, "If Ramakrishna were here, what would he have me do?" If he would be against it, do not touch it. He is with us. Even when we do not see, he is always present. Incarnations do not die; they do not fade away. We must just tune the mind to their presence. When any negative feeling comes, just close your eyes and pray for his guidance and for pure devotion.

## April 10, 1975

We never truly know the meaning of loving God until we realize him.

## April 14, 1975

The only way to conquer fear, which arises from perceiving duality, is through love and knowledge of oneness and unity.

It is better to care for peace and trust and harmony than for who is right and who is wrong.

## April 15, 1975

Renunciation comes in the end, meaning, the end of worldly experiences. The monastic robe is not the point; living the life is the point. A monastery does not make a monk; one must have that quality before and throughout, inborn. The convent or the monastery only provides a setting in which to develop oneself.

## April 17, 1975

[Referring to the picture Keshab Chandra Sen had taken of Sri Ramakrishna in ecstasy:] In the whole history of the world it is the only picture of a person in the highest *nirvikalpa samadhi* state. Everything, even the heart, stops in that state. That picture is of pure consciousness and bliss, and nothing else. Sankara exactly described that state with his words, "I am the blissful consciousness, I am Shiva, I am Shiva" (*cidananda-rupaḥ śivo'ham śivo'ham*).

## April 22, 1975

Three things are necessary for spiritual experience—devotion, purity of mind, and faith.

## April 25, 1975

Faith does not demand *anything*—it is complete surrender. The two greatest examples of pure faith recorded anywhere are these: One was when Naren continued to visit Sri Ramakrishna for a whole month when the latter ignored him completely. The other was when Sarat and Latu were upstairs on Kalpataru Day and Sri Ramakrishna was downstairs showering blessings on everyone present. When they were asked to come down, Sarat and Latu stayed where they were, saying, "He knows what we need." That kind of faith is everything.

The best thing is to surrender, saying as Thakur did to the Divine Mother, "Oh Mother, I don't know anything, just give me pure devotion." Then the mind will be more free and the Light can get in. Nothing we can think or imagine can even approach the reality of it, so the best thing is just to surrender with a prayer for pure devotion.

When Swami Ashokananda said that in meditation one must try to "see" him, that means to feel his presence in the contemplative state.

Every person has his or her own individual approach. Where they are, or where they have been, or where they will be—cannot be seen from outside. No one can be compared with anyone else.

Pray to Sri Ramakrishna, "As Mother took care of everything for you, you take care of everything for me." We think we know something, but we do not know *anything*. So much is just imagination or wrong thinking; we do not know anything of what is going on. So have faith in him.

## April 30, 1975

[A disciple asked, "When you say that Thakur is always with us, do you mean in the all-pervasive sense like Brahman of Vedanta, or in a more personal way?"] It is true in a much more intense and personal way. Within the cosmic realm, these incarnations—and there are only a few—are like huge rockets which, once fired, have remained in orbit. But we must be conscious, become *aware* of their presence. The minute you think of him, he is there. Many people, lay as well as monastic, including Americans, have experienced his presence through the intensity of their devotion.

Japa helps a lot to keep the mind in a pure and undisturbed condition. The moment we think of Sri Ramakrishna, we think of God. He is purity itself.

**May 2, 1975**

[A disciple asked, "Does Sri Ramakrishna know I exist?"] As Thakur said, God hears even the footfall of an ant. Even when he was physically far away from Naren, Sri Ramakrishna knew his thoughts. No one could fool him, nor can we now. He sees *everything*, just as in a glass case. The same was true of his disciples and of anyone who merge their awareness with his; that is *nirvikalpa*.

The thing is to channel our awareness into his. Our consciousness now is limited; his is unlimited. If we merge ours with his, ours becomes unlimited also. That unlimited consciousness is why he knows all. When a child cries, the mother jumps. Similarly, he knows our everything. But he need not jump, because he is already here. His awareness of us is already present, much more than an earthly mother's. What we must do is keep our awareness focused on him. He is the fire with which to light our candle. Like a red hot iron ball, he is fire through and through. When some people asked Vivekananda to come and preach, he said the preacher in him had died long back—it was Ramakrishna doing everything. He said if you take a stick and put a turban on it and take the name of Ramakrishna, the stick will do all sorts of things. So powerful is his name.

Everything Sri Ramakrishna said about the Divine Mother is true of him also, because he is one with her. He is everything, everywhere, the inner controller. We are the machines, he is the operator. Sri Ramakrishna maintained a dualistic attitude as an example for this age. To identify as the child of God is the way for us to curb the ego. But his oneness with her is the truth.

## May 7, 1975

[Talking about Gita ch. 11 where Sri Krishna tells Arjuna that he is only an instrument:] Being an instrument is meaningful only insofar as we try to merge our will with the Divine will. That happens as we try to feel, "not me but we," "not I but Thou." We will avoid so much misery if we can learn to silence this "I, I, I." We judge everything by the standard of this little ego. But this ego is *nothing* in light of the whole world, not to mention the Infinite. We must make the "I" more inclusive—expand the heart and make it all-inclusive. Then you will cause less misery and become less miserable yourself.

[A disciple asked how to deal with anger when one is falsely accused.] If you are right, then there is no reason to be angry; if you are wrong, you cannot afford to be angry! Reflect, do not react. Under no circumstances lose your temper. Open the ears and close the mouth, rather than vice versa. Say nothing on the spur of the moment, but try to explain later in a calm way. Do not just say things, but seek understanding in whatever is said. If falsely accused, simply do not accept it. Do not say anything; just do not accept it. What is most important is to not allow for any bitterness in the heart against anybody. Say to yourself, "There is no room in my heart for bitterness." Pray for that person and pray to be forgiving. "Father, forgive them; they know not what they do." Also, look for any grain of truth in the accusation, either immediate or remote. Reflect on it carefully and calmly. But if the accusation is false, stand your own ground. Otherwise you will be like the Brahmin who threw away his calf when the robbers laughed and told him it was a dog.

Whenever you are in doubt, approach with humility one who is wise, experienced and unbiased, and follow his advice.

**May 9, 1975**

It is devotion that makes you dynamic. Swami Vivekananda's scientific devotion is no different from Sri Ramakrishna's pure devotion. It keeps out emotionalism, dogmatism, and degeneration of devotion. How many times Sri Ramakrishna prayed to Divine Mother just for pure devotion! Yet he was so open, so broad and all-inclusive.

**May 16, 1975**

The teaching, "Nature functions" (Gita 5. 14), pertains to the mundane. Conscious functioning is different; prayer falls into this category. Prayer goes deep within and touches the Ground. As Sri Ramakrishna said, an earnest prayer is answered. Just as he helped his disciples, he is helping us. But it is not abrupt, like God handing over apples and oranges; it is a process. The strength and grace are coming from within. Prayer for purity and unselfishness is answered, even though we may not see it right away. Every sincere prayer is answered.

. . .

## May 28, 1975

[The swami was asked about the fact that he talks, on the one hand, about all the promises of the incarnation, but on the other, says that realization is not a gift. He laughed and said:] There is no contradiction. Realization is not a gift, and yet it is a gift. God does indeed hold our hand, but we must walk. We must pray and struggle against negative tendencies, but he gives us the strength if we turn to him. He alone gives even the desire for spiritual life. He shows the way. He does everything if we open ourselves to him. But we must walk, we must work.

Even the Direct Disciples struggled to make their own what Sri Ramakrishna had given them. Swami Brahmananda went away for austerities 20 years after the Master's death. Swami Akhandananda sat on snow-capped mountains to intensify the spirituality Sri Ramakrishna had given him. All of them struggled considerably to make that gift their own. But the path becomes easy for anyone in any stage of life who turns to Sri Ramakrishna. Once you accept him, that is it.

Sri Ramakrishna's religion is so broad, so inclusive! Anyone who follows him and Swami Vivekananda must become like that. The whole world is our own; we must see the same God in all religions.

## May 29, 1975

Sri Ramakrishna prayed to the Divine Mother just like a little child, and we must pray to him like that. "Oh Lord, I don't know anything. I don't know how to worship or serve you; please give me pure devotion."

Along with spiritual practice we must do these things: Do not see the negative aspects of life; do not find fault with anyone;

do not hate or hurt anybody. And remember him in your work. It is only when you keep the thought of him all day that meditation and prayer become easy. Learn to feel that all work is his work; all beings are his children.

Try to see Sri Ramakrishna in all Divine ones like Jesus, Buddha, Rama, Krishna, et al.

[The swami was asked whether we are Sri Ramakrishna's in the way that children are their mothers'.] It is much more than that. Earthly mothers are only a result of certain biological connections, but we belong to him at the deepest level. We are his in the Ground itself, but it becomes meaningful only when we are aware of it. It is only when we surrender to him that he does everything. We not only are given what we need, but are actually carried by him, as was revealed to Sridhara.

Surrender is the ultimate; it does not come easily. But that is the key to his grace. When Jesus said, "I and my Father are one," that means he had connected his faucet with the water main, the Ground. We have to hook up our minds with the big water pipe in order for the water to get to us. We have to get out of the house to receive the sunshine. On the way, wavering is something we have to go through. It is like trying to put a new light bulb in a light socket. First it tilts here and there, then finally the threads get in the groove and it connects nicely. It is just like that. As we go on struggling, the feeling of oneness with him gets steady and strong.

## May 30, 1975

[The swami was asked about an incident in the *Gospel* where, seeing that Kedar Chatterjee was still attached to lust and greed, Sri Ramakrishna said, "Mother, take him away."

Kedar felt terrible.] When something like that happens, it is because Sri Ramakrishna sees something in that person which others might not see and which might be harmful to the other people around. He never did anything like that from his *own* point of view, but from the point of others' welfare.

Look at his treatment of Girish. He never sent Girish away for the things other people criticized him for. What he saw in Girish was love and compassion for people. Sri Ramakrishna knew that Girish was selfless and that he could raise Girish's mind. Selflessness is more important than any knowledge or devotion or anything else. Swami Vivekananda emphasized that always. He said that if a man had unselfishness, he had more spirituality than anyone. Unselfishness is the true test of religion. When anyone told Sri Ramakrishna that someone was spiritual, he always asked, "Does he love people?" "Does he care for people?" That is what spirituality is—to feel that all are your very own—because that is the Truth. That is real religion.

## June 1, 1975

Two things are necessary for mental health: good thoughts and good contemplation.

Wherever you go, pick out the good to see, the positive to see, and the mind will thereby be filled with those things. See only the good and the positive in people and everywhere. It is, however, true that the world presents both positive and negative, good and evil. The mind will pick up and record the bad as well as the good, and those things will be in the subconscious. Therefore, whenever you see something bad, immediately attach a tag to that: "not to be imitated." Then whenever a bad thought comes up, it comes with that tag attached and does not tip you off.

## June 2, 1975

Regarding any problematic thoughts or tendencies, remember two things. First, no problem is eternal. Second, do not pay much attention to it or brood on it. Interest and attention are what give power to a thought. Just say, "I'm not interested," and pay no attention; it will not stay with you. There should be simply no time, no space, in the mind for bad thoughts.

[The swami said he got that from Holy Mother, Swami Akhandananda and Swami Kalyanananda. They all exemplified the bliss of no faultfinding. He said his own experience had shown him that refusing to see bad anywhere keeps the mind clean and pure, and it goes into meditation as soon as you sit. It is better to be cheated than to even hear anything bad about anybody. He said people used to ask him, as they used to ask Holy Mother, if he did not see the faults in people. He just said it was none of his business.]

Just as your only concern with a lightbulb is the lighted area, or your only concern with a chair is the seat which is useful to sit on, similarly just be concerned with the good in people. Why worry about the bad; it is not my business! Make it a point not to see the bad in anyone. Yes, you see the faults, but just do not pay attention. Let the "bee" of the mind sit not on the filth, but only on the flower.

There was one young man who went to Holy Mother feeling intensely distressed over the state of his mind. He told her he was no good and started to run away. But she caught his shirt and told him, "Whenever your mind is upset, think of me." That young man later became a monk.

Unselfishness is the true test of religion and the only way to live at peace in this world. You can make anybody your own by helping them. Sri Krishna said that by karma yoga alone you can realize God.

An office assistant at MIT had a hard time getting along smoothly with people. It was suggested that she not accuse, demand or complain. She followed it and was transformed. She became happy and helpful and positive. She would say to people, "What can I do for you?" Be helpful, be positive, see only the good in people. Make everyone your own through unselfishness. It does not happen overnight; do not look for proof. Just do it.

If you want to conquer bad thoughts, pay attention to spiritual thoughts. Let God's name be like a constantly revolving searchlight for you. Then bad thoughts lose their power and spiritual ones take over. Be like a printing machine which constantly re-inks the revolving plate; spiritual thought is the ink.

Swami Vivekananda charged his disciples to give him just one life and see if they would be disappointed. With Sri Ramakrishna as our guide and ideal, we are not alone and the path becomes so much easier. Take all the help you can get from that.

## June 4, 1975

[Talking about Bhagavad Gita (11. 52-55) and the subject of devotion:] When we feel that God *is* and that there is a special manifestation, then we get unswerving devotion to our ideal. After fruitlessly trying to teach Latu the alphabet,

Sri Ramakrishna told him, "Just follow me. Repeat God's name; you will get everything through devotion and faith. But one thing: you must keep the thought of God constantly in your heart." Latu literally followed that. When Sri Ramakrishna told him not to waste the nights dozing, he also literally followed that. He used to spend the whole night walking up and down under the Howrah bridge chanting the name of God so that he would not fall asleep. He got the fullest realization, and used to solve the disputes and problems people would have when studying the Upanishads and other scriptures.

The first discipline is to love people. A true lover of God, by the same logic, loves all people; for all beings in truth are part of the One.

## June 10, 1975

Realization is in the heart. When there is a conflict between head and heart, follow the heart.

Energy is wasted on negative thoughts. The mind will be calm and serene if you remain like the bee rather than the fly (landing on flowers rather than on filth). Refuse to entertain any bad thought about anybody. "I do not know." When you see negative things, no matter how bad, just say, "I do not know what prompted that, but I refuse to dwell on the bad." Furthermore, take it as an example "not to be imitated." When you go to a garden, you notice the fruits and flowers, not weeds and manure. You do not fill your bucket with garbage. See only the good in people. Then the mind will be calm and serene. When you go to bed at night, surrender everything at his feet, saying, "I do not know anything." *Really* I do not know. Who knows what course an individual life will take? Just leave everything at God's feet.

An hour of meditation or concentrated japa is worth two hours of sleep.

## June 14, 1975

In the beginning, meditation won't be a *deep* meditation. At that stage it means continuing to think of the Divine, whether through prayer, japa, hymns, etc. The point is just to try to keep that continuity. What is most important is devotion. [The swami said he never understood why Sri Ramakrishna always just prayed for pure devotion until he had his own experience. Then he realized that devotion makes you dynamic.]

When devotional feelings come at the time of meditation, they are not just positive thoughts. You are touching the true nature of the Self, which is love, bliss and consciousness. That love is the true nature of the Divine. Dwell on that feeling just as you dwell on the thought that Ramakrishna is the full manifestation of the Divine. One must dwell on those thoughts all the time. Keep that remembrance during work and all activities; keep up the continuity of the thought. At times, because of past *samskaras*, negative thoughts do come. Therefore one must hold to him constantly as a child holding father's hand. Jump to the thought of him. We must remove all false colors to get back to the original fabric. It is difficult, but keep trying.

## June 16, 1975

It is a "precious circle" (as opposed to a vicious circle). Good thoughts make for good meditation and vice versa, and so on.

## June 18, 1975

All limitations become powerless if we put them in the blazing fire of Sri Ramakrishna. Everything is burnt to ashes there. Think of him and they cannot stay.

The secret of being able to live in a monastic setting is to forget yourself and to care for others. That is a Vedic dictum. Not 50/50, but being 100% for others. First sharing, then sacrificing. Swamis Vivekananda and Akhandananda agreed that the most important thing is to love and serve. To realize God, both the end and the means is to love and serve, for he is in all. He *is* all. Sri Ramakrishna's first question about a person's spirituality was, "Does he care for people?"

[Once Swami Sarvagatananda was walking in a garden with Swami Akhandananda and saw a beautiful fully opened rose. He commented on its beauty and Swami Akhandananda told him, "When your heart will open like that, God will enter in." He always stressed expansion of heart. That is the essence of spirituality.]

When spiritual life becomes more intense, so do the senses. They become more keen. It does not mean one is unspiritual, but that is the time to control them. It is like having good strong horses that must be restrained. You do not want dead horses, but you must control them.

## July 1, 1975

As Vivekananda said, let me forget everything I have learned. All external identification is just like a shirt that can be thrown off. We are not the doers at all. We do not create *anything*; we only manipulate and rearrange what is before us.

Life is very flexible; opinions and prejudices become our enemies.

## July 15, 1975

Our life in the world is necessary to work out our karma. Until we reach the point where we do not care where we are, whether we are thrown to the lions even, we have to go on with it. All the attraction and aversion and reaction is due to the accumulation of impressions within, and all that has to work itself out until our only prayer is that we do not care how often we are reborn or where we are, just as long as we can remember God. Like the butcher or the housewife in the *Bhagavata,* it is not the work but the attitude that matters. We must simply hold onto him. Just hold on and reflect. Do not react. That way there will be no new karma created. It is all a meaningless process; but we have to go through it, learning to do every action free from greed and egoism, with balanced mind. Those are the conditions. Just keep his name in your heart. his name and his being are one and the same. Unselfishness is the real test. A *mahātma* ("great soul") is one whose heart bleeds for others.

## July 21, 1975

Imagination can be positive or negative, higher or lower. Higher, positive imagination takes us toward Reality. Imagination becomes reality—it is very helpful spiritually. It is like imagining water when you begin to dig a well, which eventually becomes reality. Similarly in spiritual life, that which we know from others to be true, imagine that and you will *become* that. What we imagine, that we become.

The Lord is always watching. Hook up the gas line and the flow will be there.

## July 23, 1975

If you have an aversion to something, try to love it. No matter what you see happening around you, simply accept it. Do not react.

With regard to japa and meditation, work on intensity rather than time. Train the mind to leave off everything else, even if for a short time. Increase the time very gradually. Train the mind just as you would a dog.

## July 24, 1975

The mind naturally seeks pleasure, happiness, joy. But always ask the question whether the pleasure we seek will really give any fulfillment or whether we are being fooled. Seek only that which gives permanent bliss with no pain attached. For the rest, say, "No, not for me."

We enter a dark tunnel when we take to spiritual life. But we know from the illumined souls —not one, but many—that there is light at the end. So we say with all firmness and determination, I shall walk, I shall walk, I shall walk. Struggle, struggle, struggle, because a time will come as we move on— even long before illumination—that we will get some light. We will see the dawn that makes us sure that the Sun will rise.

Holy Mother says that the grace of God is like candy in the hand of a child. He gives it to whomever he wills. That is devotees' language, by way of explaining the unknown factor in the process of illumination. The truth is that everything depends upon evolution and struggle. Whoever deserves it, gets it, because it comes from within. God is not "out there."

. . .

## July 25, 1975

The first thing necessary for dynamic spirituality is the conviction that God is real. We must struggle to get it through study and holy company. We can get it through reading *The Gospel of Sri Ramakrishna,* because there we get the idea that God *is* and that he alone is real. Everything else is insubstantial.

## July 28, 1975

The mantra is given only when the student is sincere and serious. It is based on the faith that has grown in the relationship with the teacher. The mantra is not just a bunch of words. It is based on someone's direct realization of God and then is handed down. The mantra gradually and unconsciously takes hold of our mind as a most powerful suggestion of the Divine.

In the early stages, the mind may oscillate between the secular and the sacred, but the mantra is a powerful tool for raising the mind to the sacred whenever it goes down. Constant repetition will bring about a time when the mind will be set at the spiritual level. But in the meantime, mantra is the "shock" to lift the mind from the lower to the higher level. It has special spiritual significance. The name, the form, and the ideal are inseparable.

Karma is strong and inescapable. There is only one way to be free from it and that is through absolute purity of heart, meaning, total self-surrender and renunciation of the ego—to feel only, "I am Thine." Krishna's promise to Arjuna in the Gita—"I will liberate you from all evils"—is absolutely true. We see the same thing with Sri Ramakrishna, as exemplified in Girish Chandra Ghosh. If we surrender to God completely, even millions of years of karma is burnt up completely. Krishna promises in the Gita that if we surrender to him, he protects what we have and procures what we need. We get that attitude of heart by keeping up devotional exercises and prayerful attitude. Pray to him for it! If we constantly pray in a spirit of surrendering everything to him, then that surrender and its attendant freedom will come.

If a person abuses the power that comes from proximity to a great soul, the blessings of the holy man will never be lost, but they will not bear fruit until the karma from that abuse is all paid off.

Being around a great soul brings power. Unless we become spiritually set, that power is likely to be used in the wrong way to our own great loss. Prestige and money may come and be abused by us unless we keep up our spiritual practice along with holy company; only then can we digest that power. One must try to look at people in a spiritual way—neither sensually nor for seeking personal gain—and keep an equanimous attitude.

## July 29, 1975

Sri Ramakrishna used to say, "Bhagavata, Bhakta, Bhagavan." Bhagavata stands for any revelation. Bhagavan means the Divine Ground. Bhakta is the devotee. In reality the three are one. They are inseparable. The Absolute, the Revelation, and the devotee are one and non-separate.

We can discover the harmony of the basic ideas in all religions. But beyond knowing it intellectually, we must struggle to realize the source of that harmony intuitively through purity of heart. We must know that Reality for ourselves.

[One time in Kankhal, there was a special function in the shrine. The young Swami Sarvagatananda showed up in his hospital clothes, because he had been working there up to the last minute. He was hiding in a corner so as not to be seen in the shrine with inappropriate clothing. On his way to the altar, Swami Kalyanananda went out of his way to pass by the younger swami and touch him. Afterwards, Swami Kalyanananda told him that was the best clothing, because he had been doing Sri Ramakrishna's work. He said, "I don't care how you come to him. Just come to him."]

### July 30, 1975

Spiritual life can be joyful even before realization comes. Once you become settled and convinced of the goal and have faith, then you can have joy all the way. It is just like taking a trip when you know the destination and how to get there; you enjoy the whole journey.

[The swami said it was like that when he came to America. He had heard about it, studied about it, knew the way. Although there was a layover or two on the way and he had never seen the place, he knew the destination and knew he was going the right way and thoroughly enjoyed the whole trip.]

### July 31, 1975

[The swami was talking about how to transform a situation where a person may have bad intentions, like when Holy Mother melted the heart of the dacoit by treating him like her father. The swami told about a woman he knew who did the same thing when a man came to her door with the intention of assaulting her. Act without fear. Act with love. You can melt the heart of anyone with your own goodness. Every heart is filled with love; everything else is superimposed.]

## August 1, 1975

Life is all a play; there is no other meaning.

[When Swami Sarvagatananda was at Kankhal after Swami Kalyanananda's death, he once went to Swami Virajananda (then the president of the Order) to resign his position because there were so many irreconcilable differences among people in the work at Kankhal. Swami Virajananda told him that he was too attached to results and should just let things be, because he could never straighten everyone out. He must just make sure there was no difference or discrimination within himself.]

We must see all as children of God and make it a life's vow to see everyone as our brother or sister. As Holy Mother said over and over, make the whole world your own, no one is a stranger. That was Sri Ramakrishna's teaching: see the Spirit in all and hold on to that alone. Everything around us is constantly changing. We must just hold to the Truth and thereby never be lost. Put a bit of the knowledge of God in your pocket and go anywhere you like.

To feel, "How can I help?" is higher than meditation. It really purifies the mind to help others, but it must always be with a spiritual attitude. Selfishness is our worst enemy. If you have to be around a difficult person, reflect—do not react. Rather go out of your way to help that person if possible.

Just as the devotee needs God, so does God need the devotee. It is like Ramakrishna's love for his disciples.

. . .

**August 4, 1975**

It is more beneficial to learn to live with others than to be alone. The pure mind is that which is free from prejudice and which accepts others exactly as they are. All-inclusiveness at every level of existence is "Ramakrishna consciousness"—that which embraces all.

Be free from attachment to praise. Do your work for God and care nothing for results. And be free from attractions and aversions, for these things are the real source of bondage. Ignore everything but that one goal. Fill the mind with the light of Ramakrishna, and let everything else go by. A mind which loves and accepts all, and is free from attachment to praise and blame, will get such joy in meditation, even if only for 15 or 20 minutes.

**August 7, 1975**

[When the young Swami Sarvagatananda wanted to stay at Sargachi ashrama with Swami Akhandananda, the older swami said to him, "How long I will be here?" Swami Sarvagatananda said that relieved him of so much. Of himself then, Swami Sarvagatananda said, "This body is dying every day; it is just a frame. I am not the person."]

**August 8, 1975**

The first thing is to give up all likes and dislikes. Scrape the mind clean down to the surface; then you can learn something. Be all eyes and ears and no mouth.

. . .

**August 11, 1975**

If you want exclusive spiritual life, be prepared to live a life demanding total alertness, no negative opinions or prejudices, no light-mindedness or laziness.

The only way to love and understand others is to put out the "I," along with all preconceptions or looking at others in selfish terms. See others *as they are*.

**August 22, 1975**

Accept no gender limitation. Behave with dignity and poise.

**August 25, 1975**

There are two aspects to prayer. One is psychological and subjective–which means, our efforts and struggles. The other is the objective spiritual response. As Sri Ramakrishna said, if we take one step toward God, he takes ten steps toward us. If a small cloud is removed, the sun pours forth its warmth and light.

When Swami Vivekananda says that we create God, it means that our *concept* of him is confined to our own knowledge and experience. God is real; we do not create God. But we create our concept of him, and think and pray and evolve accordingly. Sri Ramakrishna is far beyond anything we can imagine or conceive. We only know what he is when we realize the highest. But when we cry to him, he hears and responds much more in kind—his ten steps to our one. He is guiding and helping us.

Whenever any doubt comes, consult Sri Ramakrishna's words. They are the last word in spiritual truth, non-contradictory to any scriptures. More than that, they are the result of his own experience. Every word in the *Gospel of Sri*

*Ramakrishna* is true. Just try to understand carefully, because sometimes Sri Ramakrishna speaks mythologically or symbolically.

### August 28, 1975

If you want to make the mind calm and steady, cultivate devotion; mindfulness/alertness (all the time—no laziness); and cheerfulness (when unwanted thoughts come, just look at them and say, "I have taken his name." The Light is within, so all dirt will go.)

Just have faith in the spiritual teacher, you will never fail in life. But our struggle must also be there. The guru can show you the way and even lead you a part of the way by the hand, but you have to walk the whole distance yourself. We must open up and yield to the teacher's guidance by giving up selfishness, getting out of the narrow little self. We have to learn that all are our own. What Christ said to his disciples is true with the guru: even as you do to the least of these you do unto me.

Learn to do everything out of love for God. Then action becomes spiritual.

### September 3, 1975

One must discriminate to overcome narrowness and pettiness. The first impulse is naturally narrowness and self-interest. So you must discriminate thus: "I have all these teachings and still I feel this way," and laugh at yourself. Then gradually a time comes when you feel for others before yourself. "Thy need is greater than mine." As Krishna said, "He who sees me in all beings...."

. . .

**September 4, 1975**

Love for God/Krishna/Ramakrishna is the most natural because we are part of him. We are not separate from him.

**September 5, 1975**

The Incarnation is one who totally identifies with both the Absolute and the relative. He is on the threshold (*bhāva-mukha*) between the two, and clearly sees and identifies with both.

**September 6, 1975**

Latu's faith was unique. He did not know anything else. Latu had total faith in the words of his guru, Sri Ramakrishna, and Latu became a saint. It is an example of Ramakrishna's wonderful power—Girish (Ghosh) on one side and Latu on the other. Sri Ramakrishna was a saint-maker, illumining Naren by his very touch. And Ramakrishna is not dead. He is alive. Just have faith in the words of Sri Ramakrishna and be happy. Think, "I am his, why should I worry?"

Ramakrishna appears so simple and ordinary but he is no ordinary man, as exemplified by his blessing to Naren. He gave Naren the highest realization by his mere touch.

**September 9, 1975**

As I love you, you love one another. That is the real meaning of love of God—not being on some pedestal out there, but to love others.

**September 10, 1975**

Be yourself, no imitation of others. There is no question of superior or inferior. People have different natures.

[In the light of Advaitic teachings, are dependence on and surrender to God real?] They are real in that they lead to Reality. As Sri Ramakrishna's relationship with Divine Mother was real, so is ours with him. He hears even the footfall of an ant. At the pre-awareness stage, dependence is psychological, in the sense that it is at the mental level. Later it transforms into spiritual awareness. But even at the psychological level of putting faith in God, the father hears the child even though the child can only say "Ba" or "Pa" in trying to say "Baba" or "Papa." The baby cries and the father picks her up even if she does not know who did it. Depend upon Sri Ramakrishna completely. Do not care for anything else. Let the world say what it will.

[Referring to Swami Vivekananda's composition of the Sanskrit prayer: *Sthāpakāya ca dharmasya* ... ] Swamiji wrote that in an inspired state, as if he had a revelation like a Vedic rishi. It is like a dictum. For years it was not even translated or printed.

Sri Ramakrishna's realizations confirmed the Vedic dictum, "All that exists is verily Brahman." It is the truth, only we do not see it because our consciousness is at such a low level. But Ramakrishna saw it constantly. He had—he *is*—full Consciousness, always on the threshold between the relative and the Absolute. Yet by choice he kept up that wonderful devotional attitude to teach mankind.

To adopt monasticism or not is not the question, but rather living the life. Most important are purity of mind and clarity of thinking. Because the Light is within all, anyone can realize it with that purity and clarity, independently or otherwise. If we do have the grace of great souls, or the path of an incarnation, then it becomes easy because the road is chalked out for us. We only have to follow him. In that case, we use the clarity of thinking for understanding him and his teachings.

## September 12, 1975

Studying the Upanishads should go together with devotion. The Upanishads teach the pure form of the Divine, but that does not contradict devotion. The Gita has the essence of all Upanishads. Krishna is the revelation. Krishna's saying, "I am that Brahman" is the highest revelation ever. Ramakrishna was that, too. He and Krishna are the same One. Ramakrishna said so himself. It was just that he, instead of remaining merged in the transcendental state, chose to remain as the eternal devotee, as a child of the Divine Mother. But his "I am the Mother's child" and Krishna's "I am that Brahman" are two aspects of the same Truth.

The leaves come and go but the tree stands. Swami Akhandananda said, "We are just the leaves; he is the tree." Sri Ramakrishna is the Truth; hold on to him.

## September 15, 1975

Dispassion comes only from experience. It means to realize that our happiness, joy and peace must not depend on anything outside of ourselves, over which we have no control. If it is something permanent, predictable and not enslaving us to anything, then run after it. But do not be attached to anything outside over which you have no control.

As long as there is the mind, we cannot be really dispassionate. What we must do is become more passionate but towards God alone. As Sri Ramakrishna said, all are mad for something; let me be mad for God. Cultivate that divine madness. Sri Ramakrishna prayed only for pure devotion. With that, everything else becomes easy because other things fall away. We must have the conviction that God is the Real, that he is our own, that he is our abode, our home. That is where we feel safe and happy. If we feel him to be our home, then naturally we want to stay with him, for nothing else belongs to us.

Pray for and cultivate pure devotion. Dispassion is a natural result of that. Yes, struggle and obstacles will be there. But as Kunti told Krishna, she wanted misery because it kept her mind on him. So let obstacles come. Close your eyes and imagine him. That is how it is to be done. It is devotion that leads to dispassion.

Try to constantly think of him in a joyful way. Spirituality and gloom can never go together. Just keep the mind on the Divine Self within, the Self which sometimes manifests outside as the incarnations. They are the flowers on the Divine plant. But it is a special plant, for these flowers are eternal, ever blooming. They are God's blossoms. It is literally true, as Vaikunthanath Sanyal experienced on Kalpataru day, that Sri Ramakrishna is present wherever we look. Now it is imagination for us, but later we will realize that in his spiritual form he is everywhere. Imagination, employed correctly, is a powerful force in spiritual life.

## September 17, 1975

Two things are necessary in the cultivation of serious spiritual life. One is study, especially of Vivekananda. We must get a strong intellectual conviction, so that we don't become dogmatic. We must avoid intellectual laziness and keep the mind clear and sharp. Read Swamiji's Chicago lectures, where his philosophy is present in a nutshell. And all of that he got from Sri Ramakrishna, even though he never mentions his name in order to avoid the accusation of dogmatism.

Naren garnered that wonderful universal ideal from the Master, and then wandered all over India for six years letting it all synthesize in his own mind, trying to understand how to present that ideal to mankind. The Chicago lectures are the outcome of that, of his own realizations.

The second thing necessary is to know how to work. Religion must help us under all circumstances and it must inspire us in our work. We must get rid of the separation between secular and sacred. Just as when we work in the shrine we do everything with utmost care and orderliness, so must we work no matter where we are. We must not avoid or hate any work (as long as it is honest), and we should take responsibility on ourselves like a master, not as a slave. Take responsibility and do whatever is to be done, offering it all to him, working without attachment. Thus spiritualize every action. As Brother Lawrence said, there are no set times for prayer. Make your life a constant prayer. Then after work, meditation will come easily because the continuity of spiritual thought is kept. However, if dishonesty or cheating is involved, then be prepared to sacrifice. I would rather starve than be untruthful.

## September 19, 1975

The mind is split into higher and lower segments. The lower mind is always trying to get the upper hand. Sri Ramakrishna called it "the rascal mind." Buddha called it Māra. Just say, "Oh, rascal mind, I know you very well." Be constantly alert and do not allow anything unwanted to get in. It is like a dam where water is very powerful. You cannot let there be any break or the water rushes through. Keep the dam intact. Say, "Oh mind, come with me for a walk to his feet." Strong feet they are!

Learn to reflect more deeply. Think of the superficiality and passing nature of whatever is external, and reflect on what is behind. Remember what you have read and heard, and dwell on those teachings. When sensate thoughts come, think of Sri Ramakrishna and take his name. Such thoughts naturally come at a certain age, but the very fact that they exist neither in childhood nor old age reveals the superficial and passing nature of it. Do not identify yourself with that. Objectify it and turn the mind to something else. Avoid agitating environments and create a new habit. We are hypnotized to look at things in a sensate way; now we must de-hypnotize ourselves.

Do not be frightened when these things come. Just watch the dirt come out, as you would watch it come out of a cloth you are cleaning. Be glad it is showing up and coming out rather than lurking within. Keep up prayer and meditation and pay attention to the meaning of it. Then it gets into the subconscious mind. Japa is the powerful dirt-remover. Be calm and prayerful and reflect, do not react. Discriminate, rather than reacting to temptation, and just turn to his name. Find the thoughts or words that help most. M used to pray to Rama to save him from worldly delusion. Sri Ramakrishna himself prayed, "Oh Mother, give me pure devotion." In the Brihadaranyaka Upanishad there is the story of Yajnavalkya, who says it is for the sake of the Self that we love husband, wife, etc. It is true that bodies are just dead without the Self within. So why love a dead body? Rather love the one Self within.

As Krishna said in the Gita, he who can conquer lust conquers everything. You must just be able to stand it and conquer it. Then you have conquered everything. These things come and go, but the wonderful thing is that the Self within is never tainted.

**September 27, 1975**

The more important thing is to say, "I shall give up hatred, I shall give up selfishness." Beyond that, one should have contentment as regards small pleasures. Sri Ramakrishna made Swami Akhandananda take betel. Swami Vijnanananda made one brahmachari smoke a cigarette. So do not ever allow the mind to get depressed. As Sri Krishna says, do not torture the Self within.

**September 30, 1975**

As Sri Ramakrishna said, God is to be found in the heart of the devotee, just as the shrine is the heart of the Center (referring to the Vedanta Society). The altar is the heart of the shrine, and it is there that we meet him. It is a meeting place until we come to the state where we can see him everywhere. We have things like flower vases to create an atmosphere, and then we feel the same atmosphere which we create. The spiritual feeling of such a place is not imagination.

At the same time, imagination is necessary for realization. People who say, "It's all imagination," do not understand the meaning of imagination. The more we can imagine deeply and clearly in meditation, the more we will progress, because we are imagining the Real. Later on that imagination becomes reality.

Suppose an illumined soul tells us that Sri Ramakrishna is full of the light of God-consciousness. So we put faith in the words of one who has experienced it and then we imagine it. Finally it is realized as a reality. The thing is that we are putting faith in and imagining that which we have been told by those who have experienced it. If we were to give up that faith and imagination we would miss so much.

The important thing is to keep the Divine as the center of our thought and activity. Doing things like work in the shrine helps us to keep our mind on the Divine until we become like Brother Lawrence, who did everything with that consciousness. At the same time, we must not get so wrapped up in the paraphernalia that we leave no time for prayer and contemplation.

It is all right to accept on faith something like the sanctity of the shrine, even though we cannot understand, because of whom that faith is grounded in. When we have faith in the words of someone who has experienced the Truth, and who loves us totally with utter selflessness, and who has nothing to gain personally by telling us these things, then that faith is not blind. It is like Sri Ramakrishna saying he loved Naren, though Naren could not even afford to buy salt. That love made Naren obey Sri Ramakrishna telling him to go to Mother Kali in the temple even when Naren did not believe in that.

Reason is a good servant but should never be the master. When there is conflict between reason and feeling, follow the feeling. If we reasoned everything, then logically we would find no meaning in anything and we would do nothing.

Sri Ramakrishna himself realized everything through that absolute faith. His method was to have faith, then follow it and find out what was essential and non-essential. Then he handed that basket of his realization to Naren, who proceeded to verify it through his own experience and then explain it all through pure, scientific reasoning and present it to us that way. The two together are a beautiful blending of absolute faith and pure reasoning, putting truth in a light which shows that truth is absolutely non-contradictory. Their truth is all-inclusive. One who studies and imbibes it feels at home in any church, mosque or temple. How fortunate we are to have it put before us! Vivekananda said, "Give me just this one life!"

## October 1, 1975

The important thing is to *feel*—to feel for people. Love is everything. Vivekananda said that *jnana* and *bhakti* are like two wings, necessary to each other, and balanced by *raja* and *karma* yogas. All the four—thinking, feeling, acting and restraining—must be harmonized for perfection. Be cautious when reading Vivekananda, because one minute he extolls this and then extolls that. One boyhood friend told Vivekananda that he had praised different aspects to the skies, but one could not tell what he really felt himself. Where was the real Vivekananda? That was when he wrote, "To a Friend"—love and love and love alone. That was the real Naren, who felt such love for all.

If you can have that unselfish love, you will never be disappointed in life. Every great saint and incarnation is like that, filled with all-inclusive love. We all have it within to the fullest extent; we just have to unfold it. Open up so the faucet can receive the infinite supply from the reservoir. There is no limit to the inclusiveness of our love.

Just see the good in people. When you go to a garden, just dwell on the beautiful flowers; similarly with people, dwell only on the good. You may see the dirt and the weeds, but you must dwell only on the flowers. Then a time will come when no matter what you see, it is all good. When a gardener sees the dirt, weeds and flowers all together, he has no aversion; the filth may be a wonderful fertilizer. It is all just part of it. So when we reach that point where we become the gardener, we see everything, but nothing is bad. Sri Ramakrishna could not see anything wrong with Girish. That is Divine love, to accept everything with that selfless love.

## October 4, 1975

To clear doubts and obstacles there is no other way than to surrender. Doubts are not always cleared right away, so just surrender to Sri Ramakrishna. There is not anyone nearer or dearer. Who else do we have? Take refuge in him completely. Even more so in Mother, because at times she was greater than Sri Ramakrishna in her all-inclusive love.

Sri Ramakrishna is always present; you have only to close your eyes and see him.

## October 7, 1975

We get many thoughts just from what we see, hear and imagine. They are not all ours. Even if they are, it is a case of having thought that way in the past, even in past lives. Learn to say, "Not now, not in this life."

Reactions depend on what value you give to what you see. Learn to separate yourself from unwanted thoughts. Shankara asks us to discriminate between the real and unreal. You fall in love and think the circumstances under which the attraction came will never change, the person will never change, and you run after the person. But that which is constantly changing is unreal, so you are a fool to bank on that. Reflect on what value you give to what you see.

Just pray, "Mother, make me like you, make me like you." Let other things come and go, remain above them all. Sri Ramakrishna, Mother and Vivekananda are a trio of whose greatness we understand very little. They are like the sun; we feel the warmth according to our distance from it. Different planets get different light and heat according to that distance. But do we have any idea of what light and heat are actually in that sun? Similarly with them; we have no idea of what they really are. The encounter, the meeting and exchange between Sri Ramakrishna and Mother is simply marvelous, so great they are. So just think of them and let everything else come and go.

Women used to go to Holy Mother and tell her that the Master spent so much time with the devotees that he never had time to see and talk to her. "You never get to talk with him," they used to say. "Why should I," Mother would reply. "He is my husband and I am his wife; he knows me. So why should I run to be with him and talk with him?"

It was that same faith that Swami Saradananda showed on Kalpataru Day when he did not run to be with others to get the blessings that Sri Ramakrishna was showering. "He knows what we need," he said. It is that unshakable faith that he knows me, so why should I run to beg?

Ramakrishna, Krishna, Buddha and Christ are like so many openings or gateways into that sublime realm. They are so many faces of the one loving Godhead. Some gateways are very big. Read Sri Ramakrishna's life, teachings, sayings, think about it, imagine it. Think of the teachings of the Upanishads and Gita, then put him in that context and imagine what he is. That will intensify devotion. He is so deep and so broad. He is the incarnation supreme. Vivekananda said so. His name will fill your being.

Whatever it says in the Vedas and other scriptures is all true, but Sri Ramakrishna has swallowed them all. He includes all. Say with joy, "I have taken his name." Never be gloomy, but cultivate spiritual joy—not merely light-mindedness but spiritual joy. This much effort we must put, to connect the faucet with the reservoir. Then we must keep the faucet clean and pure and whatever is in the reservoir will be ours. All thoughts will come, but just know that they are natural, whether lust or pride or jealousy, etc. Do not ever lower yourself and think that you are weak or lowly. No, just discriminate, and with faith in his name, turn the mind to higher things. All young people have to contend with passion and possession, as well as anger. Overcome these and you have conquered the world.

While working also, keep the thought of Sri Ramakrishna strong in the heart. At the same time, put your mind into the work and do it with all efficiency and thoroughness for him. It is all for him.

**October 16, 1975**

Regarding fear of ego trips, be glad someone has told you about them so you can be cautious. It is like traveling on a road where someone tells you there is a landslide. You know where it is and so you are cautious. Pray that you will be safe from those things. Just be cautious and pray and there will be nothing to fear. Be like Sri Ramakrishna when he rejoiced that he had taken Mother's Name.

**October 17, 1975**

Real 100% faith that the Chosen Ideal is God comes only after realization. In the meantime, our 100% faith is in the words of those who have seen. Have faith in the words of Ramakrishna's direct disciples who realized what they said about him. We must have that faith.

. . .

## October 21, 1975

One glance and touch of his can turn a base metal into gold.

Purity of mind is when you see everything but you do not make an issue of it. You see things as they are, without the coloring of the individual mind and personality interfering. Yes, you see the faults of others, but you know they are passing things and you see deeper than that to the truth of that person. No saint is a fool. Holy Mother saw everything as in a glass case. She saw more deeply into people than surface faults. We just have to look more deeply.

## October 23, 1975

Gita 12. 12 says that renunciation of the fruits of action leads to peace. Always feel that I will do everything the best I can but I will not expect anything. No expectation, no disappointment.

The next verse mentions having no ill will. We can never have peace as long as we harbor any ill will toward anybody. A grudge only hurts *us*. If we hate someone, we really hate God. If we hurt someone, we hurt God. He is not *out there*; he is within everyone.

Renunciation is like flying. You cannot sit down and rest the way you can while walking. When you fly, you fall down if you stop.

## October 25, 1975

Study not for the sake of accumulating ideas, but for what will help you to live well and learn selfless work.

. . .

## October 27, 1975

One day Gandhi will be worshipped and there will be a Gandhi religion. But these are the ways in which men like Gandhi differ from those we call Incarnations:

1. Incarnations present the Truth in its pure spiritual form. It is more direct and forceful in its spiritual aspect.
2. Christ, Krishna and Ramakrishna actually said, "Take refuge in me—I will liberate thee." It is absolutely true. Sri Ramakrishna said, "Those who come here will be liberated." His life showed he could illumine others by his very touch. His samadhi state is proof to the world of what he taught. To the incarnations we can surrender ourselves. Their power of attraction is so great that people will renounce everything for them and take refuge there. They are all extremely high peaks. This difference is only at a very high level. They all manifest the same Divine, but the *manifestation* in incarnations is so great. Those peaks we can see directly from where we are, whereas we have to go higher ourselves to be able to perceive what men like Gandhi are.

The Incarnations do not come to earth because of karma. They come out of compassion and with a specific purpose—to help mankind. Most important is that there are so many factors which we do not know or understand at our human level. Our reasoning does not touch at all the whole truth of it. The beauty of it is that regardless of how or why Sri Ramakrishna came, he did come, he did and does illumine people's hearts. Let us just thank God for the opportunity to be close. Let us not miss this opportunity. We get the faith and conviction about him through prayer.

God is within us. He is not out there. He is inside *every* one of us. He is the Self existing equally in all beings. "He who sees me in all..." (Gita 6. 30). But how to touch that Ground? Through prayer, meditation, self-denial.

God is a term that says so much more than we can put in a word. He is in all. If you hurt anyone, you hurt God. If you hate anyone, you hate God. God is not a thing or even a he or a she. God is the Ground of all. The more we love God, the more we love others. The closer we are to God, the closer we are to others. The closer I am to God, the more I love you. The thing is to touch that Ground. If we dive deep, we can get a glimpse. Then the deeper we go, the more we understand.

## October 30, 1975

The whole aim of religion is to make everyone your own. What we are seeking to attain is the feeling Holy Mother expressed when she said, if you want peace, do not find fault, but make everyone your own, because no one is a stranger. Swami Kalyanananda loved Mother so much. He understood who she was.

If we can maintain the feeling that everyone is our own, we will never go wrong in life. We must learn to give up fault-finding and see people apart from their faults. Think honestly and sincerely, "Why is this person like that?" and, "How can I help?" Never find fault with anybody; rather learn to straighten yourself. Instead of finding fault, learn to make everyone your own. That is how Holy Mother was from her very birth.

When you do work at the Vedanta Center, go out of your way to make others feel happy and at home. Get outside yourself. Make every work a form of service and worship. Think of things like selling books, etc., at the Center as a means of serving and helping people. Feel, "I am just his instrument." That will help keep egoism from getting in.

**November 5, 1975**

There are defects in any institution or organization. Power and politics inevitably come where there is money and management. But we must look more deeply into the higher spiritual values and not condemn individuals or the whole organization. If you are in such a situation, always feel, "How can I help?" One can often help most by not saying anything. Often things can be resolved by the individual if he is simply aware that someone knows the problem and is watching.

The love and unity that held Sri Ramakrishna's monastic disciples together at Baranagore in the early years of the Order is something marvelous. Vivekananda said that to get God realization is easy; to get a teacher like Ramakrishna is easy; but to get a brotherhood like that is rare. Spiritual brotherhood or sisterhood is what helps us spiritually at the unconscious level. It is like being carried along by the movement of a crowd. If you can live in an atmosphere where people share commitment to a spiritual ideal, then everything you do becomes sacred rather than secular. Your work, meditation, prayer, even eating—everything becomes sacred in the light of that spiritual love.

The truth is that Brahman is present as Atman in every one of us. The same spark of divinity is present in all. That is the essence of every religion. The whole message of Christ is in what he said at the Last Supper to his disciples: "As I have loved you, love one another; as I have served you, serve one another." That is religion.

There is no other purpose but to make everybody our own. Knowledge of Oneness is the end and the means. It comes automatically with realization, but in the meantime we must practice it as a discipline. Then the mind begins to open up. In the beginning our minds are closed, but as we practice giving up all faultfinding and try to make everyone our own, gradually the mind opens up and we can then meditate easily.

Then all worldly thoughts begin to lose their power. Such thoughts will be there—we cannot get rid of them—but as the mind opens up to the spiritual light, these worldly thoughts get no attention, no food from us, and they no longer raise their heads. When they come up, simply pay no attention, turn the mind to a spiritual thought. Sri Ramakrishna and Holy Mother are so powerful that to turn the mind to them makes all other thoughts powerless. The thought of them will take over the mind.

We must expand to include all. Yes, we have ego identifications with different things, but we must be able to detach ourselves from all of them. We must seek in all these different identifications That which is the constant awareness in all of them. We must seek for what this "I" really is. That same Substance is the One who is present in every individual. That real "I" is the same Self in all. It is what we seek. That in fact is our discipline.

We must refuse to harbor any negative feeling. If we see negative things, we just brush them aside, knowing that they are just temporary and have no meaning. They are just little passing things. Instead we focus on the Self within. We have to keep our minds fixed on that Substance within everyone. The Atman is in all, without any qualification or identifications; it only appears to have them.

One who has realized the Truth, actually sees a different dimension, even with eyes open. In deep sleep, the mind has gone to another world as it were; because we can be in a room where people are moving and talking but we do not perceive them at all. But in the state of God-consciousness, the realized soul still sees all the multiple perceptions, but the mind also goes up and perceives another dimension, what we call God. It is not just intellectual; it is actually awareness, God-consciousness. Until we get to that state, we have to practice it as a discipline. The wonderful thing is that as we practice like that, even long before realization, we get the joy of living and seeing things like that. We have the philosophy behind the practice; we have the discipline; we have the grace of the Teacher; with all this, we practice the means that lead to the same end.

## November 6, 1975

Christ was also the mouthpiece of God. Sri Ramakrishna said so, had a vision of him, and absorbed him into himself.

Good and bad things are equally our teachers. It is just like driving down a road and seeing a big hole; we just avoid it. We must pray as Sri Ramakrishna did, "Oh Mahamaya, do not delude me with your maya." Pray to Sri Ramakrishna like that and put absolute faith in his name to destroy delusion. Keep taking his name and all past tendencies fade away.

Everything we see and hear, just think, "What have I learned from this?" And be absolutely fearless in his name.

Feeling is the most important thing in prayer. We need not say anything. It is just like going to a fire. We do not say, "Here I am, please keep me warm." Just turning to God we need only feel his presence. Sri Ramakrishna said that God hears us and knows long before we utter a prayer. Simply go to the fire and you get the warmth and the transformation.

Whatever we think about and meditate on, that we become. That is the meaning of the imitation of Christ. We actually take on the quality of that on which we think and meditate constantly. So think of him more and more and you will be transformed.

When you see the many forms of egoism that come up, just pray and put faith in his name. Even when you do not see them, just keep taking his name and that itself will destroy all delusion.

## November 10, 1975

The tendency toward cultishness is unavoidable if you have devotion to an ideal. But those who have seen Truth as it is are less likely to make dogmatic statements. If they do, they reflect later on the fact that it is the same Light manifesting through different personalities. The wonder of Sri Ramakrishna is that he realized so many different aspects. The Order has a heavy responsibility to not make itself just another sect or personality cult.

Sri Ramakrishna's phrase, *kamini-kanchan,* really means passion and possession. If we can give up those two, we have conquered everything. The first is reaction to external stimuli; the second is the sense of "I and mine." These are the two bondages. If we can learn not to react, and can give up "I and mine," then we are free. But we feel so helpless. The whole secret is to put the burden on Sri Ramakrishna. He knows the Truth. He has seen the Light and he can take us across the ocean of this world.

The only way to get out of this cycle of birth and death is to listen to the voices of the Incarnations, prophets, saints, and sages. They are so many voices calling to us, "Knock here, here is the exit, follow me, take refuge in me." All we have to do is turn to the Light, listen to the Voice, follow them. Once we turn to them and discipline our lives according to their teachings, then we are on our way home. When we feel bewildered, we should lay the problem before a man of wisdom, just as Arjuna prayed to Krishna to tell him what was decidedly best for him. We should not just go off in a corner and accept the obstacle. Put it before them. Take refuge in those who know the truth.

Human limitations will be there, but they are only for the time being. It is like driving a car. Obstacles will be there on the road and there will also be internal problems with the car. What counts is how you handle them, how you drive the car. Obstacles will be there along the road but we simply have to drive very carefully. The only thing that counts is to keep the mind on Ramakrishna. Whenever there is a problem, just think of him standing beside you and what he would tell you to do. Think of his teachings and what his disciples have said, and with that feeling try to think and act like that. At least you can try.

. . .

## November 14, 1975

Be serious and serene. But never be holier-than-thou. Be humble and kind and just meet others with straightforward dignity.

## November 19, 1975

Community life is important because before we can feel, "Not I, but Thou," we have to learn to feel, "Not *me,* but *we.*" The real meaning of spirituality is the feeling of oneness, that all are our own. As Holy Mother said of one person whom everyone condemned, "He too is my child; how can I ignore him?" We have to perfect secular life before we can enter upon real spiritual life. That means sharing with others, feeling for others, loving all. "Love thy neighbor as thyself" is as great a commandment as "Love God." Mind will never get into deeper meditation until we give up the ego sense, the "I" that separates us from others. "Forget yourself, care for the rest." Why? Because the Truth is that there is only one Spirit behind all this matter. The Truth is that we all are One. So we must get outside this little ego, give up selfishness, and then we can enter into the realm of the Spirit.

For those who sincerely seek, God provides the right opportunities at the right time. Knock and it shall be opened to you. Seek and ye shall find. Just do not give up knocking! For the sincere seeker, God leads the way.

## November 27, 1975

We must meditate on whatever Sri Ramakrishna said about God and Spirit, and then understanding will gradually come from within our minds.

Evil is like the dark side of the moon, that which is turned away from the sun. But if you try to show darkness to the sun, you cannot. Whenever you bring something before the sun, light is there. You cannot show darkness to the sun.

**November 28, 1975**

We must always ask, "Is it true?" Satisfaction is not the criterion of Truth. We must accept for the sake of the spiritual that which is true, including our own limitations and what others say about us, if it is true.

Live your spiritual life here and now, and leave the rest in Sri Ramakrishna's hands. Let his will be done. Be just like a kitten in his lap and surrender to his will.

Faith, devotion and purity must be intensified through spiritual practice. Just think of Mother and Sri Ramakrishna. Bow down to them, put your head in Mother's lap and feel safe there. Nothing else in the world matters. Her lap can hold millions of children. Just feel happy, "I have taken his name." Pray to him for more intense faith and to make us pure and selfless.

**November 29, 1975**

Speak the truth, but speak *pleasant* truth. Always be humble rather than taking any stand on ego or prestige.

**December 1, 1975**

Develop conscious living. Learn to be alert, aware and mindful every moment, and live consciously rather than instinctually.

. . .

**December 4, 1975**

The Lord wants only an honest and sincere heart. We have to try our hardest and follow his teachings to the letter. Then alone we have the right to demand from him. If we do our part fully, then we can say to him, "You must show me." The thing is, we must come out of the enclosure to get the sunshine. His grace is always present, but we must come out of the house. Some people want to remain in the house and still enjoy the sun, but it cannot be done. We cannot remain inside even a little bit. The house is the little ego. But once we turn towards him, we may go sometimes fast, sometimes slow, but we will never miss the mark. Do not worry about when realization or his grace will come. Just go on doing your duty and put faith in his name. Be like Swami Saradananda on Kalpataru Day: "He knows what we need." Be mindful; be aware; think of that sublime and independent Divine Consciousness; and do not worry.

**December 5, 1975**

God is blissful, don't you see? But it is a trans-sensual bliss. Always keep the atmosphere joyful and congenial. Be happy and peaceful in his name.

**December 15, 1975**

There is such a huge unknown factor in whatever we see that we must never judge or condemn others. When we feel inclined to judge or find fault, right away we must turn our mind on ourselves and ask, "Do I know myself? Do I understand all my own positive and negative aspects? Do I myself have some of the faults which I am seeing?" Then we will give up judging and condemning.

## December 19, 1975

We require intellectual conviction. The blind intense faith that Latu Maharaj and Nag Mahashay had comes only when you have seen an incarnation. The rest of us probe intellectually as well and need explanations to satisfy our intellects. Study is essential for intellectual conviction, which we need alongside faith. When conviction comes, the struggle becomes easy. For us, once we get conviction, it will just be a matter of time before realization comes.

If we accept Sri Ramakrishna and his teachings, there is no fear. It is like what Christ did for those who came to him, he would lighten their burden. It is just like that. Sri Ramakrishna himself said that for those who came to him, their problem is solved. It is just as true for us as it was for the direct disciples.

It was such good fortune for the direct disciples to see Sri Ramakrishna, but blessed are we who have not seen him but still believe in him. The same realization is possible for us. If we are conscious of what we are and where we are going and live consciously, with constant alertness, and if we can accept him completely, then there is no fear for us.

## December 23, 1975

To gain complete acceptance and surrender is a process of unfoldment. It takes time because of *samskaras*. Therefore have patience and perseverance. What is most important is to discover the joy of living the life long before realization comes. And have faith that God knows what we need.

Once Latu was jumping about with great impatience saying, "This won't do!" and "I shall tell him today!" He was wild with restless impatience. Sri Ramakrishna laughed and told him that when you cook vegetables you must let them boil; you cannot eat them raw. So he told Latu to let them boil. "You will get it," he told him. Latu touched his feet and said with great joy, "Then I have already got it!" So restlessness is good, but not beyond a point. It is good to be restless but we have to find the joy of living the life and having faith that he knows what we need.

We must also make all of life consistent with meditation. Avoid all negative aspects. That is where "love thy neighbor" comes in. Just do your duty and work with peaceful, harmonious, tranquil attitude. Be soft, spontaneous, controlled, alert. Otherwise it is like not taking care of a musical instrument; every time you want to play you have to go on tuning it. But if you make all of life free from negative feeling and be always compassionate and forgiving, then when you sit for meditation the mind easily gets in. If you keep on building the positive and avoiding the negative, whatever acceptance and surrender you already have will become complete acceptance and complete surrender.

Sri Ramakrishna's mantra is "D. Gupta's fever mixture" for us. Take that medicine and the cure will be very quick. He has already done the terrible struggle and then handed us D. Gupta's fever mixture.

## December 24, 1975

The only meaning of religion is to know we are One. We are bubbles on the same sheet of water, exactly the same Spirit in all. The fruit of realization is that we find out the meaning of life.

Anger, hatred, jealousy, etc. are the impurities that cover our true nature and make us miserable. If we can learn to forgive, we will be happy and pure. Just for our own sake we must learn to forgive.

The way to overcome limitations like jealousy and hatred is twofold. One is to get the intellectual conviction that, though they are natural in a worldly way, they are no good spiritually. Then we have to keep drilling the mind until it sinks in, just like training a child. Second is prayer to Sri Ramakrishna and Holy Mother. They do answer, in an impersonal/personal way. As Sri Ramakrishna said, every sincere prayer is answered. But we have to be patient and perseverant because it takes time. The effect in the subconscious mind of a sincere prayer is immediate, but to get the cumulative effect takes time. But there is response to a sincere prayer from a Higher Power. It comes from within because he is the Ground of our consciousness.

## December 25, 1975

It is easier for women because spirituality is a feminine quality.

## December 26, 1975

The controlled mind is our best friend and the uncontrolled mind is our worst enemy. Talk to the mind who has lived like an animal for so long and coax it toward the Divine.

Mind is like a child—watch it and it keeps out of mischief. And pray, for—as Sri Ramakrishna said—every serious and sincere prayer is answered.

## December 27, 1975

Swami Akhandananda was very strong on the point of seeing the same Spirit in all. We should make it a discipline to see the One in all. That is the goal; let us make it the means—"I shall not see the difference."

**December 30, 1975**

Sri Ramakrishna hears us. It is true in an intensely personal way. He hears even the footfall of an ant. Naren experienced many times the truth that Sri Ramakrishna knew everything he thought or did. He is always present with us; he hears even our jokes.

In Gita 9. 22, Krishna says that to those who think constantly of him, harboring no other thought, he protects what they have and procures what they need. That is absolutely true and those words can also come from Sri Ramakrishna. He knows what we need, what is good for us, and he is watching out for us as he did for his own disciples. Our experience of that depends on our keeping our mind with him. It is just like keeping the faucet open to get water from the reservoir. If we do not think of him, the faucet is closed and water does not get in.

Incarnations living on in the cosmic realm with name and form are just like planets coming from the sun. Smaller ones burn out faster, but bigger ones keep orbiting around the sun for a longer time. The incarnations are of such great spiritual mass that they keep orbiting around the sun of Divine Consciousness, some more powerful than others. Or like the rockets—the bigger and powerful ones keep orbiting the earth and don't burn out. This is a divine mystery. They come to tell us to seek first the kingdom of God, to live in God here and now. Our mind goes out to other things because it is not tied to the Ground within. If we tie it to the Ground, the mind becomes like a well-fed dog; if it is well fed at home, it does not go away. So if we fill our mind with him, it will not want to run about. Fill it with spiritual food and keep it at home.

Coming to God and coming to Sri Ramakrishna are not two different things. He is totally Divine. But it is very difficult to understand, very mysterious. Sri Ramakrishna himself said that the Divine is infinite, and we can understand only so very little. When we do not understand, that itself is the best prayer. Sri Ramakrishna told one boy to just pray to him, "I don't understand," pray to him to reveal himself. Be truthful and just pray to him like that. Pray for pure devotion. And believe his words.

When you go to bed, pull up the sheet, close your eyes, and pray to him. Just talk to him, "Please guide me, give me strength, make me pure, give me pure devotion." Repeat his name. Go to sleep like that every night; pray to him like that.

## December 31, 1975

Morality means to think not in terms of good and bad, but just that people are different. Accept the difference and learn to see the unity. Accepting difference will take away bitterness and hatred.

There are two aspects to Sri Ramakrishna's life. As an aspirant, he showed us exactly how to struggle and realize the Divine. The other aspect is the perfect personality whom we worship.

# 1976

### January 2, 1976

When Sri Ramakrishna says (in the *Gospel*) that it is sufficient to know who he is and who we are, that is true. That is the mystery of divine incarnation. To know who he is and who we are—these are not two different things. Keep reading and getting that idea set in the mind. The thing to be known is the soul. We need not know everything—it is enough to "eat the mangoes."

### January 5, 1976

More important than physical closeness of the teacher is closeness of the thought. You are where your mind is. A channel may be always with you but you must tune in.

It is alright to externalize the mind for some work, but not to let it be dragged. Just bring the mind to Sri Ramakrishna's feet. He is wonderful, I tell you. Pray, "I put my head at your feet," and keep it there. Then everything will happen in time. As Naren said, he molded their minds like clay. So pray to him, "Just like them I am to you. Please mold me like that too."

## January 7, 1976

We must follow what they say. By following what they tell us to do, we thereby raise our consciousness and are then able to understand more about this world, about ourselves and about God. The most important thing is pure devotion to them, as Sri Ramakrishna prayed to Divine Mother. There is one incident in the *Bhagavata* where the gopis say they do not even want to hear about how Sri Krishna is the Supreme Brahman, etc. Only one kiss from him is what they want—kiss meaning spiritual oneness—on that they meditate and are fulfilled.

What we need is the devotion of a child to the mother, where there is no calculation, just love and surrender. When we approach them with devotion, the more we are purified and the more the spiritual warmth we get. When we go to a fire for warmth, we do not care to understand what is fire; we just want the warmth. The same with them—the more we get that warmth, we do not even care to understand what they are. Even Sri Ramakrishna said he did not understand the Divine mystery; the infinity of the Divine cannot be totally comprehended. He just prayed for pure devotion to the Mother.

It is not that God is some being "out there." God is the essence of every being. But in those persons whom we call incarnations, that Divine essence is fully manifest. In Sri Ramakrishna and Holy Mother there is no human limitation. They are fully Divine. Just as a red hot iron ball is not different from fire, so they are not different from God. They are born for the regeneration and welfare of the whole humanity. Saints and sages also manifest the Divine and do good within a smaller circle, but the incarnations manifest the

Divine fully and are born for the whole of mankind. Whatever they say becomes law in the moral and spiritual realm.

Swami Vivekananda is the specially ordained bearer of Ramakrishna's message to the world. Sri Ramakrishna himself said that whatever Naren said was to be taken with great care. When there was disagreement about Naren's interpretation of Ramakrishna's message among the brother disciples, and there was argument, Naren would go to the shrine and meditate on it. When he came out in a very serene and calm state, the others could tell from his face and bearing that he was right. What he has said is for the good of the whole world.

Similarly, Holy Mother is the manifestation of that Divine message for this age. She is to be understood, not from the theological or philosophical point of view, but as a perfect practical exemplar of spiritual living. She lived so quietly while Sri Ramakrishna was alive, fully absorbing his teachings. Then when he was gone, that Divine Power manifested fully in her life.

The Divine Consciousness is fully aware of the human situation, and this Divine manifestation is Divine grace, one aspect of "Ananda." It is the nature of the Divine to be absolutely compassionate, forgiving, all-inclusive, all-embracing—that is Holy Mother.

## January 8, 1976

A swami told some younger monks to practice three things for one month and see the transformation: (1) Be truthful in thought, word, and deed. Ask always, "Is it true? Is it beneficial?" 2) Love everyone: "I shall not see the defects." (3) Serve others whenever an opportunity comes.

## January 10, 1976

In spiritual life prayer has a great meaning. Mother knows that the baby has to be fed at 8:00, but if the baby cries at 6:30 and keeps crying, Mother will feed her earlier. Prayer hastens the process. Is any art learned in a year or two? This is the spiritual art. Be patient.

## January 14, 1976

When we serve at the center/temple, we should always think that everything we do or give is for Sri Ramakrishna and everything we receive is from him. There is no personal obligation to anyone else. Anyone devoted to him deserves everything. Material giving has no meaning. Devotion is the only offering. The more we let his Spirit move through us, the better it will be. *Ramakrishna-gata-prana,* "life set in Ramakrishna."

The marvelous thing about Vivekananda is that his presentation of religion is all-inclusive and related to the totality of life.

## January 28, 1976

Swamis Kalyanananda and Akhandananda picked out only the very best in every religion. We should be like that in the way we look at people. See a lamp—the whole thing is dull; the light comes only from one tiny wick. But it is at the light we look, not at the rest of the thing. So always look to the merits, to the light.

We must never hold a grudge, for the sake of our own peace of mind. We must never react. Thereby we grow, through reflection. If we react and indulge grudges, our mind is pulled down. When we go to a garden, we look to the fruits and flowers, not filth and fertilizer. Similarly with people, we must see only the merits, accept and imbibe that. Be like the bee that sips only honey, and not like the fly that sits on filth as well.

When someone said that Holy Mother never saw faults, she said they were all busy finding fault, so, "Should I join you?" We must struggle for that equanimous attitude. We will fall and get bruises in the beginning—it will be a struggle—like in learning to ride a bicycle we fall in the beginning. But once you learn to ride, you can ride easily. So we struggle for some time and then we begin to feel the joy of it. A mountain of karma can be burned up by one spiritual thought, just like one match can burn up a heap of cotton.

### February 6, 1976

The key to overcoming any obstacle is to give the burden to Sri Ramakrishna. Keep a prayerful attitude. Think more intensely of him, pray to him, take his name. "Please bless me, please grace me, keep me straight, keep my mind towards you." The obstacles to be overcome are lust, anger and greed. When these three are conquered it will be wonderful.

### February 11, 1976

To want to feel, "I am God's child," is born of spiritual truth, not psychological need. I am telling you, and all the great souls have said it, not just one. If you really want to feel it, the way is complete surrender, giving up all worldliness. "I don't want anything; I am Thine." That is the way to completely become his child, or to know it. For that, pray to him, repeat his name, think of him, try to feel, "I don't want anything."

That is our true nature, only somebody has to tell us. It is a long journey to that knowledge, but we are on the road.

## February 13, 1976

Time is an important factor. But pray, meditate, live a pure life; that is the way. If you take a dirty cloth to your mother and say, "Mother, I have soiled my cloth," what does she say? "Oh, don't you worry; give it to me, I shall clean it." It is just like that. Give your heart to Sri Ramakrishna, put your mind before him just as it is and he will clean it. But *give* it to him, do not hide it. If it is given, he will do the rest. *Śaraṇam tava caraṇam bhava-haraṇam mama Rāma*. M. used to repeat those words with folded hands: taking refuge at Thy feet destroys all my mundane limitations.

## February 15, 1976

Freedom does not demand. Freedom does not hurt others. Freedom gives freedom to others as well. Have freedom with dignity, poise, and modesty.

## February 16, 1976

Prayer is communion of the soul with the Power beyond itself. It is the breath of the soul. Keep praying; it touches our consciousness and illumination comes from within. Prayer gives peace of mind, human understanding and illumination.

## February 19, 1976

There is no difference between God personal and God impersonal. It is the same Reality. Some sections of the Gita, like chapter 13, are philosophical. But then Sri Krishna goes on to say to take refuge in him. Sri Ramakrishna has the last word when he says how water, ice and vapor are all the same.

The man under the tree knows the whole story about the chameleon that takes different colors and can also be colorless. Sri Ramakrishna said that the highest is the formless aspect of the Divine Mother. Swami Vivekananda said the same of Sri Ramakrishna in the Khandana-hymn: *nirguṇa guṇa-may.* In his ultimate reality, he is beyond. But to seek the Personal God is not selfishness; it is our need. The Personal and the Impersonal are not different, they are one and the same Reality. Do not miss the personal aspect of the Revelation.

**February 23, 1976**

Our faith comes from scriptures and those who know, until we get the faith that comes from realization. What we need now is intellectual conviction and faith in the words of those who have seen. There is also a subtle form of intellectual doubt, more of an emotional doubt, that comes from urges deeply embedded in the unconscious mind. When we cannot get these things to the surface, we should pray, because beneath the unconscious is God. If we can touch that Ground, the Spirit integrates the mind and resolves the knots within.

Faith in prayer and taking refuge in him are acquired through practice. Learn by doing. When doubt comes, make that too a part of the prayer.

Ill-feeling makes crying to God useless, but only if you are letting the bitterness stay without trying to reconcile it. When Christ said to first go and reconcile with thy brother, that is the truth. Otherwise it is like being on one side of a closed door and trying to shine a light to get a look at the other side. Getting rid of the bitterness means opening the door and then you can shine the light on the other side. God is not "out there." God is within. To the extent you hate anyone, you hate God. That is the truth. When there is any bitterness, look at it. Where it is your fault, pray for forgiveness. Where it is someone else's fault, pray that they be forgiven. Reconcile it at least mentally. When sitting for meditation, cultivate a positive and loving feeling towards all.

The unconscious mind is constantly unfolding new things, so there is a constant process of integration and reintegration. The only way to do it is by invoking the Divine Ground. It is the Light beneath the unconscious that can integrate all this. We can never solve all mental problems at the mental level; new and bigger ones will just keep coming. But if we go to the Source, then we touch the Ground and get the Light that resolves everything.

The wonderful thing is that when we once touch that Ground, then we realize that the same Light is within everyone. The way to have peace and blessedness in this world is to do what Sri Ramakrishna said: "Keep a bit of the knowledge of God in your pocket and then go wherever you like." It means that if we can live in the world with the consciousness that we are all brothers and sisters, children of the same Godhead, we will have peace. That means a lot of sharing and sacrifice, and that will bring us peace and joy.

Do not be frightened that the path is like walking on the sharp edge of a razor. Sri Ramakrishna will keep us straight. The only way is to pray to him. *Tasmāt tvam eva śaraṇam, mama dīna-bandho,* "Thou alone art my refuge, O friend of the lowly." Even a man like Vivekananda, who had gone everywhere and tried everything, came to that conclusion. The only way is to go to the Source, to bring fresh water. Just go to him and ask him to keep you straight.

## February 25, 1976

In Gita 18.66, "Giving up all duties" does mean renouncing the world. A time will come when you want to give up everything to be set in That. Arjuna did that after the battle. He and his brothers renounced completely the spoils of war and gave up everything for the sake of spiritual attainment. But prior to that he did his duty, for the sake of righteousness, without any selfishness or attachment. You cannot rush that renunciation. It comes naturally as an outcome of spiritual discipline. Otherwise, as Sri Ramakrishna said, if you pluck an unripe fruit, it merely spoils. You have to let the ripe fruit fall off the tree naturally. It is like driving to New York. You have to drive 55 mph. Then you will have a safe and successful trip and reach the destination. Just have faith that he knows what we need. Believe, "he knows." Accept the ups and downs of the road. A time will come when you get close enough to see the buildings of the city and then the whole mind will be there. Do your part as far as spiritual practice and struggle and leave the rest to his grace.

## March 5, 1976

You need not call on any God outside—simply look within. It is we who choose to turn within, as a result of the wisdom that comes from our own experience. Our running about in the world, indulging in this and that, and only turning within sporadically, is our own making, the fruit of our own minds. But if our consciousness turns within, nothing can stop us. Spiritual hankering will be fulfilled because that Consciousness is within us. We are really playing with ourselves in this world. It is our own struggle that will take us within. It is a combination of our struggle and prayer to Sri

Ramakrishna. If we sincerely desire to understand him, it *will* open up.

**March 6, 1976**

Swami Vivekananda's taught us to think, "I am the infinite, omniscient, omnipresent Self." He also said we should realize: "I am nothing; Thou art everything." Both these statements are true. But in this age it is better to follow the path of devotion—to pray and to feel, "I am nothing; God is everything." Do not feel confused; just be patient. The ocean is very turbulent, but keep going up, and finally you reach that polar region where it is frozen and calm.

**March 10, 1976**

Purity means to have only one idea.

The most important thing is conscientious consciousness. Every now and then withdraw the mind and remember who you are and where you are going.

Constantly guard your thoughts. When you find any negative or unhealthy thought coming, reject it immediately—"No, not for me." If you remain alert like that constantly, within a year your mind will become very strong. Now it has to be trained into the philosophy of "No." It is hard for a plane to take off; it is a little unsteady in the beginning. But once it reaches a certain level the pilot can set the switch and move about freely. Once the mind gets into the habit, it will be the best friend. If any bad thoughts are already there, when they surface, reject them in the same way—"No, not for me." They will then go away.

Never be frustrated if spiritual intensity wanes. Just keep a prayerful attitude. Pray to be able to keep up spiritual feeling throughout. If we keep up the thought, it will gradually percolate from the brain to the heart, and the *feeling* of his nearness will come.

## March 11, 1976

Don't waste time analyzing dreams because we are consciously evolving creatures, not static. So don't waste time on what comes up as mind unfolds. And don't be frustrated. As Sri Ramakrishna said, the world is a mansion of mirth for one who has taken Mother's name. So with us, "I have taken refuge at the feet of Sri Ramakrishna, why should I worry." Maintain a happy and positive feeling.

## March 12, 1976

There is no high and low before God. Be alert and stop any thought of vanity and egoism as soon as it comes. If you forget him, then all troubles come and it doesn't take long to fall. Just keep the thought of him constantly, like a child holding father's hand. Be humble and think of serving others: "How can I help?"

Similarly, any praise we receive is his. We must know constantly that we are nothing without him. He is the fire that keeps the vegetables boiling.

Accept others just as they are—don't just *tolerate,* but *accept* them as they are. It is not for us to expect something of others, nor for us to imitate others. Be yourself; accept others; don't compare or imitate. We don't know how others are struggling or what is within them. So the things to be done are: (1) make everyone your own; and (2) rather than finding fault, look within and see your own faults. At the same time, it is good to be self-critical, but not too self-critical.

The first step in spiritual life is to never talk about others. Be like the bee and not like the fly. Learn to dwell only on the positive and never on the negative. Dwelling on the negative and talking about others only hurts ourselves.

It is natural that at times when we sit for meditation we feel vacant. All things come—dryness, disturbances, etc. There are many inner reasons for this in the unconscious mind that keep the heart from feeling what we strive to feel spiritually. It takes time for the heart to feel. A purely intellectual approach is not good. That is why we must pray for pure devotion.

We must have the intellectual conviction that there is no high and low before God. We are all just so many bubbles on the same sheet of water. Sometimes we think we are special or feel superior, only because we fail to see the specialities in others. Do not judge high and low on the basis of what we see; deeply spiritual qualities may lie beneath the surface. Always feel, "I don't know anything." We really know nothing; we see only superficially the tip of the iceberg. We don't know what is inside. We must feel we are nothing special, all bubbles, no high and low. Don't take the appearance for the reality. Pray to him to keep awareness in a humble, pure and spiritual way.

## March 17, 1976

Once having accepted him, it gets into the subconscious mind and is there even when we are not feeling or aware of it.

Sri Ramakrishna's play with the direct disciples was a great cosmic play. He was just giving them finishing touches.

. . .

**March 29, 1976**

When we meet with obstacles or mystifying elements in spiritual life, give the responsibility to Sri Ramakrishna. Say, "I don't know," and surrender to him. Just like a child with father: "I have to ask my dad." As Thakur was with Divine Mother, so are we to be with him. Have faith and surrendering attitude and leave the responsibility to him. "I don't know."

**April 1, 1976**

The unity of Guru and disciple is in Thakur. Without that it is like branches without the tree and the roots. No matter how close the branches are, they wither without that. The Guru is just a little ray of Thakur, part of him, non-separate.

Thakur is Isvara and Brahman to us because he had reached that level, that height. He is all gods and goddesses put together. He is the current coin, international coin. We accept all in his name.

**April 3, 1976**

Fill the whole mind with the thought of Sri Ramakrishna. While the hands are working, keep the mind busy with the thought of him. Then a time will come when the *whole* mind is filled with him; no other thought can gain entrance. I can tell you this from my own experience. The "I" in me is dead; it is all he inside. That is why the direct disciples also said, "I am not the Guru; he is your Guru!" It is because only he was inside them. It is like Jesus saying, "Not I but the Father in me." If you fill a container with honey and show it to someone and say, "What is this?" they say, "honey." Similarly fill the mind with him and a time will come when the mind is filled with nothing but him. Struggle for that.

## April 5, 1976

From us you get a little warmth but Sri Ramakrishna is He. Like the sun; there is no comparison. You must keep the thought of him constantly. Even Vivekananda was hesitant to try to say anything about him; same with Swami Akhandananda, who said that being with him was indescribable.

## April 6, 1976

If you want anything you must have both interest and attention. If you have interest but don't pay attention, you get nowhere. But if you have interest and pay attention, then you gain knowledge and wisdom.

Turn all emotions and passions towards God. Suppose someone tells you to turn the thought to God as soon as a negative thought arises—if you do it honestly and sincerely, the negative thought becomes powerless. Thoughts are all so superficial, superfluous. If you pay attention, they gain strength; if instead you turn towards God, they become powerless. His light burns them up like nothing else can.

The wonderful part of the path of devotion is that you can have joy from the start in practicing his presence, imagining his presence, worshiping him, praying to him, repeating his name. You practice devotion as you feel from within. Nothing can be superimposed; it must come from the heart. There was one boy who was a disciple of Swami Akhandananda. The swami always told him, "Pray to Thakur, pray to Thakur." But the boy told him that his mind always went to "Baba," that is Swami Akhandananda. He automatically called on him as the one closest to his heart. Swami Akhandananda told him that was all right, and the boy later became a monk. He had to struggle a lot but he always called on Swami Akhandananda, talking to him inwardly. That was his way. He said later on that he could then understand calling on Sri Ramakrishna.

Turning the emotions towards God makes the path of devotion easier than the path of knowledge. You can cultivate detachment by reminding yourself, "I belong to the Lord." You can practice seeing him in all beings. Even if there is evil, you can see it as ignorance and know that the Lord is there too.

### April 7, 1976

Keep any thought that purifies your mind.

*Tamo-guna* (darkness) is powerless before his light. That light falling, all negative thoughts vanish.

### April 11, 1976

The mind goes on creating karma by getting upset when things go wrong. Take the time to think; be detached. The way to be free from misery is to be detached, to realize the Self. It is a struggle in the beginning, but later on it becomes easy.

Just tell him, "I don't want this mess," and he will pull you in. It is just like when a baby is no longer satisfied with toys. Just turn towards him; just knock. All we have to do is extend the hand to be pulled in. Saviors reach out and pull us in. We only have to turn.

His acceptance is for us all, but "those who worship Me are in Me and I am in them." He is *akhanda,* indivisible; howsoever we approach him, he reaches us. The devotee's heart is the drawing room of God. Seek his presence in your own heart. Meet him there. All you have to do is purify and he is there. You don't even have to ask him to come. Why is the devotee so happy? Because God is in his heart. It is like Hanuman showing Lakshmana that he didn't have to pray because Rama was in his heart—"I have imprisoned him."

The only thing that matters is to give him the mind. No matter what else we give, the only thing that matters is to give the mind and heart to him. Even while offering other things, be feeling mentally, "I offer my mind."

## April 15, 1976

The best way to open up the heart is to not find fault. Finding fault raises walls. We see the world through the prism of our own minds/*samskaras*/psyche. Therefore we should never find fault. When the mind becomes pure and we see things *as they are,* then we may see faults but we pay no attention. Rather we pay attention to the Kingdom of Heaven within. The first step in spiritual life is not to see the difference; give up all likes and dislikes. Then the heart will open up gradually to the spirit of love and service.

## April 16, 1976

Thakur is the vine and we are the branches. This is true in a more particular and immediate way than the Vedantic or cosmic sense. Christ, Thakur, etc. are all one vine. They appear as different for the devotees' sake. But we do not create them; they already exist.

The ultimate truth is that God is formless. The forms are from the standpoint of the devotee's mind. Yet in the relationship with the Personal God, it is a two-way traffic. Just as we love him, so he loves us. In fact, if we take one step, he takes nine. His love and concern for us are stronger than ours for him. As we are devoted and love him, he feels the same, only more so. He loves us in that same personal way. He can't help it.

## April 22, 1976

Regarding interpersonal difficulties, don't try to understand; just love everyone. Even with God, we can't understand; just love him.

The feeling of distance or blockage comes because of subconscious contents of the mind. Bring them under control and learn to direct the flow yourself.

## April 23, 1976

Overcome jealousy as Rakhal did. First get the intellectual conviction that everyone is God's own child. He is there in the hearts of all. Learn then to be more considerate, thoughtful, forgiving, no matter what anyone says. Just feel that they do not know. Spirituality demands self-same attitude: no differences, no discrimination. Learn to look on others with a pure eye.

## April 24, 1976

Devotion to God is all that counts. Things like selfishness and egoism will not stay if devotion is there. Pray for that and keep the mind on that and other things will go away. What matters is who we *are,* not what we *do.*

## April 26, 1976

Never let the ego swell. Be yourself first, but feel one with all, knowing we are all one before Sri Ramakrishna. As he was the child of the Divine Mother, so be his child and just say, "I don't know anything."

## April 29, 1976

Ups and downs of the mind will naturally be there. But remember one thing: you can clean up thoughts from the past, but let nothing happen now which you will regret later on. Prayer helps a lot.

True renunciation is renunciation of the ego.

## May 2, 1976

While absolute unity is the ultimate Truth, at the existential level we need God and his grace. We only have to turn towards him. It's just like a baby with mother. She knows what the baby needs as soon as the baby looks at her face. It's just like that with us and Sri Ramakrishna. Just take everything to him. We are one in him.

## May 7, 1976

It doesn't matter what work you do; what matters is the attitude with which it is done. Dedicate everything to God. Keep the attitude of helping people. Objectify the work itself; at the same time be concerned and try to help people. We can convert others with our pure attitude. Everything can become spiritual if you spiritualize it yourself. It is all subjective. The more you fill up your mind with spiritual thought, the less trouble you have with other things. It is like pouring cement —keep pouring and gradually the ground becomes firm and you can walk. As Sri Krishna said, bow to him, pray to him, worship him constantly. The road may be covered with pebbles; it may be like walking on the razor's edge. But the alternative, if you leave the road, is the ditch on the side—one ounce of joy for a ton of misery.

. . .

**May 12, 1976**

Leave everything to Sri Ramakrishna. God loves us more than we love him. The God of devotion is true. Devotion and knowledge are not contradictory. The epitome of that harmony is in Sri Ramakrishna's teachings. He includes everything, the Revelation Supreme.

Use mental exercise, discriminate, but leave the burden to him, don't take it all on yourself. Surrendering is the best thing. "I don't know. Reveal yourself to me."

The Self is given to us on lease, as it were. But we can own it. How? By becoming God-like ourselves. The easiest way to become like that is through devotion. The best is devotion that includes knowledge, never knowledge without devotion. How to be God-like? Love and sacrifice.

**May 13, 1976**

The moment we surrender, he accepts it, but our struggle is to keep turned toward him and never to raise walls.

Sharing is the thing; no hatred or jealousy, but sharing.

**May 14, 1976**

Be generous with others, in his name. If you see all people as his children, then you become more broad and don't oscillate between attractions and aversions. Instead you generate love, which is the most powerful force. Be like Holy Mother—all are your own, or at least all are his children.

Just pray, "Mother, lift me up. I want to be spiritual."

## May 19, 1976

Take it literally that Sri Ramakrishna is your mother and father.

## May 21, 1976

The thought of Sri Ramakrishna is a spiritual detergent. As you fill the mind with that thought, a new *samskara* is created. But you must be patient and perseverant. You can do anything in his name. As we fill the mind with the thought of him, other thoughts become helpless.

Incarnations are born already perfected. They struggle for our sake. This cannot really be understood until we get the Light. The best is just to pray, "I don't know, reveal thyself to me." "Avatar" means "descent." It is the total descent of God into man. Incarnation is one who has no human limitation, totally divine.

## May 24, 1976

To love and serve purifies the heart faster than anything.

The psyche is one's own knowledge and experience, unfulfilled desires and ambitions. Behind that is the Pure Consciousness. The psyche is nothing more than the coloring or scent that remains in the form of smoke after burning incense. What we have to do is resolve all the impressions that form the psyche. It can be done. Things may cling to the mind for some time but they can be resolved if we keep turned toward God, knowing they are there, but jumping with that awareness toward God.

We can never destroy Life. Life is one. Only body is destroyed. When the mental impressions are all resolved, there is no rebirth.

If we keep three things in mind, then all negative tendencies stay down. (1) Who he is: He is our Ground. (2) What the temple is: It is his place, the body of Ramakrishna. (3) Who we all are: All are his children.

Keep the thought that you are doing his work and then there will be humility and a feeling of oneness with all. When you come and go from the temple or the Vedanta Center, stop in the sanctuary and think of him. Create a spiritual psyche.

Swami Akhandananda said they never felt bad if Thakur pampered Rakhal or Naren. They all knew they were one with him. If the branch is one with the vine, then how can there be any question of high, low, this, and that?

Regarding negative tendencies, like desire for power, etc., devotion to God is like a protection on which they bounce off. It's like how we aren't afraid of lions in a zoo because the partition is there. Similarly, the negative tendencies may be there in the mind but don't be frightened when they show up. The name of Ramakrishna is the partition. Even bad thoughts will go away if we keep up his thought.

## May 30, 1976

The highest experience means no loss of individuality, but the individual becomes the whole. The finite becomes the Infinite. A salt-doll melts but is not lost. It becomes one with the ocean, it becomes the whole, *purna*. Every realized soul is infinite.

But a realized soul becoming one with the Infinite and an incarnation becoming one with the Infinite are not the same thing. Something happens in an incarnation's oneness with the Absolute that cannot be explained. It is so beyond the capacity of human explanation. The cosmic power manifest in Sri Ramakrishna's giving the highest experience through mere touch is something possessed not by saints, but only by saint-makers. Madhusudana Saraswati described Krishna's Vrindaban play as the Absolute playing and dancing. Same with the Divine play of Sri Ramakrishna. He is still alive.

The soul realizes oneness with the Infinite when there is absolute purity of mind—no urge, tendency, modification, nothing. But in the process don't be frightened by negative thoughts, because they do not touch or taint the Self. Dark clouds come and it seems as if they will never go away. But hold on, the night is passing. That is our hope! Be patient, be persistent. Progress may be slow but hold to the ideal. Negative thoughts are the real obstacle in spiritual life. The way to overcome them is to surrender to God. Every promise of Krishna in the Gita is literally true. Whoever thinks of him with no other thought is saved. His devotee is never lost. Blessed are those who believe in God.

## June 2, 1976

More important than any external penance is the feeling of togetherness and "we." When we say Sri Ramakrishna is our Ground, it means that he is always with us, watching us, not as some judge "out there" but as our own inner guide. Feel one with all, move as one with all, but the inner content is different. The more you have that feeling of oneness, simultaneously you will feel more indrawn.

When negative thoughts come, turning the mind towards God means giving the mind an outlet. You don't stop its flow or build up pressure through suppression. Rather you turn its course and give it an outlet in a positive direction.

Swami Vivekananda's ideal—"for the illumination of oneself and for the good of the world"—is a new ideal, not the old ideal of monasticism.

## June 3, 1976

Just pray if you want to become like a child before Sri Ramakrishna, as he was before the Divine Mother. Devotion and relationship must be cultivated. You must add fuel just as you do to a fire. In this case the fuel is regular practice. Once you have that, nothing else can bother you; all obstacles fall away.

To be the child of Thakur, Mother and Swamiji means to accept the whole world with a loving feeling.

## June 12, 1976

Monism is true, and for the monist his only strength is to stand on his own Self. But the personal God is true too, and it is the truth that if you take refuge in him, he takes full responsibility. Look at Sri Ramakrishna's life. He practiced dualism —did he lack anything? No, he got everything. Even after *nirvikalpa samadhi* Thakur called it "the absolute form of my Divine Mother."

## June 16, 1976

How to gain self-surrender? Don't plan or scheme. Just take one day at a time and leave everything in Sri Ramakrishna's hands. Say, "I don't know." Never judge; be constant in prayer. Do work with the idea of renouncing everything to him (Gita 3. 30). It is not what you do that matters but what your motive is. He sees that before we do any action. In a garden, we dig and plant and pluck the flowers to offer to God in the shrine. Similarly, wherever you work, just think you are doing your part and give the fruits to him. Especially if you work at the temple or the Center, consider everything you do within those four walls as his work. Put everything on him.

And do it with self-same attitude (again Gita 3. 30). That is, don't look down on anybody. Rather make everybody your own. Keep a smile and a loving heart and remember him constantly. Again, if you are working at the temple or place connected with the Center, remember constantly that we are his representatives. We must try to present his ideas and ideals in our own words and actions. Never say one negative word. Learn to be silent. Don't let any negative thought touch the heart. Look to the good in everybody and then love will come forth in the heart.

Be flexible; learn to adapt and adjust to every situation. Then you will be free from the anguish in the heart that comes from being too rigid.

Surrender comes from always remembering Thakur and Mother and thinking, "What would they want me to say or do?" Think of Mother's complete acceptance and love for all and try to become like that—like when Christ's disciples felt, "Not I, but Christ that liveth in me."

Be responsible and willing but not rigid. Be flexible. Know that others are trying to serve in their own way, as we are in ours. Never compare or compete. He alone sees the heart. We don't have to prove anything to anybody else. Just remember him and do everything for him.

We must learn to hold on to Sri Ramakrishna. He is our eternal support. We have to know that everything else, including the Guru's physical presence, comes and goes. But as Sri Krishna promises, "My devotee is never lost." Do not fear anything. Sri Ramakrishna is our Guru, our support, our security. We feel fear because mind clings to a lower level, but if we go higher and cling to him there is absolutely no fear. The thing is, if you are true to him and if you make everybody your own, you will never be lost in life. As we are standing here talking now, he is hearing! And that is in more than the Advaitic sense. With the incarnations it is true in a more personal sense.

**June 22, 1976**

Never argue with anybody. Spend the time thinking. Rise up through yielding. People are more important than efficiency. Ask yourself whether you care for things or for people. Care for people and never on any account hurt anybody. Care for people, not the results. If you have power, don't exercise it. Never be enslaved. Always ask yourself the question whether you are enslaved or enslaving. Never be light-minded. It is the worst enemy. Don't lose yourself.

**June 23, 1976**

The best prayer is to pray to Holy Mother, "Mother, please make me just like you are."

Always be objective and detached. Then you can know the truth about anything, including the Self. Without that objectivity no scripture can help you. With that, you need no books at all.

Be detached by giving your whole heart to God.

**June 27, 1976**

It doesn't matter whether mind tends to think of Sri Ramakrishna in concrete form or whether it tends more toward the formless or transcendental. Whichever way it moves, just keep the idea that they are not different—just like water and ice.

If you are working at a temple or ashrama, whether you are cooking, cleaning or whatever work, you must remember that it is all his work and think of him or else the work loses its meaning. Don't mind what anybody says, praise or blame. Simply give or offer whatever you can and don't compare or compete. Just remember him and consider it as his work. No work is unimportant.

### June 28, 1976

We don't actually "please God"—it's just that divine love makes the whole being naturally flow towards him.

### July 1, 1976

The beauty of Thakur and Swamiji is that there is no contradiction in their teachings between impersonal and personal God. When reading *Jnana Yoga* or Swamiji's *Complete Works,* wherever he says "Brahman" or "Absolute," you can put "Sri Ramakrishna" there and find no contradiction.

### July 2, 1976

Self-analysis and trying to correct oneself is good, but not self-condemnation. Tell your mind not to think negatively; do not look down on yourself. Pray to Sri Ramakrishna to shower his special grace.

Duty is only the midday sun scorching the soul (said Swami Vivekananda) when it is at the mundane level. But if you spiritualize duty, then it becomes karma *yoga* instead of merely karma. Krishna laid the highest emphasis on duty but it was in a spiritual sense. Duty is not a question of what is thrust on us but what we accept, what we promise and therefore must fulfill. "I have accepted this duty, therefore I shall fulfill it." It is at the level of conscience. It is not *what* you do, but *how* you do—not quantity but *quality* of work that matters.

## July 5, 1976

Philosophically, Swamiji's, "I am That," is the truth. But emotionally and spiritually it is best to feel, "I am Thine. I am dependent on Thy grace, Thy mercy." Thakur himself never once said, "I and my Mother are one." He always kept up that wonderful attitude of devotion of the child.

When we pray to Thakur and Mother, yes, it is imagination. But we are imagining based on somebody's experience—not false imagining, not pretension. It's like digging for a well—you have to imagine the water first in order to start digging, and then imagination becomes reality. And they (Sri Ramakrishna, Holy Mother and Swamiji) were here not too long ago. We pray based on the experience of those who have seen them. They illumine us, but we have to stretch out the hand and ask for it. Ask and it shall be given, seek and ye shall find, knock and the door shall be opened. But we must stretch out the hand and ask. If our hands are closed tight then nothing can be given.

## July 6, 1976

Tension comes from inner conflict, like seeing a dichotomy between spiritual and secular. Negative things are always to be avoided—lust, anger, greed, etc. But when it comes to work, do whatever comes to you. "Whatever needs to be done, I am there to do it." Just be spontaneous and natural and relaxed. Spirituality is simply making natural life *more* natural and perfect. It is nothing separate from the rest of life. Creating separation causes tension. Spirituality is in the mind. The same mind with which we move in the world, that mind we offer in meditation. So if I want to offer this flower of the mind at the feet of Sri Ramakrishna, I must keep it pure constantly, now and forever. Be alert and let no dirt fall in. Any spot coming, clean it right away because I have to wear the same dress in meditation.

He (Ramakrishna) is in Jesus, Krishna, Buddha. Any divine picture you see, he is there.

## July 8, 1976

It is not possible to understand the divine mystery of an incarnation until we realize God. We should pray for only two things: (1) that he keep us free from divine illusion, from maya—not even to understand maya, but just to be free from delusion; (2) for pure devotion to him.

Those are the things Sri Ramakrishna prayed to Mother for and that is all we should ask from him. In reality pure devotion is everything.

Just as when we approach the guru with love and surrender, he reaches out and accepts us, it is much more so with Sri Ramakrishna. Anyone who reaches out to him, he accepts in an individual way. Just as Sri Krishna says in the Gita, "Howsoever they approach me, even so do I reach them." Just pray, "Please reveal thyself to me," "Help me to move towards you." That is all we can do. We cannot penetrate the Divine mystery. We can only struggle to purify our minds and pray for pure devotion.

. . .

## July 12, 1976

The story of Ramlala, like many other episodes in Sri Ramakrishna's life, is a Divine mystery. It is a fact, but it cannot be explained with logic. We can only accept it on faith because it belongs to a realm of an intensity of devotion which is beyond our understanding. Similarly, the relationship between Thakur and Mother is also a Divine mystery. Only when we rise to the realm of that pure love can we understand that Divine play at all, that wonderful love between them.

We must always have conscientious consciousness. Keep the consciousness of your spiritual purpose in life. Don't identify or lose yourself in the environment. Keep your individuality, raise your mind up, never let the mind go down. It is a habit we have to create, a new pattern for the mind.

Surrender completely to Sri Ramakrishna. Just put everything on him instead of worrying about things. The mind is such a mystery, yet it is also so simple—in the sense that it is absolutely pure before we put so much junk into it. Now, instead of trying to clean it bit by bit, just pray for devotion. That is like knocking down a building with one blow. Pray for devotion and leave everything to him. When you work, periodically dip the mind in devotion so that it doesn't become dry.

Always have a positive approach, both to others and to yourself. Even if the worst thoughts come, just say, "They will go away," and never be dejected or depressed. Be joyous and peaceful. Never find fault with others; when you see your own, say, "I'm glad I have seen it," and then clean it. If dirt falls on your shirt you simply clean it right away; you don't cry over it.

When working anywhere just be careful to remember Sri Ramakrishna. *Be* good rather than trying to *do* good, and then good work will follow naturally. Never try to please God by doing work; just try to *be* good.

## July 13, 1976

Surrender is a matter of free will in the sense that it simply means turning the mind towards God. The same mind that we have given to mundane things, we must now turn towards him. Don't worry about things. The whole world is covered with mystery and it's best just to feel, "I don't know," including when the worst thoughts come. Simply say, "I don't know," don't worry, but give the mind to him. You won't get to the East by turning to the West! Learn to leave everything to Sri Ramakrishna. If the mind is filled with the thought of him, old *samskaras* get resolved in his Light.

What does a child do? It wakes up in the morning, lies there and waits for mother to come and feed her, bathe her, clothe her. We must cultivate that same childlike faith in him. Faith means, "This is it." When we have that, we must just pray for pure devotion. When faith enters we have only to wait, and it is devotion that makes us dynamic.

The thing is to make our devotion pure, unmixed with other things. We must discover from within, with the teacher's help, what is the nature of our faith and then nurture that relationship with God. Whatever faith and surrender you have, nourish and strengthen it. Whatever comes to you to do, just fulfill it, free from mental fever, and leave everything else to him. When such a big support is there, why should I worry? It's like if there is a big ship and you want to get aboard and there is a rope hanging down. You hang on and climb up. He is that ship, the mantra is the rope. So hang on to that and you will never be lost. *Sri Ramakrishna arpanam astu,* "I surrender everything to Sri Ramakrishna." Conscientious consciousness means to keep up that thought always.

The most important thing for peace of mind is to turn towards the positive, in myself and in others. Never find fault or poke holes. Be like the bee that seeks only honey—look to the best, to the positive. Let a thousand people say a thousand things—just say, "I don't know"—refuse to look to the negative in anybody, for your own peace of mind. Let the dirt be on the road but not on me. Dirt may be there but let it not get into my heart. And never compete or compare. The fingers on one palm don't compete or destroy each other, and together they make a wonderful team and a very firm grip, with the little finger being very powerful in that grip. Also, never compare, do whatever you can. I shall be me. Do whatever comes in a calm, peaceful, loving way and leave everything to him.

## July 14, 1976

Be simple and natural in prayer as if he is just right there. Reading is good but at the time of prayer put off all big ideas, philosophy and theology and attributes. I don't know and I don't care! Whatever Thakur's children have told us, that we accept and that is our faith. To that faith we must add devotion and move towards him. His children told us, we have seen them, and that's that. We take it on authority actually. Put everything else off, just turn to him in a natural way and pray for pure devotion, for surrender, for selflessness. That's all. We don't know anything except that the love in our heart flows towards That.

. . .

## July 29, 1976

Surrendering really comes when we realize the real meaninglessness of temporal things. We come into the world with nothing and we leave it with nothing. Look squarely at it and cultivate the intellectual conviction of the meaninglessness of everything. After conviction we begin to feel that he is our only support, and then real surrender comes.

## August 1, 1976

Put desires squarely before the mind. Look at it and have the mind look at the consequences along with the fulfillment of the desire.

The whole secret is conscientious consciousness, to keep the mind with us, constantly alert. We must keep it where we want it ourselves. His name is our only support. Just say, "I don't know anything, I take refuge in thy name." Then repeat his name with that consciousness. Pray to him that as he touched Naren, as he touched Vijnanananda, "Please touch me."

We must imitate Holy Mother's attitude in life. She accepted everything—all that work, all those people—as part of a process and she felt that all were her own. That comes from total identification and no individuality. We are to try to feel the same.

## August 7, 1976

(The swami calls this his "spiritual codification.")

- ADC: Never accuse, demand, or complain.
- LRC: Love, respect and cooperate.
- DDD: Devotion, detachment, dedication.
- SSS: Seek, surrender, serve.

**August 10, 1976**

In spiritual progress we gradually move from the physical to the psychological level. In the thought-world we must resolve all modifications, urges, tendencies—gradually empty the mind of all thoughts through concentration on Sri Ramakrishna. In contemplating him, it is not as if he is a thought. Rather he is the pure Brahman Itself. Form is just for the purpose of our contemplation or we couldn't think of him at all. Form is but a mask covering Pure Consciousness Itself. Slowly all other thoughts die down until it is just him.

We must have detachment. Real love is detached love. It broadens to a wider perspective, there is less thought of self.

Most important is to feel that he is the way. As we drive on the road there are mountains and ditches on either side, but if we keep our eyes on him we will go straight to the goal. That is the meaning of Jesus' saying, "I am the way." Sri Ramakrishna is the way. All we have to do is to keep our eyes on him.

To open the heart, first we must feel, "I don't know anything." Then, to feel, "Thou knowest everything."

When we lift the ego and put everything on him, we feel so light. No burden, worry or anxiety. We become like children and enter the kingdom of heaven—childlike and guileless.

If you complain you will never become one with him. If you want to become one with him, never complain. Understand and adjust. Forget yourself, care for the rest.

**August 15, 1976**

We are just like the direct disciples to him if we can say, "I love you, I take you to my bosom. I shall constantly think of you. I shall keep that promise and you do the rest." Put the mind on the Fire and the water will boil, but it takes time. Don't worry, keep his thought constantly, in every action, every thought, everything, and leave the rest to him. And keep off all selfishness. Always feel, "It is thy work I am doing."

There is nothing like God's name to purify the mind. Pray for the surrender of the kitten. No matter how much junk is in the mind, if we apply the detergent of his name and the thought of him, everything must come out. Let the bad thoughts come. Just say, "I have taken your name, I shall not be afraid of anything." Pray, "I don't know anything," and leave it all to him—our part is to keep his thought.

**August 17, 1976**

Take ten pictures of yourself at different stages of life. Looking at them, try to know what is the constant "I" through the changing body and mind. That constant, that Ground, is That which is in Sri Ramakrishna. He represents that Light. Just as canals are fed by a river—you may not see the river but that is where the water comes from. We are like canals fed by water from the Divine River, and That is what Sri Ramakrishna is. Through *nirvikalpa samadhi* he had become one with It. He was always on that threshold. It is like when Jesus said, "I am the Life." Sri Ramakrishna is that Life within every being, the same Life, the same Light within all. Yet he is both personal and impersonal. To the extent that we can't understand it, just pray, "Please reveal thyself to me."

## August 20, 1976

There is a turning point when the mind can see what it doesn't want. As to where we are going, pray to Thakur, "Please reveal thyself to me." We will be safe if we hold to the ideal of Thakur/Mother/Swamiji. But don't take anything for granted. Most important is to be constantly alert and conscious.

Leave everything to Sri Ramakrishna. When the mind has trouble discriminating, just pray, "I don't know anything; please make me the way you want it to be."

Cultivate the attitude that everything we do is for his sake. Do everything in his thought, renouncing everything to him, and then life will never be monotonous. Pray constantly. "I know what is right but I don't do it; I know what is wrong but I can't avoid it; please be seated in my heart and guide me. I make mistakes day and night. Please guide me constantly. Don't leave me alone."

Thakur and Buddha reveal the exact same Truth. Buddha from the point of mind; Thakur from the point of Spirit and God. Thakur is God and nothing but God. Wherever you touch him, you touch God.

## August 26, 1976

We are all radii, all branches, but some know and some do not. Until we realize for ourselves that we are on the Vine, it is like branches and sub-branches. Then finally we realize there are in reality no branches at all. For us now the guru is real and we take God on faith. Later God becomes real and the other becomes apparent. We are all in That actually.

Whenever we try to understand, we don't understand anything. Only one thing we need to know: He is our everything. We don't know who he is. In the Gita, Krishna leads Arjuna to the point where he says he is beyond all dualities. It is the same with Thakur. Only pray to him for pure love; we don't understand anything. Who he is, who we are, what it is all about. Pray only for pure love; pray to him for what he prayed to Mother. The goal of life is to become one with him and then by the same logic we become one with all.

## August 30, 1976

Pray to Sri Ramakrishna. He can work miracles. He worked miracles while he was alive. He worked miracles after he died. Just pray to him for pure devotion. That is the best prayer and the only prayer.

We are all one. To possess means to enslave and be enslaved. Rather love and cooperate with all. "Whatsoever you do to the least of these, you do unto me."

## August 31, 1976

Give up all likes and dislikes. Whatever comes, do it with joy. It is all his. Whatever you do, remember it is his.

A man like Tota Puri, through great one-pointedness, could have the knowledge of transcendence without having attained the knowledge of the immanence and manifestation of the Divine. The real knowledge is to know both. The man who knows the Divine becomes fearless and all-loving, equal to one and all. He who knows only transcendence doesn't understand and may fear the world. But he who knows the immanent as well isn't afraid of anything, moves with fearlessness in the realm of maya. He doesn't grow two horns but becomes all-loving. Those who know only the transcendent must come back; they are not yet perfect because there is still isolation and separateness.

**September 3, 1976**

Just keep his thought constantly and everything will work out. Don't worry, just turn to the positive. Don't find fault but see your own faults, but not in a negative way. Loosen your hold gradually, through detachment.

**September 5, 1976**

The emphasis is to be on sharing and cooperation, never on comparison and competition. As Holy Mother and Thakur accepted all with their individual approaches, so those who are close must be like that too and that will help his cause. "The more the better"—sharing and cooperation.

**September 6, 1976**

Keep Sri Ramakrishna's name on the lips and keep Holy Mother before your eyes.

**September 9, 1976**

The high water mark of our closeness to Sri Ramakrishna is our acceptance of others and trying to help all according to individual needs.

Never, never react. Cultivate perfect calmness under all circumstances.

Sri Ramakrishna's religion is one of joy and mirth, never gloomy or dry. Be peaceful and happy. The more we are close to him, the more we feel joy and peace.

Be constant in prayer, in alertness—every minute, just like when you are driving.

Incarnations are like huge rockets of tremendous spiritual mass, orbiting around the Sun of Divine Consciousness. The name and form are Truth itself because the incarnation is the Ground itself—God and nothing but God.

Thakur used to stammer so sweetly, out of fullness. He would take the boys walking and tell them what is what. They hardly asked any personal questions because with him it was like all doors and windows opened and he saw so clearly—he answered everything without their having to ask. They felt they were walking with God himself. There was no room for any doubt. Even when he was so sick, they were just aware of his divinity. After he died, the feeling of separation was only momentary. Like Mother did, the boys realized he had only passed from this room to that room. They visualized him when they wanted to and sometimes even without trying. The real resurrection is his continued spiritual presence, in name and form in the spiritual realm—a whole different realm, more real than the world of the senses.

## September 10, 1976

Pray always as Thakur prayed, "Oh Mother, give me pure devotion. I don't want anything else. Give me pure devotion—You know the rest." Pray for that and leave the rest to him.

Everything in this world is relative. The only absolute is God. So be tipped off by nothing in the relative world. When things come, say firmly to the mind, "Oh mind, you belong to God!" And don't move away from that. We take false steps when we take our eyes off the goal, off the road, and look to other things. But if we keep our eyes on him, then nothing else tips us off.

Always act with the thought, "What would Mother do?" If we think of her in that way we partake through her grace and her being.

Most important is to let nothing negative get into the mind. See the dirt but don't take it into the mind. Just say, "I don't know." If someone else does wrong, pray for them and feel also, "I may be wrong." But don't put anything negative on others, on the person. Be loving and accepting, no matter what. Don't accept anything negative.

Just by living the life, everything comes naturally. If you want to go to New York, simply follow the directions and drive carefully. But if you just say, "I want to go to New York," and don't accept the process of getting there, then you never get there. Same with spiritual life. Follow the teacher's directions, live a pure life, be constantly alert and prayerful, and you are bound to reach the goal.

We are all zeroes actually. Only the One is. As Mirabai said, we are all *prakriti*; there is only one Purusha.

## September 12, 1976

We cannot put down egoism and pride ourselves, unless we humble ourselves before him. We can't do anything without that Pure Consciousness/God. As Thakur prayed, "Mother, I do what you make me do, I say what you make me say." It's like boiling vegetables; they boil only because of the fire beneath. We can't overcome any of our negative tendencies without humbling ourselves before God. When pride comes we must think: from the subjective standpoint, I can't do anything but for God; from the objective standpoint, I can't accomplish anything without the help of others. But the main emphasis is to feel, as Thakur did, "Mother, I am nothing without you." He could have said as Sri Krishna did, "I am That." But he chose to remain the child of the Divine Mother. With his constant awareness of the Divine Ground, he always had the awareness that nothing could be done without Mother.

Consciousness and space are interwoven. As you can't think of any object without the idea of space, similarly with consciousness. As you can't separate heat and light from the sun's rays, so you can't separate consciousness and love from the Divine.

As we feel we are children of Thakur and Mother, so we must feel that all are their children. Then the heart expands. It is true because That exists in and through all. We are all one in truth. There is in truth only one mind. But we feel separate due to individual knowledge and experience. That constitutes individual minds. In a room there is only one space. But if you burn three different types of incense in different parts of the room, for a time there are three separate smells, but only for a time. When knowledge and experience are resolved, the individuality merges in the One. Resolve it by feeling, "I don't know anything." And that is the truth—our knowledge is far surpassed by our ignorance.

## September 15, 1976

In *Ramakrishna the Great Master* it is explained that Sri Ramakrishna was in the state of *bhavamukha*. Incarnations, established in *bhavamukha* as historical personalities and confined to one time and place while alive, become *sarva-*

*mukha* when they die. Released from physical name and form, the historical being becomes a cosmic force, the all-pervasive spiritual essence. Anyone who comes out of the enclosure, including people of other religions who come out of the sectarian enclosure, can realize him.

Though our true nature is divine and God is within seeking to illumine, it is an unanswerable mystery why it is so perilous to tread the spiritual path, why it is so hard to keep straight. The only way is to strictly and exactly follow the teachings of the illumined souls—no deviation according to the use of our own intellect. The only way to God is through these revelations. That's why they say, "Follow my commandments," or as Thakur said, "Just do what I say." We must follow their teachings as best we can.

### September 16, 1976

When any negative tendency comes, be aware and be prayerful. You need not do anything else. Don't be afraid when they show up. Just be glad you are conscious of it and be prayerful. They are the enemies of the wise.

The way to become selfless is simply to care for others. Feel that others come before me.

### September 17, 1976

When we are trying to see the Divine in all and we see someone ugly or evil or vulgar, know that it is like water in the ditch. It appears to be mixed up with the dirt, but in reality the water is pure. If you distill it, no dirt is mixed in. If it evaporates, the sun's rays take up the pure water, it goes up to form the clouds, comes down as rain, and we drink it. When it evaporates, the dirt is left behind. If they were really mixed up, you couldn't separate the pure water. The Self is just like that. It is never impure. Divinity is never lost. Any soul can be purified now through spiritual intensity (e.g. Girish). God is present in everyone. The negative is just in the psycho-physical complex, which is always changing. God alone is real and unchanging.

Swami Jagadananda used to say that everyone is realizing God. That is, there is in reality nothing but God. Therefore everything we see is God. With every pulsation of thought we realize God, only we do not know it. The thing is to know it. Knowledge is power and that we gain through spiritual struggle, by putting our mind on him. Finally we go beyond his name and form and realize that everything is God.

Everything is a beautiful blending of *purusha* and *prakriti*, spirit and matter. But as Sri Krishna said in Gita, he is the Knower in all. We are separate from the point of the psycho-physical complex but the Knower is one, the same in all.

The man of realization sees the same world we see, same diversity, etc., but he sees it in a different light, as he sees the same Light in and through everything.

## September 22, 1976

The more we turn to Sri Ramakrishna in our struggles, the more strength we receive from him. All thoughts come because we have past impressions. But whatever comes, simply put it at his feet. Say, "I don't know *anything*," and pray for pure devotion.

The meaning of religion is that the same One is in all. Differences are only temporary and superficial. Realization is to know that no one is different from me.

Sri Ramakrishna and his disciples, and their disciples, and so on are like a tree and its branches and its sprouts. We get the sap through that connection. What we receive from the Guru comes from that tree. We need have no fear because the Source is eternal. Thakur is in touch with the Cosmic Force and is eternal. The force of an incarnation is tremendous.

## September 30, 1976

At times we are open to God but then we close up again and feel so miserable. The way to keep open is through prayer. But the opening and closing is part of the process. We simply have to bear it, just as Sri Ramakrishna did in his struggle. Just keep praying to open up and to *keep* open.

## October 1, 1976

Don't let anything get you down. Just hold on because every problem that has a beginning also has an end. Forbear. Forbearance is most important in spiritual life. Only one thing has a beginning and no end and that is Enlightenment. Even that in reality is not a beginning; rather it is something we forgot but now we remember.

## October 6, 1976

The best way to gain pure devotion and the feeling of being the child of God is constancy. That is also how to avoid having a leaky jar. We lose devotion because we put the mind on other things. Only if we keep water on the fire will it eventually boil. It's very scientific. Keep the mind on him and everything comes. Therefore constancy, constant thought of him, is most important.

. . .

## October 7, 1976

You can't always have holy company. Therefore cultivate the practice of God's presence because he is the best company. We must be able to have that peace and joy when we have no company at all.

When you feel drained or dry, use hymns to cheer the mind.

If you have to work in the world, know that it is not the nature of the work that counts, but the attitude. The whole universe is his and so is your work. Just feel that it is Sri Ramakrishna's work. If the work itself feels somehow out of harmony with you, objectify it, be detached, look at it objectively, even with humor: "See what a thing I must do!" It's all a part of evolving.

Most important, while at work or anywhere, is to keep the thought that everything around is a constantly changing pattern, so don't be attached to anything. Just think of the Ground and don't get attached to the changing patterns. Above all, be detached.

To think of God as Mother is not making something up; it is simply thinking of God in terms of what we know. We are imagining on the basis of what we have read or heard from those who have experienced. Blessed are those who can imagine. Gradually our imagination becomes realization and then we find that not only is God Father and Mother but much more than that. The psychological becomes the spiritual.

## October 9, 1976

When the mind is agitated and you can figure out what you don't want but can't get hold of what you do want, the thing to do is pray for guidance: "I know what is right but I can't do it; I know what is wrong but I can't avoid it; please be seated in my heart and guide me."

Or, "I don't know what is right for me; please guide me." The more we sincerely open up and feel the prayer, the more inspiration comes from within.

When surrender and feeling don't come, we simply have to keep trying. It is like squeezing a tube of toothpaste to make it come out. At times the passage gets blocked by mundane or sensate thoughts; we must keep trying. As we sincerely pray, karma gets worked out through that prayer.

Devotion to God can burn up anything. Look at St. Augustine and Girish.

Shift the burden to him. "I have taken your name—you are responsible." I don't know anything; it is for me to pray for guidance with sincere feeling.

## October 11, 1976

While it is true that "nature functions" and functions according to law, it is also true that there is Divine intervention beyond nature and its laws. We have seen examples in Sri Ramakrishna's life. He did it and is still doing it. As far as consciousness goes, spiritual laws are operative and they are different from natural laws. In that realm, we have to exactly follow what he says. Follow the commandments, and leave the results to him. We are to surrender like kittens. Just pray and keep praying and then let Mother do her job.

Detachment means don't identify with anything but God.

Holy Mother said that for those who come to Sri Ramakrishna, "Everything is finished." That is true because it isn't easy to come to him.

Whatever is left of *samskaras*, simply pray to him to burn it.

## October 25, 1976

We must not let go of the control of our mind even for a second, because if it goes off the track, then we are lost; we can't think at the crucial moment. But if we keep control constantly then it is like trained horses who can be controlled at any moment. We have to be the driver of the mind and senses rather than being dragged by them.

To gain intellectual conviction we must study avidly, especially Swamiji's *Complete Works,* because an unconvinced mind cheats us. We must keep the mind constantly awake, alert, mindful, and try to gain conviction about what we are seeking. Where there is a gap in our conviction, due to past *samskaras* and uncongenial environment, then we have to recognize the limitation of our intellect.

At that time, say, "I don't know," and surrender. We have to learn to shift our burden to God. Self-surrender is not easy, but it comes in the beginning on the basis of the experience of others. We take their word, on the basis of what they have become by surrender to him, and we try to surrender like that. Don't rush or be hasty; just pray for surrender. Confess any weakness to him and pray to him for that surrender.

## October 27, 1976

"Enter into thy closet, shut the door, pray in secret." Take it easy and be natural and spontaneous in prayer.

Time factor in meditation is not the thing; intensity is what matters. Don't waste time in the shrine. If you can't meditate yet, mix japa, prayer, and hymns. Just try to keep the continuity of the thought, and that in a natural, spontaneous way.

Feel that you have all the time in the world. Feel free and relaxed and then talk to him as a child with mother. You can say anything—have no fear—even make demands of him. Pray to him to help you cleanse your mind, like a blowtorch does. See the thoughts and pray, "Why do you put these things in me? Make me pure and clean now!"

If there is dryness or tension simply get up and read a book. Never drudgery or monotony.

Don't harbor any negative thought even for a moment, especially about others. We just don't know. Refuse to see anything but the good. Keep the slate clean and fresh and be inclusive.

## November 1, 1976

The way to overcome any negative or unwanted thought is to renounce it through detachment. Tell the mind, "Not for me —I don't want that." Tell the thought, "I don't want you."

## November 2, 1976

Holy Mother says, make everybody your own. Thakur says, nobody is your own. Between these two statements rests everything. Nobody is your own because we never know when the bell will ring for us to get off. But while we are here together, we can live in peace by making everybody our own. When we realize God, then we know that in truth we are all one. Really, no one is a stranger.

Thakur is an unlimited ocean that can take away the sins of all. But he will make us bleed. It's like a rich man saying he will pay off your debts. You will not be arrested, you are freed from bondage, but he makes you work then. We have to earn every bit of it through our spiritual living.

The point is not whether he takes our sins and suffers on our behalf. The point is that he has shown us how to help ourselves, how to follow the spiritual path. The only thing required is attentiveness. One careless moment and we can fall to the bottom of the stairs. When you walk on the road in the rain, you carefully keep away from the curb to avoid being splashed by a passing car; in the same way, when you have to move in the world with worldly people, you have to be constantly alert. You have to be strictly set internally as well as externally. Any sensate or worldly thought coming, you must nip it in the bud immediately. Be alert, be mindful. Then you are safe. With a few years of that mental training, you will be safe anywhere.

The best prayer to Thakur is to give him the mind and say, "You color it just according to your dye." We may not know how the mind is to be set. So just ask him, "You color it just as *you* want it to be." Surrender to him completely.

Avoid possessiveness or else the spiritual becomes personal and you lose the ground. There must be sharing, acceptance of all as our own.

Like the bee who seeks only honey, refuse to pick up any negative thought. Refuse even to listen to anything negative, because those things get into the subconscious and later on allow you no peace. Don't secularize the mind. Keep the spiritual goal alone always in the forefront and let everything else come and go without letting it touch the mind.

Thakur, Mother and Swamiji are the new Trinity—Thakur to straighten the Spirit, Swamiji to straighten our thought, Mother to straighten our life.

What a wonderful divine mystery are Thakur and his disciples! Each one was so unique in his own way. It's as if they were close to the shore, so he pulled them in and then sent them to pull others out of the mire.

**November 3, 1976**

Austerity means denial of mental and physical enjoyment. It means to minimize your wants, to be satisfied with whatever you have.

Meditation means to hold the mind and to observe the mind.

Absolutely avoid all light-mindedness when with people outside the spiritual atmosphere. Keep in mind constantly what you are and what you are for. You must keep the ideal bright before your eyes always or else you will be lost. The more you have to go out in the world, the more you must keep the mind within.

**November 7, 1976**

It isn't that the mind *changes*; it gets *purified*. If we turn the mind to God every time our negative tendencies show up, they gradually lose their power. The thoughts remain but become powerless. The best prayer is, as Thakur prayed, "Oh Mother, please give me pure devotion." Devotion to God can burn all negativities. What is needed is renunciation and detachment. We must open the heart to God, turn towards him, and then his Light can get in.

**November 8, 1976**

There are three things common to all devotional mysticism: (1) transcending the senses, (2) unity of existence, and (3) going beyond time, space, and causation.

You must break the cycle with strong will-power and detachment.

Apply Occam's razor to life: cut away all non-essentials. Reduce all wants to the barest minimum, whether material things or knowledge or anything. Waste not, want not. Those who have faith in him will never lack anything.

**November 9, 1976**

Serve and sacrifice for others, in the name of God. That is true religion.

**November 10, 1976**

Whenever you want to straighten the mind about something, pray deeply. Our prayer dives within and reinforces the subconscious mind. Thakur said that sincere prayer is definitely answered.

When you take God's name, remember what he represents; remember that this life is unreal, God alone is real, and that he dwells within us. It's like having a million dollar check that you can cash at any time, but it only helps you if you remember it is there.

When you come and go from the center/temple, remember and keep the continuity of the thought, "I come here only for God."

**November 14, 1976**

Sometimes when we try to overcome an obstacle we get an intense reaction. We struggle, the cloud becomes darker; but if we continue struggling without giving up, the cloud goes away. The best thing to do is repeating God's name (*mantra japa*). Mantra means "protective thought" and it will protect you against negative reaction. Repeat Thakur's name with alertness and feeling. Keep his face before your mind and feel, "Where else can I go? What else can I do? Please keep my mind at your feet."

God is our Ground, he is our own. But it is hard to believe this fully until we realize God. At present we depend on our faith in his words and in the words of others. Turn the mind to God and the clouds will go away. Say to the negative thought, "I know you are strong but not as strong as God." Then repeat Thakur's name, picture his face, and feel as if he is looking at you, and place your mind at his feet.

## November 17, 1976

The more we open our hearts before God, the more our bonds are loosened, our mind becomes more pure and selfless, and our contentment grows. It is like coming out of the enclosure to bask in the sun. God knows our prayer even before we pray to him. He is much more anxious to give than we are to receive. We take one step and he takes nine towards us. It is like baby asking mother for something she is already preparing. Mother is more concerned for the baby's welfare than the baby is. She prepares food for baby even before the baby cries with hunger. God knows what we need before we ask.

The other most important thing is: as you pray, so must you conduct yourself. If you pray for purity, then act like a pure person. Don't just ask Thakur for help; try to be like him. Combine your prayer with corresponding conduct.

## November 24, 1976

Let God talk to you. A drowning man simply lifts his hand and looks up. All we have to do is look up and God takes care of the rest. Just close your eyes and picture Thakur and Mother. Repeat his name, keeping everything else off from your mind.

### November 25, 1976

The more we love God, the more we understand him. To love is to know; to love is to realize; to love is to become one with him. And when we become one with him, by the same logic we embrace all. When a fire burns high, it also expands horizontally. So also with love of God. But we must love him intensely, under all circumstances. For that we must pray. It doesn't come right away. Pray as Thakur prayed, "Oh Mother, I don't want anything; just give me pure devotion." In him are both *nitya* and *lila*. Worship him and you will understand both the Absolute and the Relative very clearly. But what is required is to love him intensely.

### November 27, 1976

It is true that renunciation comes due to God's grace, but we can receive that grace by opening our hearts to God through prayer. Not necessarily aloud or using words, but simply to turn the whole being towards God in silence. To be a child and feel, "Here I am before you, I am helpless, I don't know anything, please make me pure." Prayer means to simply turn the whole being towards God, or to Thakur, or to the Divine Mother—whatever comes naturally to us.

### December 2, 1976

The silent prayer is not contradictory to the usual prayer in which we use words and talk with God. But sometimes a child just goes to the mother's lap and looks up at her face and doesn't say anything.

Sometimes we have a spiritual ideal and we know through reason and are logically convinced that something is bad, but still part of the mind goes there. It is because of the instinctual portion of the mind, based on past habits. Superego is the ideal; id is the instinctual; ego is in between and is lost if swung to and fro aimlessly. But if the spiritual ideal is there, the ego (conscious mind) can hang on to that. The thing is that as we intensify spiritually we also intensify past *samskaras,* the instinctual part. All we can do then is hang on to the spiritual ideal and bear it. Devotion to God can burn everything.

## December 3, 1976

Pray for just one thing. First admit, "I don't know anything." Then pray to God to be with you and help you keep your mind at his feet. That is the best prayer.

One demon (*asura*) tried to run away from Krishna because he dreamed that Krishna would kill him with his *chakra*. But everywhere he ran he saw that *chakra* coming at him. So at last he ran to Krishna himself and took refuge at his feet. Where else could he go? Pray again and again, *Tasmāt tvam eva śaraṇam mama dīna-bandho* ("You alone are my refuge, O friend of the lowly"). Repeat this again and again.

Struggle hard, pray, surrender, and leave the results to God. What you do now will determine your future.

## December 11, 1976

Struggle will be there, the fight will go on, because things have to be worked out, but don't fight alone; fight along with God. Just be careful. We can't afford to look to the negative side of anything. Look only to the positive.

To be alert and careful is good, but don't be worried or anxious. Obstacles will come, but don't complain. Don't pay attention to them. Watch out for them and be cautious, but then drive on. Just follow the road. Equip yourself well according to the instructions given; drive well and drive carefully. Let all things come, just keep driving straight. Right now we take the ideal on authority, on faith, because we haven't seen it. Even some of Thakur's disciples didn't go to him in the beginning for God. They went because they were drawn there and didn't even know why. They were as if dragged irresistibly.

**December 16, 1976**

We can base our spiritual life on Sri Ramakrishna's life and the fact that he told Naren, "Yes, I see God more clearly than I see you." It is Thakur who fulfills what Krishna said about how few there are who know God in reality. Not only did Ramakrishna know God, but those who followed him experienced God too, and others are continuing to do so.

In spiritual life, negative thoughts do come. The old *samskaras* come up and resist being put down. All we can do is repeatedly say, "No! Enough! Not now! Not for me!" Pamper the thoughts and they become strong, but continue to say no to them and they realize that they are not welcome here. We have to use discernment and dispassion (*viveka* and *vairagya*), which means to keep saying, "Not now, not for me." The only way to do it is to be constantly attentive to the Divine.

If you are jealous of someone and want to overcome jealousy, the best way is to love that person.

Holy company is like being baked in divine warmth. Unconsciously we are lifted up and protected.

### December 20, 1976

When *prārabdha* karma comes up, it cannot hurt you, but it can threaten you. When it comes up, it is like four lanes narrowing down to one; there will be roadblocks and obstacles. But that doesn't mean you have to stop or risk falling down. You just need to go slowly, follow the signs to the lane that is open, and drive slowly and carefully. You may be delayed a little. Be awake, alert, mindful. That means constancy in the thought of the Divine.

### December 21, 1976

Thakur said to a disciple, "You have the grace of your Guru. Why should you fear? Take courage. He who has the grace of a guru cannot be drowned in the ocean of worldliness, even though storms of craving may arise. The Guru will lift him up." That is more true than anything, especially the grace of an Incarnation of God. If we stake everything on that, we can never be lost. If we have that help, we can bank everything on it. That is for sure.

### December 24, 1976

Purity of heart means wholesomeness—that means, no separation. Only impurity causes a feeling of separation. Purity of heart means to feel that all are One. When Jesus says, "Seek ye first the Kingdom of God," he is asking us to feel that all are children of the same God.

"Blessed are the peacemakers for they shall be called the children of God." Here "children of God" means those who are completely selfless, those who have no thought of themselves.

"Righteousness" means that which is good for all which, even when universalized, is still for the good of all.

We have no peace until we seek peace for all. If we seek peace only for ourselves we may get momentary satisfaction but then we soon become miserable again. But if we seek the same peace for all, then we enjoy real peace. Don't say "me," say "us."

Always think that God is by your side. Be absolutely fearless. Don't be afraid of anything. Be like the bee; pick up only the good and the positive everywhere.

## December 28, 1976

Like physical pain, any mental suffering—worry, anxiety, tension—is an indicator that something needs to be attended to. Find out what it is. Ask yourself if you have control over it and what you can do. If it is something over which you have no control, because it depends on something outside yourself, then find a way to adjust with it. Never must your peace and joy depend upon any object or person outside yourself. If they do, you become a slave. Suffering is better than slavery. If it is something over which you do have control, then cultivate that control and firmly tell the mind what is what.

The way to keep away a holier-than-thou attitude is to always remember Thakur. Everything is really his. That thought keeps egotism away.

One day at Baranagore, Swamiji argued in favor of non-dualism in the morning and in favor of dualism in the afternoon. But with regard to Thakur, we are all pure dualists because no one, not even Swamiji, could say, "I am one with Thakur." It is a dualism beyond non-dualism.

There was one monk who read only the *Kathamrita* ("Gospel of Sri Ramakrishna"), nothing else. If you have faith, then even one book—whether *Gospel, Gita* or *New Testament* —can deliver you. But if the intellect demands satisfaction from all angles, then you need other things as well. Swamiji's *Complete Works* contain the world's wisdom. Thakur is our "President," Swamiji is the "Commander-in-Chief.," we are his soldiers. He is our hero. If we find him too demanding, we can go to Mother.

## December 29, 1976

You can do Thakur's work throughout your life without losing your ground (1) if you have devotion to him and (2) if you work with a humble and detached attitude. Stay out of petty and political matters, and keep the mind on the spiritual. Have no personal attachments. Be kind to all, but in an impersonal way.

# 1977

### January 1, 1977

When there is a "dark night," pray to him, "Make me your own," "Please be with me." The dark night will pass.

### January 2, 1977

[From a lecture on "The Mystic Touch of the Divine," in honor of Kalpataru Day] Their touch lifts our consciousness, their highly charged Divine touch. It is not confined to that time alone. Those Divine Beings remain forever in the cosmic conscious state. To receive that touch there must be preparation from our side. What we have to do now is knock, seek, think of him, face him, fill your mind with that Divine Personality and you will receive that Divine touch. Jesus said, "I will come again."

Not only do they touch and illumine people, but they also leave behind certain instructions to follow in order to receive the Divine touch. Thakur said, "Whatever I say, do it." Jesus said, "Follow my commandments."

Holy Mother's raised hand is always present. Just move towards that, bend down and you receive her grace.

Even now Thakur is here in our very presence—not out there, but in our hearts. Residing within us, he will touch us, but we must first become humble and deny ourselves, and then we experience his touch. Therefore Kalpataru Day is meant for us all. Let us go to him, seek him, and make ourselves humble. He is anxious to illumine every heart. In every soul he is present. Look within, keep away from all negative aspects, straighten your mind. If you take one step he takes nine steps toward you. But we have to turn the mind inward. His is a mystical touch, it is a fact of experience. Start the New Year with that God-consciousness. Like the devotees who went to Kashipur, go to him and re-create that scene in your mind.

The living God is right here in our own shrine. All we need do is go to him, bend down and humble ourselves before him. He is present everywhere. Where three are talking, he is the fourth. We need to only turn our minds toward him and seek his grace. Thakur is the embodiment of all gods and goddesses. All spirituality is present in him and in Holy Mother.

The word "nun" should be spelled "n-o-n-e," because to become nothing is to become something. We must deny ourselves, humble ourselves, give up all ego and give up vanity of learning. What is most important is introspection, contemplation, prayer, diving deep and living a spiritual life.

## January 5, 1977

To be spiritual doesn't mean to be dry-faced and morose. On the contrary, it means to be happy and cheerful. It means to be natural, but in a positive way. Be happy, do anything, but keep in mind the wonderful example of Sri Ramakrishna. Religion is simple. It simply means to feel one with all. It is that which binds us together and makes us feel as one. When someone asked Sri Ramakrishna how we know if someone has realized God, he said, "Does the person feel for people? Does he love all people without any selfishness?"

Religion manifests in our actions. Karma yoga is not a discipline on the fringe of spiritual life. No, it is at the very center of it. Meditation, devotion and discrimination are meant to enable us to act unselfishly. Holy Mother's life was the demonstration of that. We have to learn to *live* spiritually, not merely read and think about it. Make everyone your own. Don't find fault with others. Whenever you see any evil, just pray, "May I not be like that," and see what you can learn from it. But don't condemn the person. If we hate, we imbibe the hatred.

Avoid any idea of self-importance. It's not that *we* are needed; rather we need *him*. It is for our own spiritual benefit that we help in the work at a Vedanta center. Thakur doesn't need anybody. The work will go on without anyone, but it is for our good. So do your own work, contribute in whatever way you can, and leave all the responsibility to him. Be very humble, because we are all equal here. We are all his children. When you go to work outside the center, that is his work too. Detachment comes in feeling that it is his, and therefore you should do the best job you can. Always feel, "How can I help?" When you help others, you really grow.

## January 8, 1977

Keep the attitude that others have done their work, what is left is now for me to do. Take responsibility but don't treat it as a burden. Practically speaking, it simply means to set priorities and do what you can. There is no unfinished work. Whatever you do will purify you. At the same time, every work has some imperfection, so don't ever think that what you have done is perfect. To avoid egoism, keep a prayerful attitude and surrender everything to Sri Ramakrishna. As for help from other people, blessed are those who come and blessed are those who don't come. Never be upset; always give others the benefit of the doubt and take everything in a positive way. Find joy in doing your own duty.

**January 13, 1977**

Never be a slave to anybody. Never try to please others for a smile or a favor. Never expect anything from anybody. If there is no expectation, there will be no disappointment.

Love all, care for all, but in a detached, impersonal way. Don't do it in order for people to like you or for them to do you a favor. That's the way to slavery. Always feel, "I don't expect anything from anybody," and don't be a slave to anybody. The best way to guard against this is to be always alert. If you are slavishly trying to please others, then forget about God-realization. How can you surrender to God if your mind is elsewhere and you are selling your soul to them? Constantly ask yourself: "What is my motive?" Carefully analyze whether you are seeking some favor and thereby making yourself a slave. Be the slave only of God. Seek to please only God: "I am Thy slave." He is a jealous God. Give your whole heart; if you don't, he feels, "You don't really want me," because you have surrendered to something or someone other than him.

Swamiji's surrender to Thakur meant so much because Swamiji was so strong. He found fault with everyone else, but in Thakur he not only found no fault, but he found the fulfillment of everything—and in Thakur he found tremendous love. As Thakur placed his doubts before Mother, place your doubts before him. Things can't be understood merely through logic.

The way to enlightenment is to love him. And we *can* love him even though we don't know him. Many loved before realizing and *then* the realization came.

## January 16, 1977

In spiritual struggle one must exercise one's will, which is the power of assertion. On the rational side we have the ideal. But 90% of the mind is in the emotions wanting to go down. At such times, exercise the will. When the mind is torn, objectify it and ask yourself what you would tell your best friend, and then follow it. Or think what Thakur would want and follow that. We have to be conscious or else the will slips off unconsciously until we get a slap.

The mind becomes sensate if it focuses on the body, but it becomes spiritual if it focuses on the spirit. It is for us to decide where to place the mind. We have the power to do as we will. If you exercise the will, you gain great strength and rise ten feet tall. Summon the will through prayer. Pray for strength of the will and for pure devotion. If we summon the will through prayer, through surrender and seeking and resignation, we get grace from him and that strengthens the will, until finally we realize that he is within us. Be strong in the thought, "I have taken his name," just as Thakur felt, "I have taken Mother's name."

God and God's name are one. This is discovered by the illumined. Hence mantra is powerful, sacred and secret. It leads us to the Spiritual Ground. The beatitudes are mantras, they are the revelations of Christ. They protect us, they help us to grow, harmonize, and become one with the Ground.

**January 18, 1977**

To get over the obstacle of ego, which is not as simple as it sounds, the first thing is to analyze the ego and to realize how fictitious and temporal are the identifications that we make. We have to try to gain the intellectual conviction of what we really are, behind and beyond all these little identifications.

Cultivate the sense of "we," prior to the state of "not I but Thou." Try to get the feeling of being the child of God, and most importantly, that *all* are God's children. There is no room for envy, jealousy, feelings of inferiority or superiority, power-seeking, domination, etc. To feel that all are the children of God is to feel that all are exactly the same, regardless of the differences, which are only apparent. The truth is that all are exactly the same divine essence. Jiva *really* is one with Brahman, not just in imagination.

**January 19, 1977**

Even when you positively resolve to overcome an obstacle, it does take time to resolve it, especially mental obstacles. But the most important thing is to hold on to the devotional aspect. If you keep devotion to Thakur above everything, then everything will straighten out. Just feel, "I love him, not anything or anyone else."

**January 20, 1977**

Comparison, competition and jealousy creep in when we forget why we came to spiritual life. The goal is to be close to Sri Ramakrishna, period. If we look to anything else, we are gone. We forget why we came to spiritual life because of lack of discrimination and spiritual living, thus we slowly slip from the ideal. We must keep looking straight at him, keep the spiritual ideal strong and not lose ourselves in secular thoughts.

## January 21, 1977

If you keep putting your mind at the feet of Ramakrishna, he will build up the bedrock of spirituality in your mind. Just keep up the attitude of surrendering everything to him. Feel, "I don't know anything." Confess your ignorance and your lack of strength before him and surrender to him. You can't go wrong if you put your mind at his feet. As long as there are missing links in your conviction, just pray. "You know me better than anybody else; please guide me. Please give me strength. Please keep me pure."

## January 26, 1977

To root out attachment we should always ask if the thing that is attracting us will bind us. Can it give us any permanent joy and satisfaction or is it just momentary? Look at the consequences.

The main thing in spiritual life is to live your daily life working in a humble, egoless way. We don't know *anything*. The only way is to surrender constantly to God and leave the rest to him. Let any obstacle come; just hold onto him and it will pass away. We don't know how he does it. Just look at him: "Here I am. I surrender to you. Please make me the way you want me to be. Keep me in you lap. Keep me clean. Away from you I may become dirty. Keep me close to you. I am Your child!"

. . .

## January 28, 1977

When we call on God—even when we don't know who he is or how to think of him—he knows every bit of it because he is Consciousness. Not only that; he responds through his love. *Sat-chid-ananda* is a term full of the meaning of who God truly is—Consciousness and Love. If we sincerely turn to him, cry to him, he responds through his Love. He purifies us from within. His grace will bear fruit in time. It doesn't matter if we do not know—*he knows!* He hears even the footfall of an ant.

## January 31, 1977

Cultivate humility by having respect for your superiors, love for equals, compassion toward your juniors. Humility comes if we learn to see the same divine spark in all. The differences we notice are only superficial. We have to learn the art of seeing all as equal, as one.

Just as Thakur said he could never become unconscious by thinking of Mother, who is Consciousness itself, similarly we will never become unconscious by thinking of him who is the instrument of purity and divine Consciousness itself. Those who always think of Sri Ramakrishna will never go off track. Just do the right thing and leave the results in his hands.

## February 7, 1977

We cannot afford to be negligent. We must keep our mind on the Divine. The two things necessary are intense devotion and constant remembrance. We may be moving in a dark tunnel, but we should move fearlessly with full faith in him. He is calling us from the other end. Be happy in his name; don't worry about anything.

The only way to practice spiritual disciplines, as explained in the Gita, is the path of surrender. It is like going on a journey. If there is no marked path, you may go here and there, or in circles, and be lost. But if someone has made a road and painted white lines on either side, you can then follow it. The road between the white lines is what is called the path of surrender. The incarnations are like the engineers who have made the road and reached the end. Then they look back and ask us all to follow them. That is what is meant by, "I am the Way." They have trod the road, realized the goal, and call us to follow the path they have chalked out.

If we have the spirit of surrender, we can surmount any obstacle. No matter what threats or temptations present themselves on either side of the road, we can stay between the lines by keeping God in our minds. But we must keep our attention there constantly. We should never forget the goal or allow anyone to tempt us off the road. We should feel, "I am not stopping for anything—I know where I am going."

When mind is tossed up and down, all we have to do is turn to him. *Tasmāt tvam eva śaraṇam mama dīna bandho.* Remember that constantly. Intense devotion and constant remembrance constitute the path of surrender. Don't worry about anything. Depend upon him and commit to him totally.

The pure mind is like a perfectly clean glass. You can clearly see the picture behind, the Pure Consciousness behind the mind. Purify the mind through devotion to God and complete detachment from every person, thing, idea. None of these things belong to us. They come and they go. Look only to the object of your devotion and move towards that. Keep that thought consciously and constantly.

## February 16, 1977

God is s*at-chit-ananda,* Pure Truth, Consciousness and Love. This is present everywhere. Only our instrument of perception is not pure and therefore we don't see it. In Thakur it is manifest in its fullness. He is Pure Consciousness and Pure Love in its fullness. His Light can work miracles, as when he touched Naren and gave him the experience of nondual consciousness. His Light can illumine our hearts.

## February 23, 1977

When we are initiated in Thakur's name, our responsibility becomes his responsibility. His name is our refuge. The way to overcome egoism in any form is to pray to him constantly. Close your eyes and look at him or at Mother, and confess, "I don't know anything. I am confused and lost. *Tasmāt tvam eva śaraṇam, mama dīna bandho.*" We have to shift the burden to him.

Spiritual life is a commitment. He himself said, "Whatever I say, do it." In every situation we must give up our personal likes and dislikes, and think, "What would he want me to do?" We must merge ourselves in him and follow him. Make the ego his servant. Just look to him like a helpless child. Or at times with blissful feeling, "I have got you; why should I worry about anything?" Be detached and look at them, look at yourself, even laugh at yourself. Keep praying and turn the responsibility over to him.

## March 1, 1977

How we see the world depends on our own mental projection. [To women monastics]: In dealing with men, look upon older men as father, equals as brother, youngsters as son or little brother. At the same time, minimize contact because in the early years, old impressions may lead us unconsciously into trouble. Protect the mind with the thought of Thakur.

When there is conflict between head and heart, follow the heart. Realization is in feeling. Devotion brings purity of consciousness. At the same time, intellectual conviction is most important because it strengthens the will. When the will is aroused, all other temptations disappear.

Thakur's birthday is the most meaningful day to those who have come into his orbit. His birth is more real to me than my own. Because of his Light, all this is lighted. Because of his Consciousness, all this is conscious. He is everything to us.

Our intellectual conviction so far is based on testimony. With that conviction, cultivate discrimination. Always think, "Where does it lead me? Will I lose my ground if I follow this?" Keep up the spirit of freedom and drive carefully; stay within the white lines means to keep the mind on Thakur.

"I am the Way," means that we should keep straight by keeping the gaze on him. It's like a mother teaching her baby how to walk. She moves away a little bit and then stretches out her arms and says, "Come on," and then baby moves a few steps and falls into her arms. It's just like that. Yes, there are many traps on either side of the road—this is meant not to frighten but to alert us, so that we will be careful to stay in the lines.

## March 2, 1977

[The swami said he learned two things from his mother which helps to keep the mind clear and calm.] One is to never judge, especially on the negative side, but to feel, "I don't know," and, "I may be wrong." Let no negative thought taint the mind. Second, never eavesdrop, because we hear only part of the whole story; we know only 1% and we imagine the remaining 99%.

If any negative impulse comes, say, "I don't know, I may be wrong." Don't entertain any negative thought but turn the mind to something positive.

**March 7, 1977**

The most important thing is loving consciousness and to feel one with all. When we repeat his name, we should feel that we are all set in him. We are all his children. Behind all apparent differences is the same pure, untainted Consciousness.

The way to cultivate Divine love is to try to love whoever you dislike. The way to improve loving consciousness is to feel for others. Never bear any negative feeling toward anybody. If someone hurts or displeases you, say to yourself, "They don't know," and pray for them instead of feeling hurt or negative.

God's love is a lot more than even mother's love—and this is not simply in the Advaitic sense. God's love is conditioned by our surrender to him. It is personal. God's love is not from the impersonal Absolute. It is him, Ramakrishna. We leave everything for his sake and, in him, everything is fulfilled. Unlike all other loves, God's love is all-inclusive. As we grow, we begin to feel that his love is greater than anything else and that whatever light we have is due to his grace. Holy Mother always used to say, "Pray to Thakur." Manifestation is "the Way."

**March 8, 1977**

Be God's child simply by praying constantly, "I don't know *anything*. Please guide me. I don't know what life is, my mind runs here and there, I can't hold you. Please hold me." Like a kitten, not a monkey: I can't hold you, *you* hold me. Go to bed at night with that prayer: "Please take away from me all ego, pride and vanity. Let me serve you, may I see you in all beings, let me be your child, hold me." Holy Mother said that those who have taken Thakur's name, consciously or unconsciously, are his children and he never forgets them.

**March 10, 1977**

Whatever happens in your life, tell that to Thakur. That is what is meant by opening your heart to God. That is how the heart is purified, because it is like putting everything in fire—everything is burnt. Tell him everything—good, bad and indifferent. As Sri Krishna says, "Offer everything to me." Once Girish was rude and vulgar in Thakur's presence. When he came to his senses, he bowed before Thakur, put his head on Thakur's feet, and said, "What else can I offer you—this is what you have given me!" Just see, Girish offered to him just what he was and Girish was purified. Girish gave the whole responsibility to Thakur. We must shift the burden of everything to him. Direct everything, passions and all, to him and everything will be deified.

**March 24, 1977**

[Regarding some spiritual seekers who were dry and gloomy, the swami said that one reason such a state comes is because of lack of higher expression.] Higher expression is to see life and people and events in a wider, higher way, never in a petty, narrow way. It means to be detached but to be concerned. Try to heighten the consciousness. Positively, this means intense devotion to God. Negatively, it means to withdraw the mind from the non-Divine and make it one-pointed.

At the highest level self-control is necessary because we have to give the whole mind to Sri Ramakrishna, not even one fiber sticking out.

Thakur's is the ideal life. His life with Holy Mother, his attitude toward his own earthly mother, everything was ideal. [The swami said he could not find any spot of imperfection in Thakur or Holy Mother. He also talked of the miracles Thakur had done in his own life.] Trust in Thakur's grace, everything will be alright.

## March 29, 1977

Thakur is our real Mother and Father and everything. The best vow is devotion to him. Be like the bee who picks up only honey, never anything negative. Don't see anyone's faults, see only the merits. You may *see* evil, but don't *pick* it up. Real religion and spirituality do not consist in how much you know but in how you live every moment of your daily life. It means to feel for others, to be broad, generous, loving, compassionate, concerned, forgiving. It means to have the ability to forgive and forget, and to love those who don't love you. If you keep that positive outlook, then you will have good meditation.

[Kedar Baba had told swami that the more we cry to God, the more he loves us and takes us to his bosom.] Mother cannot keep quiet when the baby cries. We cry when we feel our helplessness: "Mother, I am lost in this world, save me!"

Evolution is a big struggle between the conscious and the unconscious mind. The way to resolve and control the unconscious contents is to be constant in the thought of the Divine. Then nothing negative can get in. The negative thoughts bounce back and become helpless. Every time any negative thought comes, turn the mind immediately to Thakur. Cling to him constantly and turn to him the moment any negative thought arises. Then those thoughts become powerless.

**March 30, 1977**

God keeps quiet and lets us go on in our own way until we cry to him. We have to knock and seek and cry, storm the citadel of God, even demand, or else he lets us go in our own way. But as soon as we turn to him, cry to him, knock at his door and seek his help, then he responds. Then his grace and blessings pour in. Otherwise he keeps to himself.

**March 31, 1977**

Gangadhar Maharaj (Swami Akhandananda) was the first to really embrace Swamiji's concept of service. He took up the ideal of seeing Thakur in all beings, seeing God in all beings.

**April 5, 1977**

The most important thing is, "If you love me, follow my commandments." That means love, respect, service, exemplified by Christ washing the feet of his disciples at the Last Supper. Calling on God doesn't mean much unless we *follow* his commandments. "Love one another as I have loved you. As I have served you, serve one another."

Interpersonal relations are most important. Spiritual life's problems are at the human level. Spirituality is very practical. Our passage to God is blocked if we hate even one individual. We must believe the words of the illumined souls when they teach us the absolute truth that all beings are one, life is one. If we want to love God, we must love and respect and serve God's children.

### April 6, 1977

Even people who have devotion to God and proximity to great souls can miss the mark unless they struggle hard to spiritualize their own minds.

### April 8, 1977

Always think in terms of the whole—identification, not isolation.

His name is the detergent to clean the mind, where clouds have gathered on the surface. Your true nature is not the clouds. He is closer to you than your own mind. Your mind is piled up with imaginations, but none of that is in him.

Just go to the shrine in a natural, spontaneous way—not too much effort—with natural devotional feeling. Let nothing bother your mind.

### April 10, 1977

As Swami Vivekananda says, the personal God is a superstition, but until God-realization *everything* is superstition, including my own body, my own form. What Swamiji said is true from the absolute standpoint, but not from the point of spiritual development. Ramakrishna realized Brahman and came back and worshiped Divine Mother. So just as he left everything to her, leave everything to him. If the mind feels crazy, put the crazy mind at his feet. Swamiji himself said that Ramakrishna molded the brains of his disciples. So put your mind at his feet.

### April 11, 1977

Resurrection means to become aware of our own spiritual nature. That in turn means to know that everyone has the same Divine spark within. We have to cultivate that awareness. Not I, but you the Lord, and all are yours. The meaning of Christ's resurrection is that we can all be resurrected, that is, we can all realize our true spiritual nature. When Jesus says that we can get it by believing in him, it means we need to follow his commandments. Not merely to *believe* in them but to *act* upon them. This very world is heaven if we feel that all are our own, if we believe in our own spiritual nature and look to the same in others rather than seeing the differences. It is perception of variety and difference that leads to all problems.

If you have unselfish love you will never be lost in life. Trust in God and love people instead of thinking, "me, me, me." To love God means to love all. If you believe in God, believe in people. Have faith in others and in yourself.

## April 13, 1977

Keep up his thought, no matter how—whether through meditation, prayer, singing, japa, work—and try to keep his thought. Even at work, say to yourself: "I am working to maintain myself so that I can realize God in this very life." Or look on helping others as service to God. Just try to associate everything with him.

Devotion can purify *everything*. Have no fear of negative thoughts, but when they come, turn the mind immediately to God. Don't look at them or carry them even for a second. But be gentle with the mind. The mind is like a tender baby. When any negative thought comes, make it a rule to pray immediately, "Mother, I don't want anything but pure devotion to you. I am you child." God is purity itself and we have to gradually purify the mind with that thought.

The more we struggle, the more the devil dances. Like water in wood, you may not know it is there but when you burn the wood, the water comes out, sizzles, but then is dried up. So with our mental tendencies. Thakur is like a blazing furnace. Put the mind there and everything is burned up. Thakur is more alive now than when he was on earth, because then he was limited in a way by his physical body.

In the evening vespers, we sing, *Tumi tama-bhañjana hār,* "You destroy all darkness." When we pray like that, how can we ever be despondent? I have taken his name, why should I be unhappy? Rather we should always be content and cheerful. Put everything at his feet, it is his responsibility. At night just put your head in his lap: *Tasmāt tvam eva śaraṇam, mama dīna bandho*—surrender everything to him and go to sleep. Our faith now is based on the words of those who have realized. Pray for faith and surrender.

Whenever you enter the center/temple, always stop and feel, "I am entering a temple; I am a little child who doesn't know anything." Look on everyone there as part of Sri Ramakrishna. Keep that feeling that I am a child who doesn't know anything, no matter where you are in the temple.

Everyone keeps the thought of God in his or her own way. Look at Latu Maharaj (Swami Adbhutananda). He stayed at a printing press! He was absolutely free to move in his own way. But the first thing to him was when he could serve Holy Mother. To him Thakur and Ma were the same and their service came first. That was his japa and meditation and everything.

Detachment is the surest means to mental purity. Whenever a thought comes, ask yourself if it has been with you always.

No, it came at a particular time and it will go away—don't pay any attention to it.

If anyone ever told Thakur that someone was a great man, he would ask two questions: Is he unselfish? Does he feel for others?

The first thing in yoga or in devotion, according to the Gita, is nonviolence, meaning, not to hurt anyone in thought, word or deed. How to be nonviolent? Be compassionate.

Anyone coming from Thakur's shrine should feel joy, because we have put everything before him; it is his responsibility. Always try to feel, "I am happy that I have taken his name."

## April 15, 1977

When you feel lack of faith, put even that before Thakur; pray for faith. Be always happy, never feel miserable. If any unwanted thought bothers you, just pray. Remember what Mother told a boy: "Think of me." Don't feel miserable; it doesn't help.

## April 18, 1977

Never identify with negative things. Always feel and keep the thought, "I have been blessed. I have taken his name. That will burn everything."

The significance of the "five sheaths":

- *Physical:* be fit
- *Vital:* relaxation (nerves)
- *Mental:* reflection (ignore negative and move towards positive)
- *Intellectual:* co-relation (relate things properly)
- *Blissful:* all-loving

Religion means the perfection and purification of these five sheaths such that the whole being is illumined by the Atman or Kingdom of God or the Divine Spark within.

## April 20, 1977

The way to gain the feeling of taking refuge in him is to pray and pray and pray. Also, read and try to gain conviction. It is not a simple thing to gain real faith and devotion. Be positive, positive, positive.

## April 23, 1977

The way to gain humility is to feel honestly that I know nothing! Also, never be too sure about your perceptions, especially negative perceptions of others. If we see negativities in others, our vanity increases. Therefore, always feel, "I don't know." A devotee must have humility before God.

## April 24, 1974

*Advaita-jñāna,* nondual knowledge. Keep a bit of the knowledge of God in your pocket. It makes you feel non-separate; then you can't hate or hurt anybody. Keep in mind constantly that the same One exists in all.

Regarding Truth: always ask, is it true? Is it the *whole* truth?

Regarding purity: have no prejudice; keep a clean film.

Feel: (1) God is; (2) God is in all (attitude of harmlessness, compassion); (3) God can be realized; (4) I can realize God.

Anytime we identify with an existential situation, the ego swells. The ego must be *controlled*. Keep the rascal ego as the child of God.

## April 27, 1977

Spiritual life is the effort to remove all that is different from our true spiritual nature. Any other thought is not me. My true nature is divine.

You are the children of God—that is the Truth! Everything else comes and goes.

Two things we must do. One, avoid negative atmosphere and negative thoughts. Two, cultivate spiritual thoughts as much as possible and keep close to that atmosphere. The turtle is in the water, but her thoughts are with the eggs on the shore.

## May 2, 1977

The secret to mental health is organization, or systematization, of our thoughts—what to accept and what to reject, and how to correlate thoughts. Create a mental wastebasket and throw negative thoughts there. Don't harbor any negative thought. If a negative thought comes that you can't understand, throw it there and don't worry. We can't go on worrying about everything. It is like we have a big mental refrigerator. We have put rotten food there and now we are getting the smell. If you can't find out the source of a bad smell in the air then put incense there. In other words, counteract bad thoughts or unseen obstacles with spiritual thoughts.

Prayer is like removing layers of dirt above a powerful spring. The more we remove (i.e. intensify our struggle and prayer or crying to God), the more the pressure from below increases, the more response we get. And that Ground is Pure Consciousness. It is dynamic, nuclear power. The process is both psychological and spiritual. Our opening up and the spiritual response. And that Ground, that Light, is within us. We are all set in That.

To resolve negative feelings: first feel, "I may be wrong." If you are sure someone else was wrong, then feel, "They did not know; it is just ignorance." Overcome violent thoughts with compassionate attitude. The minute you resolve a negative feeling, you really move up.

## May 6, 1977

To be the child of God means to empty oneself completely.

## May 8, 1977

The best prayer is for faith and devotion. If we have faith in Thakur and Mother, that is most meaningful. Thakur's dualism was a dualism beyond non-dualism.

When faith is lukewarm, then pray for faith and thereby keep consciousness of the Mother. "Oh, Mother, I want only that faith. I will take care of myself and my mental thoughts; just give me pure devotion. I want to be your child." Don't even pray to be free from bad thoughts, just pray for pure devotion.

The real spiritual ideal is in Mother's last message to make the world our own. Don't find fault with anybody. Nobody is a stranger to you. To make everybody our own, not in a worldly way, but with that high spiritual ideal behind.

To have 100% faith in Thakur and Mother is to have everything. Salvation is assured if we want it. We don't need anything; *mukti* is nothing compared to devotion to them, their love and grace.

## May 9, 1977

In the steps to realization, the first step is to see God in Ramakrishna (or in one's chosen ideal). The second step is to realize the Beyond through Sri Ramakrishna. The third step is to see the same God in all beings. To see Ramakrishna in all beings is the highest step.

## May 16, 1977

Go to meditation in a natural, spontaneous way, with the awareness that there is nothing God does not know. We pray for the sake of unburdening our hearts, but he knows our prayer long before we utter it. The only thing is to fill our minds with his consciousness. That keeps everything else off.

You realize the Ground of your own being. At the same time you experience a vast shoreless ocean—a beautiful experience. Then you come down and realize the same divinity in all.

Obstacles to Meditation:

1. Physical.
2. Moral—you must reconcile everything. Admit, "I am sorry," if you are at fault. Pray for them if the other party is at fault. Or simply say, "I don't know," and don't judge.
3. Mental—never identify with any negative thought. *Objectify* it. Put it aside if you can. If it's too

powerful, then boldly look at it, analyze it, and then say, "Not for me."

4. Intellectual—the obstacle is doubt. We must resolve it and the way to do it is to read the lives and teachings of the saints.

## June 1, 1977

It is very difficult to understand the great divine dispensation in Sri Ramakrishna's advent. Incarnations come to illumine our hearts, for the good of the whole world. Think constantly about who Sri Ramakrishna really is.

Struggle to gain surrender and pure devotion. One moment of true surrender can burn 1,000 years of karma. When devotion comes up, along with it come humility, compassion, love, all virtues. Just pray constantly for pure devotion, nothing else. Try to feel, "I don't know anything," and surrender everything, external and internal, at his feet.

An illumined person's perception of the Divine Consciousness in all is not a visual perception through eyes. It is a feeling in the heart, as when a mother sees her son in a crowd and feels he is my own. That's how a saint feels for all people.

## June 3, 1977

Pray for two things when any negative thought comes: "Please give me pure devotion," and "Don't bind me with this māyā."

## June 16, 1977

What is needed for spiritual life are devotion, purity of mind, removal of the ego, and expansion of the heart.

Whenever we sincerely struggle and take even one step, God takes nine steps toward us, even though we may not feel it. It's like men caught in a coal mine. They know that if they make a sound, calling for help or knocking, those outside will hear and move toward them. God does respond when we are struggling and we must think like that and imagine God's coming toward us even when we can't feel it. Thakur is Truth itself and every word of his is true. So believe it when he says that God hears even the footfall of an ant, and that when we take one step toward him, he takes nine steps toward us.

### June 22, 1977

For one who is spiritually set, all individuality is gone. The only way to gain strength is through thinking of him. his name and form are one with him. So repeat his name. If any negative thought comes, repeat his name, even if mechanically at first. Then slowly that repetition becomes instinct and protects us from all negative thoughts. Negative tendencies gradually become less powerful. The minute any negative thought comes, turn to his name or prayer.

Latu (Swami Adbhutananda) put faith in nothing but his name and got illumination. When the mind wouldn't repeat, he would close his eyes and imagine himself at Thakur's feet and say, "Here I am, I am your boy; I am dirty, you cleanse me; I am yours"—just keeping himself at his feet, demanding his grace.

Purifying the mind with the thought of God is like putting wet wood in fire. At first the moisture comes out, sputtering, sometimes so much it seems as if it will put out the fire. But if you keep it there, slowly the edges begin to burn and gradually the whole piece dries out and then becomes fire itself. So when we turn the mind to God, even if we feel no results at first, keep it there and slowly it catches fire. There is no shortcut. Thakur said there is nothing like God's name. Repeat his name constantly and all delusion will vanish.

## June 30, 1977

The difference in Thakur's and Swamiji's teachings is in their approach. Thakur starts with God, helping us to understand about God. Swamiji starts with man and how to make man God—*nara-nārāyaṇa*. As for actually living the life, we look to Holy Mother—how to carry those teachings into day to day life. She is the embodiment of Thakur's teachings.

## July 5, 1977

Illumined souls see our minds as in glass cases, but they don't tell us everything they see, lest they should disturb us. There is nothing to fear. What they say, mark it. What they don't say, forget about it. Whatever they see, they have the power to purify it.

The most important thing is to surrender to God. The more we surrender, the more we are purified. The more we turn towards him, the more light and warmth we get. The more we surrender to him, the less we are troubled by what happens outside.

Accept all work and all responsibility, be intensely active, but take it easy inside. "It is all his will." The more we surrender to him, the more we lighten our burden.

Swami Vivekananda is like a huge telescope through which we view Sri Ramakrishna and all religions, philosophy, ethics, etc.

Don't try to please people. Do good, serve them, be pleasant, but don't enslave yourself by trying to please people.

Only one in a million really believes in God. Like stars in the daytime, we don't see God and therefore his existence is not real to us. Many people pay lip service to belief in God, but it is easier to reach an atheist who honestly expresses his doubt than a believer who has never thought deeply or acted on that belief.

The best analogy for Brahman is space. Like space, Brahman is vast, impersonal, everything is in it and pervaded by it. It is unchangeable. Everything in space comes and goes, but the space itself is unchanged.

Many scientists cannot accept the common idea of a God "out there" who is cast into some narrow dogma.

[The swami was asked to speak to a group of such scientists at a conference at Star Island. At first he was asked to speak without using the word "God." Having asked them what crime God had committed, the second day he spoke on "What is God." He defined God as Pure Consciousness and Pure Love, the only two qualifications of God.

God may also be called truth, but truth is only inferential, as when we peel away all the layers of paint and finish from a wooden chair, whatever is left we infer is "wood." But consciousness is experiential. We all have subjective awareness and all awareness is from God. That Consciousness is neither he nor she, but rather it. It is pure awareness. Similarly, Pure Love is unconditioned and untainted. It is spontaneous and unqualified by "if" and "but." There are no likes and dislikes in pure love; it is same-sighted and unconditional. But human love as we experience it is all conditioned. Take even a little baby—it will run straight to the mother who has held and fed and nursed it, even in the case of a foster mother. But if a foster child once finds out that is not its real mother it turns away and wants the real mother; human love is conditioned.

The swami then asked the scientists to think deeply, even to meditate, for five minutes on the idea that their own true nature, as a spark of God, is pure consciousness and pure love. After that someone raised the question, "Then why do you call Jesus 'God'?" Swami explained that one who manifests those qualities of pure consciousness and pure love we call God. We cannot understand the abstract impersonal ideas of truth, consciousness and love, but when someone fully manifests those qualities we say he is not human; he is godly; he is God. It is as if you take a cold iron piece and immerse it in fire until it becomes red hot. That iron piece is then fire throughout. Touch anything and it burns. We say, "Don't touch it, it is fire," because it performs the function of fire. So with Jesus Christ. Because he fully manifested that Pure Consciousness and Love he is identified with God.]

Vedanta teaches that the same God is within all of us. But we do not see him because of our ignorance. Ignorance is the cause of our limitations and our misery. When the Pure Consciousness within shines through our finite minds, it is distorted by the prism of our knowledge and experience, whether good or bad. We do not see clearly, do not see things as they are. We receive even the words of an illumined soul through the prism of our own minds. When Jesus washed the feet of his disciples before the Last Supper he remarked even then that not all were thereby clean. It is because man's ignorance is so deep. The time factor must work out man's evolution.

But when consciousness is purified, vision becomes clear. A man of pure consciousness sees as God sees. He sees others' minds as though in a glass case. It is like seeing through glass which has lost its glass-nature. You no longer see glass but clearly see what is inside. If you look through a dirty glass, you see the glass itself; or if you look in a dirty mirror, you see the dirt rather than the clear image. But if the glass is clear, you see clearly what is inside. But an illumined soul doesn't tell us all that he sees, lest it should disturb us; he tells us only what will help us to evolve.

## July 6, 1977

Brahman cannot be conceived of nor understood nor described. It is beyond everything. Buddha tried to understand Truth from the standpoint of two things: (1) the world outside and (2) himself. From the point of the world outside, he discovered that everything in the world of matter and mind is constantly changing. Because man tries to possess that which can never be held, he constantly suffers anguish. We feel anguish on two accounts: (1) we want to possess that which we cannot hold and (2) we fear the loss of that which we have got. But if we observe closely, we understand that we come into this world with nothing. We only manipulate that which is already here and we leave this world empty handed. Therefore, how to live while we are here together in this fast-moving train? Share, share, share. Don't deny anything to others, don't try to possess anything exclusively. We are all set in that one Truth.

Truth can only be understood through manifestation. Like all the radio waves which pervade the whole universe, God-consciousness is invisible and we don't see it. Just as a powerful instrument can tune in to any channel, we can tune our minds and experience, see, touch and even talk to the eternal Divine manifestations at the level of cosmic consciousness—Jesus, Buddha, Krishna, Ramakrishna.

Two things are needed for this experience: purity of mind and one-pointedness. There must be no other thought, no other desire than Ramakrishna. But it takes years of struggle in meditation to silence all other thoughts. Bow to him, pray to him, surrender to him, even in work keep his thought constantly. Tune the mind totally to him and you will experience his presence.

## July 7, 1977

A realized soul sees God and nothing but God, so many names and forms floating in God-consciousness. If you take a vessel made of ice and immerse it in water, there is water inside, water outside and the vessel itself is made of ice. It is just like that with God. Thakur's dualism is not the type of theology which says man is different from God. No, we are non-separate from God. He had the highest experience of Oneness but then maintained that wonderful attitude of a child of the Divine Mother. To him, God as Brahman (inactive) is the same as God the Father or Divine Mother (active, Shakti). The difference is only in manifestation or function. The same with everything—everything is Brahman—the difference is only in name and form, in manifestation.

What happened when Thakur touched Naren? That touch spiritualized his mind, lifted it from the level of sensate perception to a level where he could see the Reality beyond name and form.

In every situation think, "What can I learn from this?" Tremendous spiritual growth comes from that attitude.

When Thakur says, "All things that exist have come from this," he means not from the physical but from the infinite Indivisible behind. It is like Krishna saying that fools, not knowing his true nature, think he is confined to that form. Thakur, in saying that, is identified with the whole cosmic process.

## July 8, 1977

Faith makes the mind take the form of the object of faith, like a mold in which Pure Consciousness takes that form. As in the ocean, the cooling effect forms blocks of ice of that very water, so the devotee's faith and devotion make the Pure Consciousness take that form. What is needed are purity and one-pointedness. Mind you, ice blocks won't form if there is dirt in the water; dirt is rejected. Ice will only form of pure water. So the vision of God with form takes place only in Pure Consciousness.

## July 9, 1977

Read the *Gospel of Sri Ramakrishna* in order to help control egoism because Thakur says some strong things to bring it down. Most important in control of ego is to feel, "I don't know." Have no pretension. Don't try to please people. Be good, be helpful and pleasant, but don't try to please anyone.

Be positive. Negative thoughts will come but whenever they do, immediately pray, "Oh Thakur, may I not have that thought." If you keep the mind positive and refuse to harbor any negative thought, then you will be happy.

Avoid all comparison and competition. When anyone else gets attention or gets ahead, feel happy. Feel, "They are also mine, I am glad." Those unwanted feelings go away with the spiritual touch; pray to Sri Ramakrishna.

Read the *Gospel* with the feeling that you are there.

## July 10, 1977

The important thing is not whether people take Sri Ramakrishna's name as opposed to others who don't, but *where* their mind is, where their faith is. He is there to bless everyone, whether initiated or not. He needs no intermediary.

Japa helps a lot to purify the mind, if we do it with faith and a calm mind. To straighten the mind, when we don't even know what is bothering it, repeat his name with faith. If you want to lay a foundation and find that there are big rocks, you chip away as much as you can and then cover it with cement. Rocks may be there but they are no longer obstacles because they are covered with cement. Similarly, just bring the spiritual thought and cover the mind with that.

Pray to Sri Ramakrishna to straighten the mind. Admit first, "I don't know." Then pray to him, not in order to know what is in the mind, but just to *straighten* it. "I don't know what is in the mind, just give me pure devotion." Pray, also, as he did, "Don't bewitch me with your māyā."

Most important is self-examination. You have to ask yourself, "How is my mind working?" If it is going toward the negative, get it back where it belongs. If once you have spit something out, knowing it is not good for you, then don't put it back in the mouth.

It is true that we can have whatever we want if we have the guts to go after it. Cowards have minds full of unfulfilled desires. But be very careful about desires. Before going after anything, ask yourself those two questions: What are the consequences? Where does it lead me?

## July 12, 1977

Māyā is nothing but our minds, the contents of which hide God or the Pure Consciousness within us. The process of purifying the mind is a long and intense struggle. But once we have decided that is what we want, that I want to uncover and resolve all the contents of my own mind in order to realize the Consciousness behind, then we have to turn within, learn to be silent and introspective and constantly alert. The first step in spiritual life is silence, to look within, never to point the finger outside in criticism or complaint but to discover and purify whatever is wrong within me.

No matter the impurities, the moment you say I am sorry, I will not repeat it, that very moment you are pure.

Purification is a long struggle with its own suffering and privations. You suffer in the unwinding process just as you suffered in winding up the big ball of the mental contents. In that unwinding process you have to be extremely cautious not to wind it up again. One wrong turn and you can miss the whole thing.

How to keep from being lost in this unwinding process? "I am the Way." Revelation is the way. Hold on to God as to a big rope hanging from a ship. Examining the mental contents, seeing that devil's dance of the subconscious, keep calm and detached and hold on to God. Then you will not be lost or drift away. Go to an illumined soul who has pierced the veil of māyā and ask him, "Sir, what is the way?" Then turn within, be calm and introspective, hold on to the Divine and be constantly alert, constantly prayerful. And don't stop. Even a speck of impurity can keep us from seeing the Truth. Even if after 50 years of struggle you feel, "I have gotten nowhere," hold on and keep struggling because the mind has to be made *perfectly* pure.

Most important in spiritual life is to keep away from non-essentials. Be spiritual. Morning, noon and night, let the only prayer be for pure devotion, as Thakur himself prayed. Then everything will be alright.

## July 13, 1977

The Guru doesn't get liberation until all those he has accepted as his own attain the goal. In the spiritual realm it is when the aspirant has lifted his own mind to the spiritual level that the teacher can really help. But there must be struggle, struggle, struggle to reach that level where the aspirant can be in tune with the teacher.

In spiritual struggle we have to go through many things, sometimes fall down and get up again. Mind goes up and down, things come up, temptations are there. His name is our only hope. If we hold on to him and keep his consciousness we won't be lost. The whole bundle of karma can be burnt through surrender to God. Karma stands on ego, on self-assertion, but if we don't assert ourselves and surrender everything to him, karma becomes practically helpless.

There is no fear if we keep up his thought. Whatever we do, keep his thought in the mind. It is also true that whether we are aware or not, the spiritual teacher's heart is always with us. We need not even be near him. It is true that he continue to be so even after leaving the body. If you are spiritually sincere, that guidance will always be there and you get a wonderful feeling of the teacher's presence. It is like working in a house while someone you love is present. You may not be in the same room or talking together, but you have that wonderful feeling of the presence and company of the beloved.

The most important thing is to follow the Guru's teachings. Whatever he tells you, follow it without wavering. Acceptance must mean functioning as well as faith, not conviction but conduct, not belief but behavior. Be loving, be pure, be holy, not just crying, "Lord, Lord." Even the psychic contents can be resolved if you conduct yourself well in the social setting.

Holy Mother often said that until all her children had reached the goal she could not keep quiet.

Surrender to God. Not I, not I, not I. Then all karma will be burned. Don't try to justify your existence. Just surrender everything to God. Not, "I did this, I did that," or, "I am sorry." Put the whole burden on him. *Tasmāt tvam eva śaraṇam mama dīna-bandho,* "You alone are my refuge, O friend of the lowly"—if you can say this and keep it in the mind constantly, there is no fear.

You can prevent the return of the weeds with a fence made of the name of God. Japa has a great significance. It acts as a barrier from which negative thoughts bounce. Through constant remembrance we create a new psyche. Try for just one day. Resolve to keep the name or the thought of God constantly. You will find that many negative thoughts which usually disturb you will not get in. If we give the mind positive food in the form of the thought of God, it will not dig up negative thoughts. But we have to use great will power to keep up that thought. When we persist with the practice, negative thoughts gradually lose their power. They may come up, but they bounce back.

Holy Mother used to say, "My child, do whatever you like, but constantly repeat God's name." Slowly we discover that the mental contents are all of our own making and through our own will we can prevent becoming a victim of any negative thought. When any negative thought comes, use discrimination and renunciation. Ask, "Is it good for me, where does it lead me, what are the consequences, does it help me?" If not, that very moment renounce it. Don't harbor it even for a second. No interest and no attention; it loses its power. Turn the course of the mind. Immediately turn the mind to a positive elevating thought. Don't hate anybody, don't hurt anybody, be loving and helpful, and keep the thought of God constantly.

Asserting the ego is the cause of all our misery. Don't be a victim of your own ego. Don't let the ego identify with the wrong thing, with anything negative. The minute you separate yourself from others and assert "I" rather than "we," that moment you pave the way to hell. But if you think, "Not I, but we," you keep the ego under control. As Thakur taught, keep the "rascal I" as the servant or child of the Divine Mother, and remember that all others are the same. Remove the ego and all negative tendencies fall off; they have nothing on which to stand. Love thy neighbor as thyself means the same—not I, but we.

## July 14, 1977

Thakur's slap to Rani Rasmani was for all of us. Whenever we are in his shrine and think of anything else, remember that slap. Swami Ramakrishnananda himself, even in Thakur's presence, used to look at him and pray that he might not think of anything else. "May I not think of anything but you" —because sometimes his school examinations would be on his mind. But he was determined that when he was with Sri Ramakrishna, he would not think of anything else.

Swami Ramakrishnananda was very strict with monastics. He told them to be honest with themselves and made them get out if there was any weakness in the mind or "theft in the heart." He said, if you want to be here, don't waste time; if you don't want to lead a spiritual life, then don't waste your time here.

You may have the grace of God and Guru, but you must have the grace of your own mind as well. Otherwise, no favorable atmosphere can help you. How to gain that? Through questioning yourself, introspection. What am I seeking? Where am I going? What am I doing? Look within, and I guarantee no misery can touch you. If you feel miserable, analyze it and you will destroy it. If you can't find out, then put it at his feet. Have that faith that I have taken his name. If there is a rotten smell, put the incense of his name and it disappears.

Pray to him that you may remember him in all your actions and then everything will be alright. And constantly question within. Be serious within yourself. Be pleasant with people, but more important is inner seriousness. Be strict with yourself. Yes, the Guru will save, but you must look at him, you must knock. He takes responsibility—all concern and prayers are there, but we have to open up to him. He knows all but we have to be aware and completely open with him.

Most important is one's own thinking, self-examination, mental clearance. Otherwise we may be charmed by the externals of spiritual life but not be internally set; in that case we are gone. It is a spiritual block which is impossible to overcome as long as we have not set the mind internally. Our own conviction is most important; otherwise it is all sentimentality.

At the same time we can have joy and peace. Our devotion to the Light reflects in our joy—no gloominess or worry. Have faith in his name. Surrender the ego at his feet. Only then you get something. We are really nobody. We have to lift the anchor or we will never make it in any atmosphere.

Anyone who complains has not touched the Spirit. Pay no attention to externals. You can smooth very little externally. But look within. Set the internal and then nothing can tip you off. Don't complain. Take things as they are and do everything with his thought.

## July 15, 1977

If we heed Sri Krishna's teaching, "Grieve not over the inevitable," we can avoid 99% of our misery.

The best way to conquer māyā is to deeply probe within. Probe ego, probe ignorance, probe any problem until you get to the root of it and then it vanishes. Examine, examine, examine—deep introspection.

If you cannot understand a problem, can't get at it, then admit to yourself, "I don't know." Try to feel deeply that you don't know. In effect, then, you are not accepting the problem and its effect is minimized. It slowly melts away.

Just live a pure, selfless, devoted life, no matter where you are.

## July 19, 1977

Spiritual life means "me" must be gone. "Not I, but Thou."

You are neither man nor woman; you are Ramakrishna's child.

Never lose a heart. Always take the help of others. Cooperation is most important, never isolation, exclusion, or possession.

## July 21, 1977

Holy Mother once said, "Get your food by doing work." Swamiji's ideal is not to be a worthless beggar but to serve people, giving in return for what you receive. And there is such joy in giving.

Swamiji is the huge telescope through which to view Thakur. If we had only *Kathamrita,* we would have a Ramakrishna sect of pious shrine worshippers. He is far too vast for the ordinary pygmy mind to grasp. But through Swamiji, his teachings are interpreted to the modern mind. Holy Mother is the exemplar; she shows us how to put those teachings in practice.

- Thakur is Reality.
- Swamiji is the Interpreter/Teacher.
- Mother is the Exemplar.

One must constantly scrutinize one's motives. Everything, good and bad, in the universe is within us. It is for us to control the lower tendencies. For that we have to seriously question our own minds as to what we are seeking, why we are doing things, even though they appear to be good. Otherwise this mischievous ego gets in and slowly takes over with egoistic feeling, unconscious aspirations, and after a long period, we get tipped off without knowing how it started.

Ignore peoples' praise; he knows the heart. If people praise, pray immediately, "May I not lose my ground." Don't seek to please anybody; be true to him. Serve him. The best contribution is in living in a spiritual way, in being what you *are*.

If you question yourself constantly, nothing will go wrong. If you don't question, no God can save you. There is no safety for anyone until the end. All minds get bad thoughts. Never be frightened or depressed. Let nothing weaken your mind. But look at it, feel glad that you have seen it. Then remove the obstacle so that you can proceed on the road. If, in questioning, you detect a bad motive, don't feel dejected, just correct it right away.

**July 22, 1977**

Don't be frightened when you discover things like bad motives in your mind. Just struggle to purify your consciousness. It *can* be purified. These things do not stick to the Self, but all has to be purified before we can see the Light.

The difference between religious life and spiritual life is that religious life is externals and spiritual life is a big internal struggle to purify. Our strength is in Sri Ramakrishna's realization. He *realized* the Light and he told us we can see it and he told us what to do. There lies our strength.

**July 24, 1977**

Do work in the shrine with extreme care, as if he is there watching you. No, not "as if," he *is* watching you. Yes, in the cosmic sense he is always watching, but the Presence is more concentrated where his picture is installed. The whole ritual process at Belur Math is a real art. And that has a tremendous effect on the subconscious mind. A few minutes of intense spiritual consciousness can wipe out many disturbing thoughts and worries and also burn up much karma. It gets in and has its effect even if you don't see it right away.

Regarding egoism in the mind, pray the minute it comes. If people praise, surrender it to Thakur and pray, "May I deserve *your* praise." If unwanted thoughts come from inside, just pray right away for pure devotion. Lift the anchor. The anchor can be slowly loosened by prayer. Pray, pray, pray.

When bad thoughts come, don't identify with them. Assert your true nature as the embodiment of blissful consciousness. He who is joy, light and peace is within my heart. "If God is within me and I am God's disciple, God's child, then I should be blissful." Other things have come at a particular time and they will go away if you turn the mind to God. But one must be constantly alert that secular ambitions don't get mixed in with spiritual development. If you turn sincerely to God, bad thoughts will go away.

## July 26, 1977

When you realize God, nothing really *happens*. You rather realize who you already are. You realize that your true nature is pure awareness. Even when you leave the body, nothing really happens, because you were already dead to that, completely separate from that. But one who has followed a discipline of feeling for people may take another body in order to help people. Even as a child, then, he feels detached. He follows customs for the sake of the common good but he knows he is not all these things; slowly the light comes and he realizes.

*Nothing* is definite in the cosmos. There is change and yet there is law in the turmoil. But we can only hold on to Truth.

An incarnation is the highest love-manifestation. Free souls may take another body because they feel for people, but with incarnations, it is a mystery. They are different. Their characteristic is their love for people in the highest sense.

What you practice, that you will realize. If you practice music, you become an expert musician. If you practice detachment, you will realize detachment. At present our practice is on the basis of the conviction we get on hearing from great souls.

## July 28, 1977

After realization, meditation is natural; it is the touch with the Ground. When the realized soul is alone, until there is some interruption or some work, mind goes inside in its own wonderful mood. Until then we have to struggle to keep the thought. After preparing the mind for meditation, try to keep that thought. Think of Sri Ramakrishna within the heart, full of that joy. Or think of Light or Atman or whatever thought appeals. Push out every other thought and try to continue the Divine thought; that becomes meditation. If you can't keep it, use japa or prayer or hymns or whatever you can do to keep the thought. But keep it joyful, never monotonous or gloomy.

When we seek rest, we sleep. When we seek spiritual joy, we meditate. Meditate three times daily with the joyful feeling that we are going to think of him with our love and pure devotion. While doing japa, picture that blissful face of Thakur and how that bliss was so much that it overflowed. He is full of Divine love and joy. As we repeat his name think that we are trying to fill ourselves with That. That is our true nature.

What we are trying to do in life, in spiritual practice, in going to the shrine to meditate, is to know God. We don't know

God at present, but we do know of his manifestation as Sri Ramakrishna and from what we have heard, we believe he is the manifestation of that Infinite. So we ask him, because he has fully realized the Truth that we are seeking. He is like a red hot iron ball which performs all the functions of fire—if we want warmth we go to the burning hot iron ball. Similarly if we want God we go to Ramakrishna. It is with that purpose that we go to him, bow to him, think of him, pray to him. Think of what he was, if that one touch could give Naren the highest consciousness.

What we are seeking now is that spirituality, and thinking of him spiritualizes our mind. As a red hot iron ball gives the warmth of fire, so the thought of Ramakrishna, who is filled with nothing but God, spiritualizes the mind—every moment spent in the thought of him spiritualizes the mind. So we go to the shrine with the idea of establishing a relationship with him as the manifestation of God. We seek his grace and purification. This is a spiritual and devotional meditation, not raja yoga type meditation. Somehow keep his thought, make him the center of meditation. Pray to him to lift you up, put all limitations at his feet, tell him you have no one else, where else can you go? And he is *present* there, it is not just a picture, but the living embodiment of God.

## August 9, 1977

"Arpana" means "offering," in the sense of offering the whole being in a spirit of total dedication. For 37 years Swami Kalyanananda never looked to Bengal. He had given himself to Swamiji who, when he sent him to Kankhal to start the hospital there, told him to forget Bengal.

There is such tremendous value in selfless work—no limitation of time, space or anything—just giving selflessly. It lifts the ego and you get good meditation then.

As we move up toward God, our hearts also expand horizontally. The farther up you go, the more you see. There is only one humanity. All are one. There is no separation. Therefore we must not hate or hurt anybody—ever. If you say an unkind word, you are hurting God in that person. Similarly, any help or service rendered to others is really service to God. Most important is to feel for others. That was Thakur's index of spiritual progress: "Does he feel for others?"

Why do spiritual aspirants renounce? Not to get away but to broaden, to expand in order to include all, to be free to love all, to be a slave to none.

It is true that God provides opportunity for sincere aspirants, but then it is up to us to use that opportunity properly.

At this stage we can't go on looking for immediate response and results. Our business is to do what the guru has told us and follow the daily disciplines of prayer, japa, meditation and leave the rest to him. It is an exercise and a discipline. Follow it and quit looking for results. If the intellectual conviction is there, the real faith and devotion will slowly come. If seriousness and sincerity are there, everything will work out. The clouds of māyā have to vanish someday. They don't stick to the Self. He has made others to realize the Self —he will also make me realize it.

Prayer for others also helps, because a selfless prayer lifts the ego. When ego is lifted we touch the Ground, which is the same Ground in all, and the person in need receives fulfillment.

In the process of reincarnation, the strong positive and negative qualities of mind are carried in the subtle body to the next birth. Individual personality is not retained but the strong qualities are. The case is different with highly spiritual beings. They retain personality, completely spiritualized and of only Divine quality—like how Thakur said Ramakrishnananda and Saradananda were previously Christ's disciples. It depends on spiritual mass. And these personalities are held in orbit by the tremendous spiritual personalities we call incarnations.

When we can't understand philosophical arguments, it is alright to accept something (i.e. God has become everything) just because Thakur said it, just as a child believes, because mother and father say that it is true. Jnana yoga is good from the point of proving philosophically what the devotee says is true. But we have Thakur to call on.

If you want purity, just think of him, that's all. Just think of him and repeat his name, nothing else, because he and Holy Mother are purity itself. To think of them is purity, honestly I am telling you—even Thakur's nerves were pure, physical body itself was 100% *sattva*. Just think of him and repeat his name and then even if bad thoughts are there, they won't bother you.

## August 15, 1977

To propitiate the Divine Mother in order to escape maya and to obtain her grace means one must please God, through prayer, humble supplication—what Thakur calls weeping for God or Prophet Mohammed called crying to Allah. That is the only way because the subconscious mind is so sneaky. The thought of God protects us from picking up negative thoughts which get in if we aren't extremely cautious.

Otherwise, if we let them in in a careless way, they accumulate in the subconscious and then tip us off unconsciously later on. For that we pay a heavy price because then it is extremely difficult to straighten the mind.

Mantra means protective thought. That one word which the teacher gives, when repeated, accumulates and produces a new spiritual psyche. But negative thoughts work the same way. Therefore keep up japa while working, keep a constant prayerful attitude. If you are in a situation where bad thoughts tend to come up or old behavior tendencies come up, pray all the more. Any time an unwanted feeling comes, pray, because then the spiritual thought gets into the subconscious with the bad thought and the bad thought loses its power.

We have to be constantly alert. In the shrine also, keep the mind there. It does no good to be there if mind wanders out. If spiritual feeling wanes, read what the teacher has told you in order to rejuvenate it.

Whenever there are clouds in the mind, admit before Sri Ramakrishna, "I don't know." When doubt about spiritual life comes, just pray all the more that he will give you strength to live your life well.

Monastic life means you have to resolve many limitations. There can be no weakness. Shankara said a monk is one who has burned all his passions. You have to be alert 100% of the time, 24 hours a day, all your life.

### August 21, 1977

It is not, "Please don't bind me with your māyā," that we pray to Sri Ramakrishna, but "Please free me from all limitations." He can do it too, as his touch purified Girish. When we pray like that, we are purified by the mere thought of him, and he also responds. It's not his māyā; he isn't binding us. He is absolutely pure and embodiment of perfect harmony and universality. M. said, "You and Christ are one." But he is more than that—he is beyond all. He could embrace Christ, Buddha, Krishna, all, and not out of any social or political necessity but out of spiritual realization.

When you feel any limitation coming, move away—physically if possible, but if not, then at least mentally.

**August 24, 1977**

Don't worry about any negative thought coming. Just think of Thakur. Things come to the conscious level from the subconscious mind, but these things are all only on the surface; they don't stick to the Self. Therefore see them, even laugh at them, think, "Look what I went through." Then turn the page and don't think of it anymore. All other things were just part of the evolutionary process.

If you keep the mind clear, clean and calm throughout the day, meditation will reflect that, and vice versa. If you are agitated and edgy during the day, you won't have good meditation. At the same time, don't be too calculating about meditation. Just do it with devotion and as a routine, in a natural, spontaneous way. Put off all worries and anxieties there. The shrine is the place you have no worries. Don't calculate what has been gained, etc. Just do it as a discipline, a process.

**August 25, 1977**

Don't pay much attention to the ups and downs of the mind; just keep a prayerful attitude. Never dwell on a negative thought, because then it makes a dent in the subconscious mind. It is like grabbing a red hot charcoal. If you hold it, it burns, so you throw it off immediately. You don't carry it; you pour water right away. Praying means pouring water. You don't resolve things by thinking about them; you resolve them by praying. Then the prayer gets attached to the thought in the subconscious and, when the thought comes, the Divine thought comes with it.

Whenever you say something to people, always have the feeling, "How can I help?" "How can I make things better?" It is easy to hurt and you must learn never to do that, but always handle things gently and delicately.

**August 26, 1977**

Incarnations are beyond everything. They never lose the awareness of their divinity, even when they come down. They are always on the threshold. Thakur sometimes was lost completely in it, but even when he came down and perceived the outer world, he still had the Absolute too.

Everything perishable is like water, the Imperishable is like the beach. Purushottama (described in chapter 15 of the *Gita*) is beyond both, like the sky above—beyond, yet within —both beyond and within, even within the perishable. Therefore, though thinking of Thakur with form, think of him as the Ground of everything. Having attained that Consciousness he became conscious of everything.

**September 1, 1977**

Those who want spiritual life must be extremely vigilant because you never know when the mind may slip. Be careful *always*.

Realized souls (who have experienced *nirvikalpa samadhi*) see everything in God, like seeing fish in water. You see water above and below and all around. That is for those who have seen beyond name and form, i.e. gone beyond Christ, as Meister Eckhart said (he renounced God for the sake of God).

**September 3, 1977**

Conscience is the voice of God. It is like the gateway to our Ground, the opening, like if you poke a hole in the roof and see the sky. When we pray seriously and sincerely, as in prayer for forgiveness, we touch our Ground. That is, we touch our conscience. That is the meaning of conscientious consciousness. It is not mere lip utterance but turning inside with conscientious consciousness in the prayer. Through that opening of conscience, we touch the Ground. Thakur is there. He is everything. Everything we are saying he is hearing.

**September 4, 1977**

Did Holy Mother ever forget her divine nature? She never really forgets. A part of the mind is always aware. But at times the mind is more externalized. When the illumined ones are alone, their minds go inside naturally until there is cause to externalize. Then for the sake of others, they externalize the mind more, even say meaningless things to make people feel comfortable and at ease. But the awareness is never lost.

**September 6, 1977**

At the end of his life Swami Niranjanananda was living alone at a monastery, not of the Ramakrishna Order. He used to come to the hospital at Kankhal during the day and render some service and then he would go back. He always begged his meals, though Swami Kalyanananda asked him to take meals at the monastery. One day he failed to come and Swami Kalyanananda thought he had gone elsewhere, but when he didn't come again the following day, Swami Kalyanananda went to him and found him lying alone with cholera. He died shortly thereafter. It made a deep impact on Swami Kalyanananda and thereafter he always sent a *brahmachari* around regularly to all the surrounding monasteries to see if anyone was ill; if they couldn't come to the hospital, he would send food and medicines.

Intuition takes place once you have yourself made all preparations through your own study, reasoning, struggle, etc. Then when you have done all you can do, you must wait. And then the light flashes.

When Krishna said he is both being and non-being, that means both pure consciousness and that which is not conscious. But pure consciousness is in and through everything. In that which has no life, it does not manifest. In living beings it reflects in the eye.

Our self-awareness now is identified with the body. But when we die, what is left is our knowledge and experience in a subtle form. That gives coloring to the consciousness, as incense burned exists in space giving a fragrance to it. It is that knowledge/experience quotient which gives rise to a new birth. We take a new body to fulfill the unfulfilled ambitions, to grow, etc.

We don't remember the past because, while young, the brain is too undeveloped and, when older, the mind is covered over with new impressions. But in spiritual growth, when meditating, *everything* has to be resolved because we have to deny the ego, i.e. everything that has gone into making the ego. In that process we may remember things from the past.

Thoughts come and we don't know where we got them. Therefore never be frightened, don't suppress or repress them, but look at them with detachment, intensify your prayer and meditation, see them as last year's snowstorms and thereby resolve them. You are safe if you resolve rather than repress them.

Individuality is a myth in the sense that once everything is resolved—no unfulfilled desires, urges, etc. left—then individuality is gone. Then only the pure Self remains, the same Self in all. The only thing that differentiates one from another is knowledge and experience. When that is resolved completely, individuality is gone.

The speciality of Purushottama (Gita 15. 18) is from the point of identification. A normal human being may experience *nirvikalpa samadhi* but even that is only a glimpse in comparison. But Incarnations, even when they come down from that state, have that constant infinite awareness. They are always on the threshold and never for a moment lose that awareness of identification with the whole cosmic process. He is supreme, not only from the point of Pure Consciousness, but as a being, his awareness of what he is.

## September 7, 1977

One must be extremely careful when away from the objects of senses not to dwell on them in the mind. Be alert, constant, detached, discriminative. If you are in a situation where you can't work things out through karma yoga, the way is to put them at his feet. Surrender everything to him, empty yourself and then Light comes.

Be constant. Keep up his name and thought. That keeps negative thoughts away. That thought of him is like windshield wipers, keeping the mind clear. Otherwise, if you revolve sensate thoughts or any negative thoughts, karma is unresolved and crystallizes and then tips you off. Resolve it through sincere, conscientious prayer, prayer from the core of the conscience.

Prayer is a soul-seeking attitude, the craving of the soul for Truth, for God. It is not verbal, it is a movement of the total being and you must act in harmony with the prayer, in thought, word, and deed. If you pray for purity of heart, then think pure thoughts, keep pure speech, act in a pure way.

Why does one lead a spiritual life? What is the purpose? To dedicate totally to spiritual life. That means spiritual *living*, not waiting every moment for realization, to utilize the time well for a spiritual purpose. Problems will be there, individual and collective.

When we try to spiritualize, old tendencies resist strongly. The more we move toward the spiritual, the more obstacles will arise. The Devil is waiting inside for a chance to tip us off. Therefore we need study to gain intellectual conviction because, when we doubt, at the same time old tendencies try to attract us to the opposite.

Whenever doubt comes look at Thakur eye to eye—no doubt can remain. And never be monotonous—let the bliss reflected in Thakur's face be the means as well as the end. We must keep up spiritual joy because that will hold us, otherwise *samskaras* present a case for the opposite.

Be joyful in work, prayer, study. That on which we meditate is not dull or dead. It is full of bliss and love. Spiritual life is happy-go-lucky in the sense that devotees can have joy at every step. Any obstacle coming, put it at his feet. If Naren,

Rakhal and all those brainy boys could sell themselves to him completely, then so can we. As Swamiji said, he molded their minds like wet clay.

Make no show of spirituality. It is all inside, all secret. The best and most serious meditation is when you are alone, free, no time limit. That is the purpose of having more leisure, so meditation can be free. At the same time, don't make it monotonous. In morning meditation, if mood doesn't come, try hymns or japa or different ways of keeping the mind there. Through the day, if you sit, when you lose the feeling, get up and do something else, but keep up the trend through study or work or something, but don't give a gap. Keep up the spiritual mood always.

From the collective standpoint people misunderstand and criticize, but let nothing disturb your mind. Never react, but reflect. Be a gentleman first, then a monk. Be a lady first, then a nun. That is, speak properly, be always courteous; have love, respect and concern for all; treat all alike as friends, but always be detached and impersonal. Be neither disinterested nor exclusive. Be just like one among others, because before God we are all the same, but keep up spiritual seriousness within. Spiritual arrogance/vanity is a crime against humanity and a sin against your own soul. If you "love thy neighbor as thyself," then God will love *you*. Make all feel at home, create no friction, then you will be able to meditate, because the same mind functions in these different situations. If you hurt even one person, you hurt God; if you hate even one person, you hate God.

When temptations come, have the ability to say, "Get lost!" Once you have spit it out, don't pick it up again.

· · ·

## September 8, 1977

Dharma is that which you have publicly declared you will fulfill—you have accepted it yourself, it is not thrust upon you—and which is not contrary to virtue, that which holds us together. Once you have accepted a particular dharma—station or position or ideal in life—you may be imperfect in that, but don't give it up for something else, even though you may be able to do that other thing perfectly well. If your dharma is spiritual life, even if in the beginning you are imperfect in that, don't forsake it for something you may be able to do more perfectly.

## September 9, 1977

If you eavesdrop and wonder, "What is going on?" then the mind is dispersed. It is a reflection of light-mindedness, because if you are occupied with spiritual thought the mind doesn't wander about. If you are spiritually set, the mind is always thinking of the spiritual, constantly questioning what this is all about, what is the reality. Eavesdropping is a crime against humanity and a sin against your own soul.

First and foremost is to put the mind on Sri Ramakrishna.

## September 10, 1977

Swamiji says that monism means no Personal God to carry your burdens. This is true for the *jnani*. But so few are fit for that. Yet even for those who worship a Personal God, they must take full responsibility. Giving the burden to Sri Ramakrishna doesn't mean we become irresponsible. Yes, he is our Ground, our guide, our support, our strength, but it is fully our responsibility to follow his commandments, his teachings.

In Thakur there is no personal limitation. There is more of the Impersonal there. His dualism is something different, as Merton understood. Thakur and Sri Krishna are the Impersonal personified, without losing their impersonal all-pervasiveness, Purushottama. Swamiji himself called Thakur "supreme." We can only understand these things through our own mental purity. We have to purify and spiritualize our minds in order to understand it. Thakur is solidified Consciousness—*chidghana*. He is unified Divine Consciousness.

The mind's restlessness must be controlled. Shakti (power, energy) is there but it can be channeled into study and prayer and meditation rather than always jumping into activity. There must be regularity and you must tell the mind, "Now it is time for study," or meditation; otherwise mind will always find an escape.

When tension or restlessness come, the mind must be curbed, curbed, curbed, and trained. Don't let it fool you. When tension is there, release it through reading or singing a hymn or japa. When restlessness comes, find out the cause. Analyze the mind in a calm, quiet way—when the feeling came, what caused it, etc. If tension or depression come, ask the mind, "Why don't you take his name?" Attraction and aversion are natural, craving is natural, but never come under its sway. You have to curb it immediately. Fill the mind with Ramakrishna now. You must exert the will! You can put the mind wherever you want it but you have to exert the will.

When you see negative things in the mind, don't identify with them. Yes, mixed motives may be there. Everybody without exception has negative things in the mind, but you must never identify with the negative. What you become is a matter of what you identify with. Always identify with the positive. Yes, negative things may be there but if, through the grace of the Lord, you have got devotion, move towards the positive. Be positive. Be spiritual.

You must always be humble with all. Blessed are the meek. And never be demanding of anybody, except Thakur and your Guru in a spiritual way.

Beware of mental and physical laziness and avoidance. But when you see them, don't identify with them. Just put everything at his feet and move towards the positive and spiritual.

Put everything at his feet. That is the only way. Do everything as his work and thereby lessen your burden and gain self-surrender.

We can never say, "I don't care," about others. We are a part of the whole and must have psychosocial sense. When, later on, higher consciousness reveals, we will understand why we can never ignore anything or anybody.

## September 13, 1977

Swami Vivekananda said that the only sin is selfishness. No act in itself is bad. It depends on how we do it and with what motive we do it. God sees the heart, for he is the Eternal Witness.

## September 14, 1977

Have no problems. Just tie up the whole bundle and put it at his feet. "I am a machine. You drive it."

## September 16, 1977

Lack of higher expression in monastic life makes for gloominess. That is, we must develop the total personality and that is the beauty of Swamiji's four yogas. There must be joy in spiritual life—spiritual conversation, singing, joy in meditation. Never make it monotonous or dry.

Any negative tendency showing up, don't identify with it. It has come at a particular time and it will go. When you recognize that something is harmful to you, then strongly renounce it. Put it off or else it will linger. Truly you are none of these things. Your true nature is Pure Spiritual Ground. These things are bound to come up, but don't identify with them; just put them off.

## September 17, 1977

Man—as a human being—has no free will. As a human being he is bound by his karma. But when he begins to spiritualize his life through spiritual disciplines, there lies his freedom. There man is not the doer. He [pointing to Thakur] is the Doer. Give up all planning and scheming, just take things as they come and act spontaneously. There is no ego there. Karma is built up on the ego, but the minute you say to him, no matter what you have done, "I won't repeat it, I surrender to you completely," then karma is gone. It has nothing to stand on. You just surrender to him completely, accept things as they come and then you become egoless, spontaneous, free.

It's like St. Augustine's confessions, in that his karma was exhausted and he never repeated his lower ways. Same with Girish. Karma bound him only until he surrendered completely to Sri Ramakrishna. He who has surrendered to him should have no fear. But you must pray with absolute sincerity and earnestness. To become like that, just pray and pray and pray.

We must accept all people just as they are, whatever they may believe, and not force them to accept our ideal in totality. Sri Ramakrishna's specialty is universal acceptance. We must never make a cult of him. Let us live the life and realize the Truth. For living the life, follow Mother—forbear, forbear, forbear, as Mother asked us to do.

**September 23, 1977**

Prove your strength in purity and spirituality. Coming to spiritual life to escape worldly misery is only bad if you fail to spiritualize. Then you get into power and politics. But if you keep up study and disciplines and keep up the spiritual, positive ideal, then there is no harm in coming in order to avoid and escape worldly misery.

But beware of mental and physical laziness. Be alert! Be mindful! You must be keen to catch the thoughts that arise. Mental laziness is the greatest obstacle to spiritual life because then you unconsciously slide downhill. At the same time, never be frightened; just drive carefully. And always be aware of how your actions affect others.

**September 25, 1977**

There are two aspects to every person: (1) the child of God, and (2) the human limitation. Look to the child of God, be one with all in God. Then there will be no problem.

**September 27, 1977**

Keep alert, awake, mindful. Always beware of mental and physical laziness. And most important: never allow any negative thought to pass through your mind and arrest or attract you. Put it out immediately. The unconscious mind protests when you try to spiritualize, but you have to say a firm no. It is just like going to the refrigerator and finding spoiled cream there; you don't take it even though it is there. You have the power within to undo the whole thing but you have to strongly assert the will. And be alert. "Thine alone is the hand that holds the rope that drags thee on—let go thy hold!"

Be humble. Humble and prayerful—no argument.

## October 2, 1977

When you try to spiritualize, the struggle between the conscious and the unconscious goes on. That is the time you have to stand firm, take a stand, make a resolve, and don't yield to the unconscious. If you yield, you become a victim, a slave of it. We come to spiritual life to try to create a new psyche to help us in our spiritual pursuit. We are responsible, we have to make it.

We have to be alert and awake, and the minute old thoughts come, strongly renounce it mentally as well as physically. If we indulge it mentally, that is more dangerous than physical involvement. We have to be mindful and strongly renounce those thoughts mentally. They will come, but we have to say, "No, not now, not for me. There was a time, but not now."

We are all in a big train, moving fast. Who knows when who will get off! So while we are together, live well. Most important is to share, make all your own, and be happy together. Never lose a heart, for he is there in all. Equate yourself with the rest. Nobody owns anything, nobody brings anything into this world. Life is a lease to us and we only manipulate what he has kept ready for us. It is all God's grace. Live well and ask yourself daily, "What have I done?"

**October 4, 1977**

The way to keep an attitude of mind that doesn't resist change is to have the conviction that everything is change, everything is constantly changing. We can't hold on to any person or any externals as if they are permanent, because nothing is permanent. Yet wherever we are, we are to love all the more, be concerned, but know that everything is changing.

**October 5, 1977**

Don't have any fear. Put your faith in Sri Ramakrishna. Gita (9.22) is true beyond doubt, and tested by Swami Vivekananda too. Don't take refuge or depend on anything other than him. The way to learn it is to do it. *Śaraṇaṁ tava caraṇaṁ bhava-haraṇaṁ mama Rāma,* "I take refuge at your feet, destroyer of all mundane limitations." Put total faith in him, have no fear.

When any worldly limitation comes, don't look at it. Look at *him*. Put everything at his feet and it will die a natural death. It takes time, but you just have to do this again and again. Instead of paying interest and attention to the limitation, look instead at him.

The mind naturally oscillates between pulling you up toward higher thoughts and dragging you down toward lower things. Our job is to catch and control the mind. Instead of letting it drag us down, we have to lead it slowly and steadily toward higher consciousness.

Faith in God comes after much experience and suffering and then we stake everything on that, no matter what suffering and privation may come. A mother may be a beggar but her child stays in her arms no matter where she is. We should be like that as children of God. If doubt comes, pray all the more. Just keep up the ideal of renunciation and purity. If you want to deserve his grace, do what he would have us do. "Follow Me" means—follow his commandments exactly.

Wake up in the morning and surrender to him, surrender to him at night, and sleep in his lap.

Don't test your faith, though faith in him stands all tests. Just serve others without selfishness, narrowness or discrimination and be true to what he would want us to do.

There must be no calculation in that surrender to him. Be his child, trusting in him no matter what. I don't put any limit to that.

## October 6, 1977

When you really resign to God, nature doesn't touch you. Rather, spiritual nature functions then. As for external circumstances, you see his presence in everything. To resign to his will means always to think, "What would he want me to do?" and follow that exactly.

One boy who hadn't seen Thakur was following what Swami Akhandananda would tell him. The Swami told the boy to think of him (Swami Akhandananda) and what he would ask him to do. Then the burden would be his rather than the boy's.

## October 9, 1977

When Thakur says that for certain devotees God assumes eternal forms, that is because they don't want to merge; they want to keep the joy of communion with the Divine in that form. Of all people Sri Ramakrishna had the right to say that.

God reaches us according to our faith. When faith really deepens in a pure mind, the mind takes that mold. You see it, you can actually talk to That, and receive a response. It is a Cosmic response, you actually hear it, as Sri Ramakrishna heard and talked to the Divine Mother. That is the power of purity and devotion. It only happens when you have absolutely no other desire except to realize and visualize God in that way. Imagination leads to realization. If you understand the Ground, you do not become fanatical in your worship.

The forms of a divine incarnation are eternal. Sri Ramakrishna will exist forever. They have reached that level in the cosmic realm where they retain that name and form eternally, like planets in the cosmos.

## October 10, 1977

Sacred is anything that unites, secular is anything that separates or isolates us from the rest. All misery in life is due to separation. When we move in unison, there is peace and joy. Never lose heart. The greatest wealth is to gain hearts. But for that we must be unselfish, no axes to grind.

Exclusive spiritual life is a responsibility. Be cautious and humble and never, never react, no matter what anybody says. Don't depend on external circumstances. Take the opportunity to straighten and set the mind.

## October 13, 1977

Create spiritual unrest in the mind. Don't be satisfied with a little contentment. Swami Vivekananda wasn't satisfied with anything but the highest. He wanted to see God in everyone and everything.

Serve others out of genuine concern. Love but never be a slave to society, because society cares only for itself, not for the well-being—and certainly not for the spiritual evolution—of individuals. Worldly people only calculate how much you give and how much you take. They don't understand unconditional love. You have to be strong within yourself.

Two outstanding characteristics of Swami Akhandananda were these. One was that he was like a child in his total dependence on Thakur and he used to encourage people to rely on Thakur completely. It is very difficult to be in the world and leave everything on him, but Swami Akhandananda was like that. The other thing was his unconditional love for all people, high or low, rich or poor, no matter what. He loved all.

The high-water mark of spirituality is to love and accept all without any discrimination. Holy Mother is the only example. There is none other. She felt everyone as her own with absolutely no exception. When someone came to Udbodhan in her absence and no one gave him food, she fed him immediately when she came to know. Later she told whoever had received him that all should be fed no matter when they came. What would you do if your own brother came? Feed him, isn't it? Just like that. Treat everyone as your very own.

Don't worry about clouds. They cannot stay long. Just pray constantly to Sri Ramakrishna. Let every breath be a prayer to him for pure devotion. Pray deeply to Holy Mother, "Mother, where else can I go?"

## October 18, 1977

Īśvara is the Ground of our being. Incarnations are the mouthpiece of īśvara, who is the reservoir. Sri Ramakrishna is the huge main to which we hook up. Reservoir we don't know. We just hook up to the main and get everything. He is our only hope. No life is easy. If we externalize the mind, we are lost. But if we stay close to him, everything will work out. There is no fear. Be happy and proud, "I have got you." As Thakur had Divine Mother, so we have him.

Visions are an intensification of your own consciousness. When that becomes realization you never lose that awareness. Incarnations are the only beings that retain their name and form in the cosmic realm and can be universally experienced. Great saints may retain, but not in a universal way. You can experience their presence if you are absolutely in tune and have perfectly purity of mind.

If you struggle to lift your own mind up, you can then be receptive to good thoughts and be helped by that.

## October 21, 1977

When we offer food to God, it's not that he partakes but that he blesses. Then we take it with the idea that nothing is mine and with the idea of sharing.

## October 24, 1977

The simplest pranayama is enough for spiritual purposes. Do it as part of preparation for meditation. It gives a break from all other thoughts, as well as harmonizing the nerves.

Kundalini is Pure Consciousness behind the mind. It is coiled up at the bottom—that is, consciousness is at the lowest level—when *samskaras* are piled up on top. Then consciousness is dark and colored by sensate thoughts. As we evolve spiritually and eliminate the *samskaras*, the consciousness becomes gradually lighter and lighter and slowly moves up (that is, *kundalini* rises). Finally when everything is eliminated and even the ego is controlled, it goes to the highest, to *sahasrāra* and that results in *nirvikalpa samadhi*. This experience is the same in every yoga, every religion. You cannot but see that Consciousness everywhere if you attain that state, that absolute purity of mind.

As devotees we call on that Consciousness as Ramakrishna. He look upon it as Mother—"Oh Mother Kundalini, rise up!" We say, "Oh Ramakrishna, live in me!" And as we pray to him, we must also follow his teachings.

In all the yogas, the first step is moral perfection. For an exclusive spiritual life, this means absolute detachment from everything outside. We can't meditate if there is sensate hankering. It holds the mind, like rowing with the anchor caught in the mud. Anything outside the mind is mud. We have to be extremely careful not to indulge in enjoyment in a subtle way. That is why monks and nuns in the early stages have no external contact. Because of past *samskaras* you never know when the mind may go off. You have to deliberately, consciously, keep the mind inside. Never allow it to go out.

Be always impersonal, never indulge in personal talk and never be light-minded. Seriousness must be kept. As we control all tendencies, the mind is gradually purified and consciousness rises. That is why exclusive spiritual life requires celibate life. If you want to put the mind on something higher, it must not run out. But unless you completely control it—deliberately (it doesn't just happen)—it will always run out.

. . .

## October 25, 1977

Guru and disciple are like two bottles, the Guru pouring into the open disciple bottle. As for the bottle that pours, it isn't the shape of the bottle that matters; it is the content and that is he. Content is only he. You receive his touch by being close to him; therefore pay more attention to him.

## October 28, 1977

When the mind wavers or feels unclear about direction, just keep it at his feet and he will inspire you.

In spiritual life, never compare or feel jealous. Each is great in his own way; each finger on the hand is different. Each is *perfect* in its own way. Keep your own individual feeling toward the Guru, toward Thakur, and don't look to anything else. And feel about everyone, "They are also me." We are all one and that is the Truth.

## October 31, 1977

Lose a few points but never lose heart. Understanding is more important than who is right or wrong.

Ask the mind constantly, "What are you seeking?" Not that you are unworthy or insincere but by constantly asking, "What do I really want?" you gain direction and steadiness.

Judas and Christ are both in me, because my mind is part of the collective unconscious. And I have the freedom to choose. Physical and mental laziness makes us yield to the lower. Exercise the will to choose the higher. Evolution means will.

Always ask, "What have I learned?" If you do wrong, sin is gone the minute you realize what you have done and what you have learned. If you see any wrong or anybody wrongs you, just ask, "What can I learn from this?" That way you avoid conflict and guilt.

**November 8, 1977**

If you have a constant problem in the mind, it is like going to the doctor with a thorn in the foot which he says he can't remove; you must live with it. Therefore you simply walk very carefully, avoid bumping it; just be always extremely cautious. Socrates was very prone to anger but he never lost his temper because he was so cautious. So with any mental problem. Just be careful and avoid any situation which gives rise to it. It is good to be aware of it, accept it, and avoid it. Awareness, acceptance, avoidance. Awareness, acceptance, resolution. Put the whole thing at his feet and let him manage it.

**November 21, 1977**

Since no one but God owns anything and since we are all interdependent, we should all have an attitude of gratitude and humility and sharing toward all creation. Nobody owns anything; anything you claim, God has already claimed it.

One of Swami Vivekananda's disciples said, "Can't you just make somebody happy?" That is religion—to give help and happiness wherever you can—not to go knocking on doors but to take the opportunity when it comes.

The most important thing in a nun's or monk's life is not externals but to be self-set, spiritually set. You have to set your own goal, your own pattern, always in tune with the rest, but setting yourself within. An organization cannot give you realization. To be spiritual means to look to the spiritual side, never the secular mundane side. Always keep harmony with all because the One we contemplate daily is present in all. Therefore Mother's teaching about not looking at faults but making everybody our own is what we must try to follow. She is our exemplar. Don't be organization-minded, but strongly set your own mind on following the teachings of Thakur and Ma. What an opportunity we have got with their realization and them as exemplars!

To be honest with yourself means to ask yourself whenever any thought or urge comes, "Is it true, is it real?" "Does it help me, where does it lead me, what are the consequences?" Then you will never make a false step. All sorts of thoughts come, but with what to identify? Ask yourself those questions and then identify with your true Self. And never imitate, never compare. "I've got to be me."

**November 23, 1977**

The reason a monk or nun is far superior to any person of intellectual height is because of renunciation, most especially renunciation of the ego. First comes renunciation of externals, sensate things. Then internal renunciation of your own reasoning; you go to the trans-rational psycho-spiritual level. Then finally you renounce yourself completely and it becomes only spiritual—no identification except the Divine Spark. The first thing necessary in monastic life is to be humble. Most important is to have the feeling: "I don't know." Then you are open to receive Light.

Dedicate everything to him. No matter what you are doing, feel, "I am doing his work." It is all his work. He himself said that if one is earnest and sincere, he will help them.

**November 25, 1977**

The only thing that matters is to center all your thought in him. Alertness doesn't mean to be all rigid and self-conscious.

Be alerted to him. Just live according to his teachings. Think always, "What would he want me to do?" Or, "What would Holy Mother do?" Be filled with him. Just love him and put the burden of everything else on him. In thinking of him the will becomes strong and everything works out wonderfully well. Our prayer and study are simply for the sake of turning the mind to him. If we observe all externals but fail to turn, then we don't move at all. Leave everything to him and move in a natural, spontaneous loving way, free from all burden, anxiety, tension. And most important—be absolutely egoless. Do your work in an egoless way. He doesn't like it if ego comes up. Be with others in a humble egoless way. Keep your head at his feet. Keep your thought centered in him, whether in prayer, japa, work; whatever you may be doing, it is all his.

Just never forget your destination. The car may stall at times, sometimes you have to slow down, sometimes go fast, but you will keep moving in the right direction if you never forget your destination.

### November 26, 1977

Even if you don't have resignation to God now, you can certainly get it—if you will it. Look at how many people's attitudes were changed by Sri Ramakrishna. Just constantly assert that attitude, as he was with Divine Mother. Don't take any burden on you. Be as he was: "Mother, you know everything."

### November 28, 1977

Unconscious indulgence is due to lack of alertness and weakness of will. We have to keep the mind constantly awake and alert. Let nothing happen without your knowing it. We can get will just through complete surrender to him, as Thakur told Girish. If we surrender completely to him, we become unable to take a false step. We have to create a new spiritual psyche, through prayer, meditation, austerity, etc. When that becomes strong, it has the power to undo the mess of our unconscious mind. New spiritual *samskaras* overpower the old.

Three things to practice for peace in life: (1) Reflect, don't react; (2) Be detached, not attached, but be concerned; (3) See the same Ground in all.

In the midst of the changing patterns of life, hold onto That which is changeless.

**November 30, 1977**

Oneness with all automatically comes if you are one with God. As you move toward the center you automatically move toward other radii. But be careful not to move toward another radius, because then you move away from the other radii. That is attachment. Give your heart and soul to him. The more you give up individual selfishness, the more you move toward him. Don't worry about other things. Just repeat his name. Get the mind well set in him.

The Truth in all of us is the same. We are all nothing but the ocean of loving consciousness, the embodiment of blissful consciousness. Everything else is changing. That alone is constant.

**December 7, 1977**

The relationship between Guru and disciple is more than any earthly relationship. There is no if-s and but-s there. It is absolutely unconditional, no line of separation. Every time

Swami Akhandananda saw a picture of Thakur, his mood changed and he bowed his head down.

## December 9, 1977

Struggle is there in every life. Since we must struggle no matter what, why not struggle for what is best? Put every thought at his feet. He is our support. When we have taken his name we should never be dry or gloomy. Be like when he was with the Mother. "I have put everything at his feet; he is the boss." Relax; contentment is most important. It's not what we attain; rather spiritual life is in the living—how we live.

## December 15, 1977

The biggest austerity is his name. Austerity means restraint; how much restraint it takes to surrender to him! That is our austerity. Just keep his name and all delusion will vanish. Nothing else will be able to get in.

## December 22, 1977

Of the two commandments, "Love God," and "Love thy neighbor," the second is greater than the first. It's easy to realize God; if the mind is clean, God-realization comes of itself. But to love and serve is really something great. We are a far cry from love of God if we cannot love our own brother and sister. Swami Akhandananda said, "Hate not, hurt not." That means not to project a single negative thought ever towards anybody.

The mind gets patterned and then we think in certain ways and we don't stop to ask why we think like that. If we have conditioned our own minds in a certain negative pattern, now those thoughts are conditioning us and we think we are that. We have to stop, look at it, ask how I got this way, see how it has come through a conditioning process, uninvited, unconsciously—and then say, "Nothing doing!" That is, detachment—to look at the negative thoughts and say, "Nothing doing." Then on the positive side, practice. We ask ourselves, "What is it I want to be?" Seeing the lives and teachings of spiritual people we then try to reset our lives accordingly, try to shape our thought and behavior in that new pattern.

Never let the mind create issues. Life will be lost completely in that. Never argue with the mind. If you admit an appeal, you are lost. Don't even entertain argument. It is *will* that turns the mind, not logic. You must have conviction, based not on logic, but on intense feeling. Conviction is only 10% reason and 90% heart. When that is there, entertain no appeal, no argument, from the mind.

When you have decided for yourself, forget about argument. Friends, relatives, mental impressions—put them all out. When the urge for renunciation comes, act on it right away because that feeling doesn't always come. And then don't argue with anybody. Don't even argue with your own mind. Negative ideas will be there; there will be problems throughout, because millions of things are there, from this life and past lives. Deal with them as they come, don't dig them. Just don't pay interest and attention, admit no appeal or argument, and move on in a positive direction—by surrendering to him, being equanimous toward all, without any greed (no feeling of "what will I get out of this"), without ego, and with a peaceful balanced mind. The battle with negative thoughts is a given in spiritual life. It is not easy. So just accept that and don't make an issue of it. Work, struggle, and follow the yoga of Gita 3. 30.

. . .

## December 29, 1977

Three most important things to remember in spiritual life: (1) Keep away from all negative thoughts; (2) Keep the mind on Thakur; (3) Be active, either in work, study or contemplation.

When you have an opportunity, utilize it well. If you plan and scheme, tomorrow will never come. But if you live well in the present, he will take care of the future. Be very careful not to let the mind scheme and not to let it create dissatisfaction. Otherwise it will always go on creating problems.

# 1978

## January 3, 1978

If you want to deserve their grace, put your mind at their feet. You may have the grace of God and Guru, but you must follow their instructions. "Think of me," as Mother told Swami Tarakeswarananda. And remember Thakur's instruction to turn the course of the passions toward God.

Mother's life is the essence of all religions. As Thakur said, "I have only gone from this room to that room," so also Holy Mother.

If Thakur is the sun of which Swamiji is a ray, then what is Holy Mother? It is difficult to express, except that she identified totally with him. We may say she has the glory of the Divine Mother, but she was so hidden. But taking what the direct disciples perceived and said about her, and Thakur's worship of her, we can only imagine her purity and her stature. We can only pray that she reveal herself to us because only thereby can we understand what she really is.

In the shrine those are not mere pictures. They are living presence, all of them. When you are in the shrine you are really in their midst.

## January 5, 1978

Never be frightened even by the worst thoughts coming. It is weakness to be frightened by every little thing and no weakling can realize the Truth. We must be strong to lead a spiritual life. Don't be frightened; rather, boldly examine everything and it will disappear.

How to gain strength? By thinking of them.

1. I am Swamiji's soldier; I will be strong.
2. I am Mother's child; I will be pure.
3. I am Thakur's child; I will be divine.

Through the thought of them we become strong. The life of a monk or a nun is in strength. Swamiji always said be strong and be pure. Strength comes from purity, purity from strength. If we are unselfish we are strong. If we are strong we are unselfish. A weakling is always seeking.

## January 11, 1978

With everything that comes, ask, "Is it true?" We must have courage to stand on truth. That means complete abandonment of satisfaction, abandonment of the pursuit of pleasure or power.

With any thought, look boldly at it and analyze it, why it is disturbing you. Know the obstacle for what it is. Know it and then throw it off. "Not for me!" Like an army general, know the enemy, its strength and then throw it off.

In spiritual struggle there must be no gap. There must be constancy because mind is always ready to pounce, to go down. Any gap, and old *samskaras* come up. Moreover, unless we are really alert, there is unconscious indulgence of the mind in negative thoughts. Similarly there must be no light-mindedness because that gives a convenient atmosphere for old tendencies to come up. We must keep seriousness always. The only way is to keep the constant thought of the Divine. Blessed are those who have devotion because that is the best support. Even if there is only a little devotion, we can struggle to turn the mind more and more toward God.

## January 15, 1978

I am sold (to Sri Ramakrishna). I pray to Thakur but I demand from Mother. Try to imagine what the direct disciples thought of her, how they looked upon her. She was the perfection of universal Motherhood. All of us are spirit; she is the Mother.

We are all on the exact same wavelength at the spiritual level; no difference. One who is at the spiritual level actually becomes one with all and reaches all at their own particular level, whether child or old man. There lies the beauty of the direct disciples' relationship with each other. They were so independent, could even fight with each other, but they were all one. If real pure love is there, you can say anything and not hurt anybody.

## January 18, 1978

If you imagine in your prayers that you are in Holy Mother's presence, that her loving response is there and her uplifting influence is there, that imagination is true. Mother is true, you are true. Just as Thakur can be seen and experienced, the same is true of Mother. She is universal and eternal. The minute we call her, "Mother," she is our own Mother. She was like that then and she is like that even now.

She and Thakur definitely accept, but our part is to keep our mind on them. You begin to dig a well and you imagine water; that imagination becomes a reality only if you keep digging. Therefore keep struggling; don't stop. We will feel her presence as we evolve. Most important is to pray to her to have her spirit of love and service. Always keep up that spiritual attitude toward people in all situations and you will never be lost. Always keep the attitude that all are Mother's children, no matter what, and feel, "how can I serve."

## January 20, 1978

Restlessness arises from so many factors. Just take his name with firm faith and that will straighten everything. Also be detached from all other things. Be blissful in his name. Put everything at his feet just as he put everything at the feet of the Divine Mother. We cannot straighten everything, so let him do it. We are nothing practically.

## January 23, 1978

Even while the direct disciples are all so different, they are all united in their devotion to Thakur and Ma. To them all, there is nothing higher than Thakur and Ma, who look like ordinary people but whose spiritual attainment is so high we cannot even imagine. When Swami Brahmananda would go to Mother, he would first consult the almanac, then take a bath in the Ganges twice, prostrate in the shrine to Thakur and then go. What must he have seen in her? We can only try to imagine.

. . .

## January 25, 1978

Monastic vows mean freedom from passion and possession.

Chastity makes you pure—so that the mind won't run after the sensate.

Poverty makes you detached.

Obedience makes you humble; rainwater collects in a lowland.

What is most important is to hold on to Thakur; hold on to the Light. No matter what comes, just hold on to him.

Avoid all comparison in spiritual life. Be just like the direct disciples. They never felt jealous when Sri Ramakrishna praised Naren or Rakhal because each one knew he was Ramakrishna's own.

Have the attitude of helping and sharing.

Life and love are inseparable. Wherever there is consciousness, there is love. Saints experience it, that even in the dust of the earth there is that *madhu* (honey or sweetness—actually love). Every heart has got that love; only in some, it has been covered up, and one must be helped to unfold and express it.

## January 28, 1978

The most important thing for exclusive spiritual life is spiritual living. Don't take any burden on you. Just follow their teachings exactly—"follow my commandments"—and then, "She knows the rest." We don't know anything, we don't know how much is deep in the mind; we don't know when realization will come or when their grace will come. Just live day to day in a spiritual way according to their teachings and leave the rest to them. Don't expect anything. Live the life surrendering to them—not with tension but with ease. Don't go on questioning or wondering what will happen when. Just live the spiritual life and put the burden on them.

The whole life should be dedicated to Sri Ramakrishna. Keep the mind set with the idea that I want God and nothing but God. Don't look to either side. Keep a self-same attitude. See all people as so many impersonal images, yet all as the children of God. As Thakur said, keep nondual knowledge tied in the corner of your cloth. "I am the child of God, all are the children of God." You will be free from tension by putting the whole burden on him. Do all work as his, don't take responsibility on you. All tension is due to egoism. He is the boss; we are all doing his work.

Do everything with a prayerful attitude; without that there is the great danger of being filled with egoism, pride and vanity. We unconsciously get into seeking power and pampering the ego unless we keep a prayerful attitude.

If you read Gita daily, you will realize the Truth. Everything is in the Gita.

**February 1, 1978**

We can only understand Thakur and Swamiji if we have complete renunciation and absolute purity of consciousness. As long as we have any sensate feeling or perception, we cannot understand anything of spirituality. If we want to progress spiritually, we must get away completely from worldly things and thoughts. Otherwise we walk without moving. In spiritual life purity of consciousness is everything. Spiritual life will be a miserable life if we don't completely get away from sensate perceptions.

## February 2, 1978

Thakur is the perfect Brahman, the one who is beyond everything. Swami Vivekananda is the manifestation, the relative Brahman. Only if we understand Swamiji can we understand Thakur. All wisdom is in the *Complete Works*. Mahapurush Maharaj once said, when someone said that the *Gospel of Sri Ramakrishna* was the last word, that M. only came on holidays. Mahapurush Maharaj said, read Swamiji, that is the last word. We need the *Gospel* plus the *Complete Works*. But Thakur is beyond both, beyond all the direct disciples.

## February 6, 1978

Atman and atom—same root word. Neither can be divided. The same Self is in all. We imagine ourselves to be that which is superimposed on the Self. It can only be realized when you are absolutely desireless, free from all temptations, but it is a process to get to that state. Any desire which is unopposed to virtue is of divine origin (according to Sri Krishna in the Gita), anything which is for the good of all and does not lead to separation or isolation.

We have to discriminate in that way and give up the lower for the higher. Always ask regarding any desire, "Where does it lead me? What are the consequences?" We can avoid so much that way. Then ask, "What is it I value most?" and turn the mind toward that.

Look at your state of mind yesterday and today—one day happy, one day miserable, but I am the same. Meditate on what that "I" is that doesn't change from yesterday to today, from today to tomorrow. That "I" is separate from all modifications, tendencies, urges, impressions. Separate yourself from all the changing patterns and try to touch the unchanging Ground within—so beautiful, so pure, so peaceful.

**February 7, 1978**

The illumined soul knows us completely as we are because he sees us as me, the true self. He knows us better than we know ourselves.

We see vapor, water, snow, ice. What is the real substance of which all these are but the modifications? Same with the Self. Everything we see is its modification. Only an illumined soul knows it as it is, but he cannot explain it.

[There was 38" of snow on this day. The swami was commenting on how pure snow is.] Water can never be made dirty. Dirt may be there but the sun's rays can take out and lift up the pure vapor, leaving the dirt behind. Similarly with us—we cry and say that there is so much dirt, I can't clean it! But the illumined soul knows how to lift up the real, pure Self. He says, "You are That, meditate on That," and then as we meditate on That, other things are slowly silenced and left behind. You are never really dirty. Dirt may be there but Self is pure. I know how to pick it up. Dirt is there but Self is lifted up. That is why we must always look to the positive and never to the negative. Don't even look at it or think about it. When once you know it is bad, just turn the other way and think that you are That.

**February 16, 1978**

Always remember one thing: Keep on struggling. A struggling soul has nothing to fear. Krishna promised it. Always be happy. Thousands of things come. Don't look at the obstacles, look at Krishna. If you keep turned toward him you can conquer everything. Be happy that we have such a wonderful ideal. And if we keep struggling, the road is sure—we will definitely reach the goal, no matter how long or how slow we have to go at times. Therefore be always happy and positive and keep looking at him. "Think of me," the dictum of Holy Mother. And, "Turn the mind," as Thakur told Hari Maharaj.

We are not perfect, we don't have complete renunciation, but we are struggling toward the ideal and we will never be lost, we will surely reach the goal if we keep struggling. Therefore have joy now in living the life. No matter what comes, put it on him. Take his name and put everything on him.

Spiritual life is not in what you build or perform but in who you are as a person. Spirituality is to *be,* not to *do* and achieve. Be spiritual. That means keeping the mind turned always toward him. That requires subduing the ego and other strong negative tendencies. You have to hold them together, pull them in, hold the mind and turn it toward him.

Real spirituality (*vijnana*) is to accept everything, deny nothing, not to separate the spiritual and secular but to spiritualize the *entire* life. Wholesomeness, not separation or isolation. Holy Mother is the ideal. That was Swamiji's ideal as he received from Thakur. The heart must be opened up and purified.

## February 21, 1978

Mind is nothing but a reflection of Pure Consciousness and that reflection gathers on itself all the images gathered from outside. To purify the mind means to resolve and silence all those impressions. The only way is through detachment. You have the strength within to undo the whole process. The way is to think, "They have come at a particular time and therefore they will go away."

We become disturbed because we gather ideas without examining them and we fail to organize our thoughts. Now we must examine, analyze and properly relate them. Don't just accept the thought that comes. Look at it, relate to it, and organize it properly with other thoughts. Otherwise the mind can create a hell out of a pleasant situation. If you can learn to be detached from your own thoughts and impressions, if you can separate yourself from them, then the worst tendency may be present and it won't bother you. Let it be there, it can't tip you off.

The other thing is never to lay the blame outside. Never find fault with others. Recognize that your own deeds have raised these ghosts.

### February 27, 1978

Seeing God depends on the mind. Ramakrishna, Christ, Buddha, Krishna—they can all be seen but it requires absolute purity of mind, spotless. Don't feel hopeless on that account. Feel rather, "We are on the way." Just follow his commandments, or as Arjuna said, "I shall do thy bidding." If you follow Ramakrishna's teachings, you are sure to get it.

### March 9, 1978

Sri Ramakrishna is the greatest revelation the world has ever witnessed. But spreading his message isn't an evangelical venture. It is to be done by living the life. Never before has there been such a revelation of the unity of the Godhead, the unity of man and the world. He is like a huge flower that has only begun to open. There is still so much to unfold. The world is crying for his message of unity. His was a hidden glory, no external show. The meaning of that was to avoid any dogmatic aspect.

Swami Vivekananda understood him. His religion is so scientific. Anyone can verify its truth. Therefore Swamiji preached the ideal, not the person.

Swami Akhandanandaji once said that it is pointless to speak about the "birthday" of Thakur. Is there really a thing like sunrise or sunset? The sun neither rises nor sets. Similarly in Sri Ramakrishna, there is neither birth nor death. "Before Abraham was, I am." "I have just gone from one room to the other." He is immortal and eternal. Sri Krishna says that one who knows him "in reality" is not born again, meaning one does not return to the state of ignorance.

Yet even while he is so universal and impersonal, the personal aspect is still there. He is our very own. President Carter—as the president—may be for the entire United States, but when little Amy comes to him, he is no less the father of that little girl. Similarly, Sri Ramakrishna is expansive and universal, but he is also equally intensive and personal.

## March 18, 1978

Sri Ramakrishna's words are all so true, spoken to one's face in order to enlighten. Any little spot in the mind keeps the Light from getting through. We must give the whole mind to God. That is why Thakur used to pray to Mother to have only pure devotion. "I don't want name and fame, I don't want creature comforts, I don't want anything except pure devotion to Thee." We should pray to Thakur like that: "Just as Divine Mother gave you pure devotion, now you give me like that. I have surrendered everything to you, you can't but give me that.

If the leaks, or the "holes of desire," are present, then a prayer is the way to patch it. At the rise of any thought or desire, pray immediately, "No, may I not have that desire, I don't want it. I want only pure devotion."

Patch it up! Patch it up! The only way is to keep a constant prayerful attitude. We must find a thought or phrase to which we can constantly turn to draw his attention, to put the mind on him. Keep the whole mind in his thought constantly. We have to make it one-pointed.

We should keep that one-pointedness in everything we do. That is karma yoga. Anything to be done, put the will there and do it as a master, never as a slave. Slaves work half-heartedly out of compulsion and with no attention. But karma yoga means to work as a master and put interest and attention, one-pointedness, on every action. Do everything for him and then you don't care for name or fame or praise or blame. One-pointedness brings happiness.

Mantra is for that one-pointedness. Mantra means "that which protects the mind." It serves to keep the mind as if on a railroad track. It straightens the mind toward God. But it must be repeated with awareness of the meaning. Then it *really* protects the mind. If we struggle for one-pointedness at the beginning, saying, "No," "Don't," constantly to all negative thoughts —just like training a puppy—then it becomes self-protective later on when it is well trained.

## March 19, 1978

Those fifty years, 1836-1886 (Sri Ramakrishna's earthly lifespan), are a big, divine mystery, a divine play, a divine comedy, a big revelation. Sri Krishna says in the Gita that those who understand his divine birth and work have the highest illumination. No one can understand the fundamental why's of anything. We can only struggle for light and help others out of misery when we can.

### March 20, 1978

The thought to be kept constantly is that God is in all, all are God's children. Always remember the presence of the divine in all and in me. As Thakur said, "Keep a bit of the knowledge of non-dualism tied in the corner of your cloth and then do whatever you like." That is the thought to remember while repeating the mantra—that he is the Ground of all. That is the meaning of religion—unity and oneness. Never forget it or you will fall down and lose your ground.

### March 22, 1978

Happiness is not a small thing. If we can make somebody happy, without any selfishness, that is real service to mankind.

There is no freedom in isolating oneself at the human level because we are all part of the whole. The more we feel free, the more we renounce our own likes and dislikes and care for others. Renounce and enjoy. Give up all selfishness.

The world is not bad. There is nothing evil. It all depends on the angle of vision. The world is a great opportunity for evolution; it is a big school to us.

There is no parallel in history to Thakur, in that he really left his own shore in order to discover new oceans. He is a big revelation. Thakur will do his work; we must just hold to his feet.

One problem with Christianity is that Jesus has been too far removed from the human. The incarnation's struggle has a meaning for us. Yes, as Krishna says, he embodies himself of his own free will. But he has evolved to that level. He has had that experience in a previous life and now he comes freely. But his struggle has a meaning for us, that we can also make it through his grace.

Thakur had reached the same level as revealed by Krishna in Gita, chapter 9. But when a perfect soul reaches that level, through force of habit he may keep up the relationship by which he has reached the goal. It is his divine privilege.

**March 27, 1978**

There are five phases of Christ's life. Advent, spiritual aspirant (largely unknown), Jesus as Christ (enlightenment and ministry), crucifixion, resurrection.

There are two meanings to the crucifixion: human intolerance and divine endurance. We all participate in the crucifixion to the extent that we are intolerant. Endurance (*titiksha*) was there because Jesus knew who he was—the Christ—not the body and mind.

Crucifixion's connection with resurrection is that anyone who crucifies this body and mind can have resurrection of the spirit. Crucify the flesh; the Kingdom of God is not of this world.

There are two most important things to learn from the resurrection: (1) We can all be resurrected, that is, transcend body and mind, and know that we are one with God. (2) When these incarnations pass away, they are of such tremendous spiritual mass that they do not just merge in the Absolute. In a spiritual way they retain their name and form and can be visualized even now. You can even talk to them. There is a natural body and a spiritual body. It was in the spiritual body that Christ appeared to his disciples. Same with Ramakrishna ("from this room to that room") and the same can be experienced even now. Only two things are required for that experience—purity and devotion.

## March 28, 1978

When you are in a worldly atmosphere, learn to keep the mind indrawn. The indrawn mind is the key. Keep a prayerful attitude, thinking of Thakur and Mother. Then you will build a new psyche that will protect you in every situation later on.

## March 30, 1978

Two things are necessary: humility and surrendering attitude. That purifies the consciousness. To feel, "I don't know," and, "I am at your feet." Go to bed with positive thoughts. Mentally put your head at their feet and go to sleep.

## April 3, 1978

All we have to do is be true to him. Let there be no theft in the heart. Then we can demand grace from God. Those who surrender to him have no responsibility. The burden is all his. If we surrender to him, he has to pay for it. But we have to be true to him and do just as he says.

## April 4, 1978

Just hold onto the rope and never let go. He is the rope. But he will make us walk every step of the way. We have to overcome all obstacles ourselves, but he is there before us and he will give us strength. He will give us *more* strength as we go. If there is a thief in the heart, don't even search him out. Don't scratch it, just surrender to Sri Ramakrishna. If you put a wet cloth in a dryer, all the wrinkles and folds dry out. You don't have to keep opening it to see if each fold is coming out. That is like surrender to him. Everything gets dried up in that surrendering. We have to make the struggle blissful and pleasant, because we have got his name.

If you want peace of mind, forget negative thoughts. If you have a negative tendency, stop and realize how you got it (i.e. it wasn't born with you). Then know you can undo it by the same process. Now fill the mind with a positive spiritual thought and create a new habit, a new psyche. Hence the benefit of japa. Repetition creates a new habit, a new psyche.

## April 9, 1978

How to have the same one-pointed love for the Ishta that one has for the Guru? If you are one-pointed, you go beyond the body and mind, and see the Light behind, the spirit, his light, his spark. The Guru may become old, even forgetful, but behind the constantly changing body and mind is his Light. No, it is God actually. Satchidananda is your Guru, as Thakur used to say. "I am the Vine, ye are the branches," means that. It is the same sap flowing in every branch. "I am in you, you are in me, we are in him, he is in us."

## April 16, 1978

You must turn the mind to the positive and make it clear, clean and calm. No reaction. No attraction and aversion. When we react, it is like picking a thing up and that becomes like a pin in the subconscious mind or a bump on the road. Then we try to contemplate—there is no external vibration—but these things come up and disturb us and we can't get meditation. That is what Christ meant when he said, "Resist not evil." Don't react or resist. "From me no danger be to aught that lives." You may see or hear the worst thing but don't have any "anti" feeling. We have to absolutely avoid every negative thought or feeling.

It is the same thing with attraction and aversion. Aversion agitates the mind. Attachment draws it out. To avoid aversion, find a counter thought. If you have hatred in the mind, then find out something good in the person and tell the mind not to forget that. And attachment must be avoided. Don't be attached to any worldly thing or person. Be alert because it creeps in due to close association. Keep all relationships on a spiritual level, never on a mundane level. As soon as you get on the mundane level with its "I and mine"—"this is my friend and the other one isn't"—then you invite reaction. Attachment draws the mind away from the object of contemplation. Don't give room for attachment to anybody except God. And don't hate anybody because God is present in all; all are his children. We want to ask him to come and dwell in our hearts, so we can't have any bitterness toward any of his children.

The mind is just like a baby. It takes things as you feed it. It is simply an instrument of cognition, so we can't blame the mind for what we have put there. Whatever we have got is because we willed it and put the mind there. Now mind behaves according to those patterns, so we have to reset the whole psyche according to the same process. When old thoughts come, tell the mind, "No," again and again. It's like if you have kept your doors open for people to come and go at any time and one man is accustomed to come freely at certain times. Then you decide you aren't going to let anybody in any more. But the man comes at the normal times out of habit and even though you say, "No," he resists for some time and keeps coming. But if you keep saying, "No," he finally gets the message and leaves you alone. The mind is our slave—we can put it exactly where we will it to be. We have to tell the mind constantly, "If you don't want a thing, then why do you pick it up? Why show interest and give attention?" But we have to be vigilant because, out of old habits, the mind may bring up old thoughts and unconsciously dwell on them. We must beware of that and immediately tell the mind, "No!" when they come.

We are trying to reset our entire psyche, to make the heart clean, because we are asking God to come and dwell there. It is a combination of our struggle and his grace. His grace works through the psyche, through this psychological process. Nothing is possible without his grace. It's like the poor man who invites a rich man to come for a visit. So the rich man sends him everything with which the poor man could entertain him and give a proper reception to him. In the same way, we pray to God to make our heart clean in order that he can dwell there. Our prayer is only for pure devotion. It's simply a matter of opening up so that his grace can fill the heart and flood it with his Light. We must pray, "I am not clean, I am struggling, I can't resolve things. You please make my heart clean and fit for you to come there."

## April 18, 1978

The specialty of Thakur, Mother and Swamiji is devotion with strength. We have our heads at Thakur's feet 24 hours a day for the whole life and we are humble and modest with all, but inside we are tough like steel. Swamiji said, enough of crying and weeping. This is the time for strength and will. We have to be heroes to realize the Truth; spiritual life is not for weaklings. When I have received initiation in his name, when I have taken his name, why should I be weak? When disturbance comes, examine minutely and find out why, and then find out the remedy from within. The answers are inside.

The most important thing is not to react to anything, impulses coming from outside or inside. That is the first step in evolution. Long before we can put the mind on God, we have to make it pure. Stop collecting disturbing impressions by avoiding all reaction. Take things just as they are, without reaction.

## April 19, 1978

If we are humble and natural, we will always balance our behavior properly. Just do what is to be done and take whatever comes in a humble, natural way. Always remember the ideal of love, respect and cooperation, and you will never commit a mistake.

## April 22, 1978

For worldly people, there is happiness in the beginning but misery in the end. For us, there may be misery and trouble in the beginning but always happiness in the end. It's not a question of who is happy. It is a question of what you want. What we are seeking is something different from immediate happiness and satisfaction. We want to find out something deeper, to find out what this life is all about. We want to move fast spiritually rather than postponing what needs to be done. We have to go slow in the sense that we cannot sit down to meditate for four hours, but go fast in the sense of having strong devotion and commitment to the spiritual ideal.

To ward off troubles, keep the mind active and keep up the spirit of dedication. Beware of egoism in trying to cultivate selflessness. The most important thing is dedication, dedication, dedication.

The spiritual path is really like a razor's edge. Struggle will be there until the end. We have to accept that. We have to constantly battle different forces. But fight we must—we have to fight! Any negative forces coming, put them before Thakur. Open up to him. Run to him with everything, just as he did with Mother.

## April 24, 1978

Selflessness comes automatically if we surrender to him. If we dedicate ourselves to him totally, selling ourselves to him completely, then selfishness automatically falls off and all difficulties automatically dissolve. His thought must be kept constantly. Just do whatever comes in his name naturally—not going around consciously trying to be selfless.

We have to be very careful about egoism in spiritual life. We must always be humble, never callous or insulting. Be always mindful, alert about what you say to anyone, because his thought comes first. Personal thought must be banished.

## April 26, 1978

The more we try to spiritualize everything, the more the devils dance. They all come up and say, "You put me here, now you can't throw me out." But we have to assert over and over that we *are* throwing them out. Meanwhile, weep to Thakur for strength. Don't weep before the devils; show strength there. But cry to God for strength.

The only way is to surrender to him and take his name. Pray to him, "I don't know why these things come. I may be responsible but I don't know how to handle it. I take your name, you take care of my mind." Put the burden and responsibility on him, surrender completely to him, and then all tensions vanish. If we can humble ourselves, then the mind becomes calm. Then alone we can find out the cause of all troubles. We have to humble ourselves completely, surrender to the Higher Power, to the Supreme Will. We don't know what is going on at all, but if we surrender to him, we can get calmness and light.

**April 30, 1978**

Once you have taken to spiritual life don't look back. It's like crossing the ocean in a plane and suddenly you stop and look down and start asking if you should have taken a boat: "Oh, the water looks so nice...." Yes, it is a struggle, but it is better to struggle on the spiritual side than get into the māyā and cry. If you are committed to Thakur, he will give you strength.

**May 1, 1978**

There was a wise old man who had a book in his room that he wouldn't let anyone touch. Finally, when he died, the townspeople rushed to find out what was in it. All the pages were blank except the first page, which said, "When you realize the difference between the container and the content, you will have all the wisdom in the world."

**May 7, 1978**

When we use imagination in spiritual life, it is different from something objective, because what we are imagining is the Eternal Subject. Ramakrishna is not "out there." Ramakrishna is in me!

We are Ramakrishna's children, but at times he tests us and sends devils. But he will give us all strength, provided we struggle. There is no shortcut. The only way is to pray, "I don't know, I don't know *anything*." The only way is complete surrender. We don't know anything actually.

## May 8, 1978

[The swami was talking about the beauty of marriage vows and how one boy who said he hated marriage was unable to stay on as a monk.] The secret is that anyone who thinks negatively can never become spiritual. We must absolutely keep away from all negative thoughts. They may be there due to past accumulation, but don't pay attention to them. Don't even look at them. Just look straight ahead—the path is clear. When you drive on the road, there may be steep cliffs and deep valleys, but you don't let them frighten you; you just drive straight. So in spiritual life, don't look to negative thoughts, and when they come, don't be frightened. Just pay no attention and look straight ahead. Absolutely refuse to harbor any type of negative thought. Spiritual life becomes natural and spontaneous when you keep away everything negative.

## May 10, 1978

Spiritual life is just a matter of will. Even with pranayama, which serves to unconsciously bring the mind under control and away from disturbing thought, putting the mind on the breath is a matter of will. You have to will it. If you exercise the will, even the worst unresolved problem can be overcome, because if you will it, the mind will follow you.

## May 18, 1978

[Reading from the *Gospel of Sri Ramakrishna*] When Thakur

said he is that "hole," it is just like Christ saying, "I am the Way." Avatars are one because behind those names and forms is only one Light. Jesus became Christ. The son of a Brahmin became Ramakrishna. When they are illumined, the Light experience is one, because the Light is infinite, eternal and immortal—therefore, the same always. The closer we come to that "hole," the bigger it becomes until at last we find there is no hole—we are in him, he is in us. He is in Father, Father is in him. You can go beyond and realize that I and my Father are one.

[Talking about *Katha Upanishad* 6.4 and *Gita* 5.19, about Brahman being equanimous and flawless:] This means not to find fault. Holy Mother is the best exemplar. Blessed are we to have her as our Mother. She is our Mother eternally, nourishing us eternally.

The definition of religion is, "Awareness of the Spirit, within and without, both individual and cosmic."

## May 23, 1978

The first step in spiritual life is to give up everything negative. Even if it is true, refuse to harbor any negative thought. Spirituality means two things—unselfishness and love for all. He who has absolutely unselfish love has realized God.

## May 31, 1978

We don't know how we got into this māyā, but we know how to get out—detachment from persons, objects and thoughts. We have to be constantly alert and detached. Separate yourself from any thought coming; say, "That is not me." No thought, no urge, no impression is born with you. They are not part of you. They have come, they have to go.

In interpersonal relations, avoid everything negative. Avoid faultfinding, suspicion and complaining. Respect all people. Love, respect and cooperation with all. Especially with the opposite sex, always keep everything on a high spiritual level —absolutely no light-mindedness. Neither to tempt nor to be tempted.

God knows your struggle. God will never abandon you. But you have to work hard.

If you have faith in God, don't worry about the future. Spiritual life means to live in the present, fully and spiritually. Don't lose the present. Live well in the present and leave the future to him.

The best pilgrimage is to go to the shrine, head at his feet.

Avoid comparison, competition, jealousy. Be steady in your own.

As Thakur loved those boys, so he still loves those who surrender to him. The thing is to turn our mind to him. We can have the grace of God and Guru, but we have to turn the mind. Don't just think about it; *do* it.

Regarding detachment, if you refuse entrance to strangers who knock on the door, eventually they go away. Your family member who lives with you will knock the door down to get in because that's where he belongs. But those who don't belong there must go if you refuse entrance. Same thing with foreign thoughts, negative thoughts. Tell them they have no place here and eventually they get the message and leave you alone.

The message for spiritual life is two things: Seek ye first the Kingdom of God. My Kingdom is not of this world.

## June 6, 1978

[To a young monastic who was having difficulty meditating:] Don't worry about anything, let nothing cross your mind, just put everything at Thakur's feet. All of his disciples did that. They all said, "I don't know anything." That was the beauty of Sashi Maharaj (Swami Ramakrishnananda)—he was so scholarly, but he felt before Thakur that he didn't know anything. Nothing matters except to know him. If we know him we know everything. It is not even to know him but just to be at his feet now. Be happy and don't worry. Put everything at his feet like a child. When we need meditation, he will bring it. When we need illumination, he will bring it. We have given up everything for him. Whatever we need, he will procure.

## June 9, 1978

The way to make the mind let go of negative thoughts is to put the mind on Sri Ramakrishna. If a towel is wet, just put it in the dryer. Don't go on scrutinizing it to see where it is wet and where it is dry. Just throw the whole thing in. His warmth will dry up the whole thing. Don't dwell on it—just put the mind on him.

## June 13, 1978

We all need blessings. Keep in mind that life is not simple. Take it for granted that it will be bad, that it will be worse. 99% is pulling us outward. But Thakur is the 1% we have to hold on to. If we hold on to him, we will make it. Work without any selfishness. If the urge to become selfless is there, it will be fulfilled.

. . .

## June 23, 1978

Spiritual life requires a simple turn of the mind to resolve to see absolutely no negative in anybody. As Holy Mother said, "Forgiveness is *tapasyā*."

Don't hold on to negative thoughts. If we let them come and go and don't hold them, they lose their power. Keep them out by being constant in seeking God. Cry and be constant. "Cry" means to pray. Throw everything in Ramakrishna. He is a blazing fire who will burn every impurity. "Turn the mind," is the way, the *only* way. Be proud that you have taken his name. He has come to purify us. Harmony of religions, well and good. But most important is that he has come to purify us.

## July 6, 1978

As Thakur represented God in totality, so Swami Vivekananda represented man in his totality, the perfection of every aspect of man—no weakness in any respect. Strength and faith in oneself were his watchwords. We must accept and feel one with all in every situation. Anywhere you tend to feel aversion, tell yourself, "If God can stand to reside in the heart of that person, then certainly I can accept him!" Avoid all petty feelings. Accept everyone and try to help them in whatever way you can.

## July 7, 1978

Samadhi was not something Thakur had to struggle for. Bhavamukha means, "In the mouth of God-consciousness." That spiritual consciousness was always holding him, as it were.

Naren's testing was for our sake—it makes our struggle less. It is like that with anyone who doubts, negates, betrays, like Hriday did. From his life we learn that in serving great souls we must avoid jealousy. Bow down to souls like Hriday as our teachers.

### July 8, 1978

Vedanta includes all philosophies. It is a mine of truth in its totality, a view of reality as a whole. It is wholesome and all-inclusive, from the lowest to the highest, including dualism, qualified non-dualism and non-dualism. You can't take the peak of Mt. Everest and put it somewhere else and say, "This is Mt. Everest." Mt. Everest is the whole thing, from bottom to top. (This was by way of explaining that it is not true to say that Vedanta is only non-dualistic.)

### July 10, 1978

Swami Vivekananda's stress on missionary work was based on his seeing the same Spirit in all. He stressed the human aspect, to *feel* for others, on the basis of that spiritual oneness. Don't see and judge others on the basis of external qualifications. See them as spiritual beings and accept them totally, not just tolerate them. Love and accept and serve others as your own, as manifestations of the one Godhead.

The combination of the divine and human aspects in Swamiji is amazing. He is so broad, so all-inclusive.

### July 11, 1978

The first step for anyone who wants to become spiritual is to accept the spiritual oneness of all. All miseries come when we separate ourselves from others.

We are all *in* that Spirit. There is only one Spirit. It manifests through the body when it fulfills certain conditions. When the body fails to fulfill proper conditions and therefore cannot manifest the Atman, we call it dead. The Atman witnesses the death of the body and watches it drop off.

## July 13, 1978

Philosophically we are with Shankara—oneness, unity. But in spiritual discipline and struggle, we are with Ramanuja. We need that concept of God as separate from us, both for spiritual growth and for interpersonal relations. The point of both is that the perfection of the soul is always there in all of us.

The way to realize freedom is meditation on Spirit as separate from body and mind. It requires avoidance of the four types of laziness (physical, mental, intellectual, spiritual). And it requires complete renunciation of the physical and mental level. To struggle spiritually means to leave off the realm of the body and mind. "My kingdom is not of this world."

Anything you seek, first ask if it will bind you. "Where does it lead me; what are the consequences?" Freedom is within all, but we have to struggle hard to assert it, like the man who dug his way out of jail with his fingernails. Anything you want, you can get if you really want it.

## July 17, 1978

The Self is pure awareness. Because of its presence, we know, we are aware, we live.

If you want peace of mind, see the Self in all. Don't pay attention to faults; they come and go. But the same Self is ever present in all. Condemning people is like driving through Connecticut on a cloudy day and then proclaiming that Connecticut is always cloudy.

Any negative feeling that you have toward others, try to find out its origin and then forgive and resolve it. Don't harbor any negative feeling or any prejudice. The truth of every person is the Self. The Self is pure love itself. Its very nature is love. So if you have any negative feeling, it is a distortion of the Truth. Therefore, try to find it out and straighten it.

## July 18, 1978

Everything depends upon intensity. We have to struggle for concentration. We have to deny everything of this world. "My kingdom is not of this world." Deny every idea of the world and concentrate on spiritual, divine ideas. Spiritual life means to concentrate on that Light, or on illumined ones, putting off all other ideas. Most important is devotion to the ideal. The more we can intensify that, the more we gain concentration and everything else falls off.

The rising of the *kundalini* is a psychic process of purification. Its "seven stages" is just a rough division.

You must look within to gain self-knowledge. You must not externalize the mind. You must dive deep within. Devotion is necessary.

## July 20, 1978

[Guru Purnima] Thakur said Satchidananda is your Guru. Satchidananda is the invisible Guru within. The Incarnation who has realized the truth is the visible Guru, as are his children to whom he passes on that realization. We think of Thakur as that Light of Satchidananda within.

No learning helps unless the spiritual urge, due to one's own *samskaras,* is there. Then, even if there are limitations, that innate spiritual urge makes you live the life.

The Guru must have absolutely no tinge of worldliness.

Even if you haven't realized God, someone who has been leading a really spiritual life can guide others—"Come on, let us go." You may not have been to some place, but if someone has told you how to go there, you can also tell someone else. Ask them to go with you, since you have been told the way.

Two things—character and spirituality—must be caught, not taught. Your mind must be open to catch what a spiritual person or place has to offer.

## July 21, 1978

Freedom means release from the little "I"—the real feeling that I am nothing, God is everything. The individual is dead. That is the meaning of real love.

To love all is the first and foremost experience of real spirituality. You may see evil, but it is absolutely impossible to hate anybody. You see multiplicity, but in and through all you see that one continuous Self.

It is because of desires and ambitions in the mind that we don't have that all-loving consciousness. The Light comes through only a tiny bit, once it is filtered through our subconscious mind. But once we begin to purify our minds, we feel that love more and more. More and more light comes and our hearts expand.

We need detachment from worldly ambitions, we need devotion to God and dedication. We can overcome much of our worldliness through discrimination. "Where does it lead me?

What are the consequences?" We have to turn the mind, examine the mind, restrain it from indulgence in worldly desires and turn it toward God. We have to learn the art of turning the mind.

## July 22, 1978

The key in living itself, what to speak of religion, is acceptance of all.

## July 27, 1978

In leaving everything to Thakur, be absolutely egoless and leave all responsibility on him. Then just accept whatever comes. To give one's life to Thakur means to give it to the public. Love God, love thy neighbor—no separation. But that, too, with detachment. Don't be lost in service—no personal equation. Dedicated to God and loving service, but keep a distance too.

In spiritual life there is no "my" way. It is all "our" way. It means to love and accept all, to help wherever you can, to forgive when one does something wrong. There is no, "I love Thakur but I hate people." No, we must love and accept all but with no personal equation.

## July 29, 1978

When once you decide to become a monk or a nun, that means total dedication to God. It means you must spiritualize all of life—no division between sacred and secular. There is no difference between hours of meditation and hours of work and service—same mind, same attitude. Every act we do must be spiritual.

. . .

## August 2, 1978

We are seeking something non-material and non-mental, that is, pure Consciousness. Spiritual feeling is, "Not I but we," "Not me but us." Consciousness is full of love. To know is to love, and vice versa.

The human being has freedom, reason, self-consciousness. Properly used, one evolves fast. Use them to discriminate, evaluate consequences, and feel, "I shall not be the slave of any person, thing or thought."

Examine everything well. "Is it true?" Avoid all attachment, aversion, and reaction. They make you a slave. Keep your spirituality through detachment. And be detached from thoughts. Like seeing ditches by the side of the road or tigers in a cage, know you are separate from them and don't identify with them.

Don't identify with anything outside yourself or depend upon anything outside yourself. Learn to be yourself always.

It all depends on looking at life from a very high level, like Holy Mother. She only blessed everyone.

## August 4, 1978

You must always be conscious of what you are for. With that consciousness of your spiritual ground, you will never lose your dignity. Most important is to be serious, never light-minded. Then people will respond to you accordingly. Never mind if people misunderstand you. Be fair, friendly, but firm. Give absolutely no leniency. Always have the feeling that you are doing Thakur's work; everything we do anywhere is in his name. Keep a spiritual attitude, an attitude of helpfulness.

Have no selfish interest in work; it is just for us to spiritualize it.

## August 5, 1978

[The swami was asked if Thakur actively helps us and has active love and concern the way the Guru does.] He really does, even more than that. To say he hears even the footfall of an ant is no exaggeration. It's just that we can't see him now. But it is just like Holy Mother experienced—Thakur told her that he had just gone from "this room to that room." He is hearing our conversation right now, but we fail to realize his presence because our minds are steeped in the world. When we honestly want nothing but him and have no other thought, we will realize his presence. To imagine his love and concern, think of what he was like when on earth. Just as he touched and graced Naren, so he is now with anyone who completely surrenders to him. But we have to really mean it.

Incarnations come and they do not go away. God is like a big Light covered by a dark dome. But in that dome are certain holes through which we get that Light. The holes are the Incarnations. Right now we are close to the hole called Ramakrishna.

Before a rocket is launched you have to tie it down with chains on all sides. But when you are going to launch it you cut them all—not one can remain. So with spiritual life—we have to be detached from everything—not one tie remaining.

Life is like a big circle, evolving from our place in God in a big circle away from God and then back around until we reach him again. But monastic life can begin at any point on the circle and you go straight. You cut it off altogether and go straight to him.

To say that Ramakrishna is here hearing our conversation is true because it is our own Pure Consciousness. How we perceive that depends upon our devotion. Thakur, Christ, Krishna are not separate. They are the mains from the one reservoir. The same water pours through each of them. It depends on how we tune our minds, which faucet we turn on. If you press Ramakrishna, then you get it as Ramakrishna. It depends on devotion, but the Reality is one.

The way to escape the clutches of māyā is simply to stay in God. Māyā is nothing but that which is outside of God. So stay in him and you are safe—like a snake in a hole; if he puts his head out he may get blows.

## August 8, 1978

Spiritual life is really so simple. We have to know only two things: (1) this world is no good and (2) God is everything. Knowing that, simply turn the mind. He is standing here before us. We have only to turn the mind. Don't stand in the fire, shouting that it is hot and you want to be cool. Get out of the fire. That means turn the mind toward him. Mantra protects the mind, even in the worst situation.

## August 15, 1978

Being a nun or a monk means you stop living in body and mind, and start living in that which is beyond them, the Self. "Swami" means, "He who is himself." That is, he knows himself as the Self, having nothing to do with body and mind. Unwanted thoughts come more when you try to spiritualize. When they come, just pray to Guru Maharaj. We have to gain that consciousness that we are neither male nor female, and stay away from any situation that raises that consciousness in us. We have to gain that spiritual consciousness through a disciplined mind.

Never be the slave of anybody and don't be a slave to likes and dislikes. It is slavery to keep the company of those who love you and avoid those who don't. When you do that, you are not yourself.

## August 17, 1978

The essence of Buddha's teaching is harmony, unity and love. In his eightfold path he uses a word which is translated as "right," as in, "right thinking." The word really means "harmonious."

Don't let your love be confined to wife, family, etc. The key is to expand your heart. First sharing, then sacrifice. "Not me, but us." Then, "Not me, but them." Or, "Not I, but Thou." Beyond that there is no religion. Yes, we have to be detached, but also to love all, expand the heart, love and serve.

When you react, you become a slave. When you reflect, you are free.

"One and all," is the key—not what I need or what I want, but what we all can have.

Two things are required for exclusive spiritual life: no individuality and no complaints—love and accept all just as they are.

## August 18, 1978

Buddha's morality has taught us what we need in life: within —unselfishness and self-control; without—compassion and service.

"Prayer is useless" (per Swami Vivekananda's teachings on Buddha) refers to, "God, give me this and that." But Buddha's teachings are full of the real prayerful attitude.

Exclusive spiritual life means you have to constantly deny your littleness—constant self-control every moment.

## August 22, 1978

Perfection means to realize the ultimate oneness of existence. Purity means wholesomeness. Impurity is separation.

## September 1, 1978

The real friend is he who scolds, not he who praises.

Avoid egoism, pride and aggressiveness through self-control and prayer to Thakur for humility.

Never react and never judge.

No personal involvement, i.e. likes and dislikes.

## September 5, 1978

What we need is dispassion and detachment from everything outside, devotion to Thakur, and dedication, which makes us dynamic. Thakur is standing before us as the Way and will save us even now if we simply turn towards him. He is the Truth in its totality. Swami Vivekananda is the interpretation of it. M. was the recorder of it. Mother lived it perfectly. Where can we get such an ideal? We can only pray to him that we don't know who he is, we don't even have real faith, but something tells us he is the only way, that there is nothing else, and so we pray for pure devotion.

The key to the beginning of spiritual life is to detach yourself from all thoughts. I am not the thoughts, not the temptations, not the memories. I am the unchanging Light inside and everything relative is really a dream, always changing.

Always put the bold question, "Is it true?"

In order to understand anybody you have to come out of your little ego.

**September 7, 1978**

Only two things we must always remember. Never allow any worldly thought to pull you out (detachment and dispassion). And think of Thakur constantly (devotion). Always keep his blissful image in the mind. Then everything will be taken care of.

All intellectual attempts to understand him are just so many words. We will be able to understand everything if we gain purity of mind. That means, being unselfish and non-sensate. That is our struggle in the beginning—to detach the mind from everything non-spiritual.

There are two phases of being filled with Ramakrishna. One is after realization. In the struggling period, it means to look constantly to him and his teachings for guidance. What would he want me to do or say or think? As he sees my mind, what would he tell me?

By reading about Thakur and Naren, and how Thakur could give and withdraw the highest experience by mere touch, impress your mind with what Thakur must be. As he could do that to Naren, he can also do something for us—even to turn base metal into gold. The more we think of him, the more we spiritualize our minds and it burns all old *samskaras*.

· · ·

## September 12, 1978

The real goal of religion is to see all beings as one. To know and put that into action is the meaning of creation. To be aware of the spirit, individual and collective, is religion. But how to know that we are one? We have to realize the Ground and that is the difficult part. It requires detachment, purity of heart, and selflessness.

Swami Vivekananda has made the goal and the means the same. Realize it through following the path of service to mankind. Give medicine to the sick. Give food to the hungry. Give education to the illiterate. That is our worship and our discipline.

## September 15, 1978

Put all responsibility on Thakur. We can't do anything ourselves unless he gives us strength. To deserve that, we have to keep the mind at his feet.

The only sin is selfishness.

## September 23, 1978

The mind is the instrument of cognition. It simply cognizes, perceives, things outside and brings the perceptions in to the *buddhi,* the decisive faculty. The *buddhi* takes a perception and checks back with all previously stored-up experiences in order to catalog that perception. If it is something familiar, it says, "Oh, it is this." If not, it puts it in a new slot in the mind-stuff, the *chitta. Chitta* is simply the storehouse of all our thoughts and impressions—everything we have ever thought, heard, experienced, dreamt, imagined, seen, read, etc. Ego is that which identifies itself with all this.

Mind, as simply the instrument of cognition, is separate from thoughts. This is the great secret, because when mind cognizes something, *buddhi* categorizes that perception on the basis of old thoughts and impressions stored in the *chitta*. And ego reacts on the basis of that previous experience. Now suppose someone tells us, or we learn, that our previous experience is not true or not the whole truth. Then we can discriminate and put the old thoughts aside and purposely bring in new thoughts. For example, let's say someone hurts us. When mind cognizes that person again later on, *buddhi* checks in with previous impressions in the mind-stuff and decides this is a person to be careful of. We identify and react negatively. But if we are trying to spiritualize, we discriminate, put the old thoughts aside and say, "Let me forgive; they did not know; let me see the good and not find fault." We can decide not to entertain old thoughts, bring in new thoughts and thus create a whole new psyche, a spiritual psyche.

We can clearly see that we have the ability to put thoughts out at will by the fact that when an urgent necessity arises, for example at work, we are able to put all other thoughts out and concentrate on the matter at hand. So also, we can put all negative and sensate thoughts out and bring spiritual ideas in.

## October 2, 1978

Swami Akhandananda was very dynamic. He used to bring everything alive wherever he went. Even at Belur Math, when Swami Akhandananda came, Swamiji and others had a wonderful time, and Swamiji's strictness gave way to his love and joy in Swami Akhandananda's company.

Swami Akhandananda would start schools wherever he went. He would wear half-pants and identify totally with the boys in order to stimulate in them the thirst for knowledge.

He called Sargacchi an ashrama rather than an orphanage. He made wonderful plans for the place. He used to learn all crafts himself so that he could teach people. He also ran a night school for people who worked. He became the central figure of the community and everyone came to "Baba" for everything.

his whole mind was at Sargacchi. The orphan boys there really felt it was home and looked upon Swami Akhandananda as God, teacher, father, mother, everything. The boys, unlike the other swamis even, had the privilege of absolutely free access to him. One little boy wanted glasses, so Swami Akhandananda had him try on a pair of super-strong lenses (to cure the desire). The boys kept the ashrama very meticulous. Swami Akhandananda was full of fun and taught through jokes too.

He was a man of the people and really made everyone his own. He was utterly unselfish and full of the same spirit as Vivekananda. He insisted on brahmacharya when he gave initiation. He told the monks that in Thakur's place, there should be no problem. If you remember Thakur, all problems are solved. If you forget him, all problems arise.

## October 4, 1978

The more we try to spiritualize everything and the more concentration we gain, the stronger the internal enemies become. They have all been superimposed and they will be there until the end. The thing is to cage them, don't look at them, and then they can't hurt you. If you open your mind to Thakur, he will work the miracle. The best thing is a humble, prayerful attitude. Bow your head before Thakur and seek his grace. He will work it out. Repeat again and again, "I am nobody, I am nobody." Be strong like a lion, but know that it is his strength. Be strong without any pride or vanity.

### October 10, 1978

We have to be convinced ourselves that spiritual life is the highest. Problems, difficulties, temptations will be there until the end. But we have got a path: "I am the way." When thoughts and temptations come, simply don't pay attention. When we see a mountain in the distance and see no road, we may think it is an impossible obstacle. But no, "I am the way." There is a path on the side of the mountain—keep on moving. Sometimes it seems joyless and we feel miserable. It is because we are struggling. That is the time to stand firm and put all your faith in Thakur.

It is that ideal of identification with every individual, like when Swami Vivekananda said that if one man went to hell, he would go too; if one man was not liberated, he would not accept liberation himself.

Swami Akhandananda once brought a practically abandoned, retarded man to Sargacchi. They bathed and fed and entertained him, and he smiled for the first time.

### October 17, 1978

Spiritual life is not the pursuit of immediate satisfaction. There is no joy in spiritual life like what you get in sensate life in an elated but temporary satisfaction and pleasure. It is the end result we are seeking—to know our own Ground, the truth of life. Therefore we must never compare our lives or happiness with anybody. We have to be firm in the conviction of what we want and not waver in that.

We are holding on to Thakur but he is holding us also. Only we must be conscious of that constantly.

Spiritual life can be one problem after another, but we have to accept that. Not to pay attention to the negative but constantly to turn the mind to God, who is "the Way," the path through all difficulties. His name can break all bondage if only we take it with real faith and devotion. Everyone had to go through this struggle but we must be prayerful, strict with ourselves, firmly set in what we are seeking—no doubt, no looking in other directions. Be alert and awake to positive spiritual direction. All thoughts will come, all difficulties, but just don't identify or carry them. Turn the course of the mind.

## October 18, 1978

Swami Akhandananda rarely spoke personally of Sri Ramakrishna. He rarely said his name even, referring to "he" or "him." He was very particular that people not use Thakur's name lightly, because the direct disciples of Thakur were so full of him, and his thought was so sacred to them. Someone asked Swami Akhandananda how to meditate on Sri Ramakrishna. He said you can meditate on him in any way you like, but just keep his thought in the mind.

Thakur is Satchidananda. We have to strengthen that conviction in our heart, not just intellect. Realization is in feeling. We have to *feel* his presence.

Someone asked Swami Akhandananda if Thakur came, like Christ, as a savior of mankind. Swami Akhandananda asked how many people the man knew whom Christ had saved, the point being that we have to work hard ourselves. We have to *follow* the enlightened ones. Nothing just happens. But they do come and flood their grace so that many minds can catch it. We have to keep away from passion and possessions, name and fame. Control the passions, control possessions, and be very, very humble. The more humble we are, the easier it gets to catch his light. Before him we are absolutely dumb kids. Our knowledge is actually nothing when we stand before him.

Establish a relationship with him. Be with him as he was with Divine Mother. He is not different from her, as Mathur experienced, and as Holy Mother said when he passed away.

Some of the direct disciples were so full of him that they could not work, like Swami Niranjanananda. And they were in no way less. Someone asked Swami Kalyanananda if Swami Niranjanananda had helped in Kankhal. Swami Kalyanananda replied that his presence itself was enough. Swami Niranjanananda didn't come to the ashrama at all. He had come to Hardwar with only a stick, nothing else, not even an extra cloth, and he had come from a very good family. Swami Kalyanananda used to prepare hot food and take it to him.

### October 25, 1978

In meditation on Thakur, to think of his form is to think of God himself. When his disciples touched him it was like touching a hot pad. Even his flesh and bones were illumined. Therefore, meditate either on his form or the thought of him, or both, anything to keep the continuity of his thought. Most important is to have a feeling of relationship. It is relationship and prayerful attitude that bring about transformation.

. . .

## October 30, 1978

People in this country can overcome competition, comparison, and jealousy if they really spiritualize. That comes through surrender to God. When we feel we are nothing before him, we not only lift ourselves up but we automatically feel one with the rest, because the ego is leveled down through submission to him. We must overcome jealousy through identification with all. Thakur has brought us a religion of harmony, unity, acceptance of all. All are my brothers and sisters. If I really surrender to Thakur, I automatically begin to love and accept, and overlook faults and differences. Pray to be like that and his grace will work the transformation. Buddha's first precept is wholesome view—no separation, but harmony and unity.

## October 31, 1978

Whether we realize God in this life or not, we are so fortunate to have such a high ideal as that of Thakur/Ma/Swamiji. The most important thing is to live the life. Leave the question of realization to him. Pray only for pure devotion; the results come automatically, but leave that question to him. It is only for us now to live a life of truth, love and unselfishness, of devotion, dedication, detachment.

## November 1, 1978

When we struggle spiritually, it is like an unwinding process of the whole bundle of mental impressions that we have wound up. We see the same desires in the unrolling process. But whereas we rolled them up with the desire to enjoy, now we see them with an attitude of self-control and detachment. We have to see the whole thing come out, like washing dirty clothes. Therefore we should never be frightened. The more detached we are from them, the faster they fade. The stronger the thoughts are, the longer they take to go. They argue with you. But it's like a bunch of thieves got into the house. You call the police and they have to get out. You see them leaving but you are not frightened because you know they are getting out. Similarly, Thakur has come, so now they all have to go. The whole key is complete surrender to him. All *samskaras* pile up on the ego, but surrender destroys that ego-foundation and they have nothing to stand on. Just as a child runs with all problems and hugs the mother, so also we should hug the feet of Thakur and watch the unwinding process with detachment. Everything has to come out, but when you see them, don't identify with them—be detached.

Complete surrender is most important—to God, a saint, or the Guru. If we surrender completely to an illumined soul, obeying implicitly even in secular matters, that attitude carries into spiritual matters. There is so much we don't know. We are trying to enter a realm we know nothing about. The only way we can move forward into that is surrender to higher power, higher wisdom. Our worldly wisdom doesn't help in that realm. If we argue or use our logic, even in secular things, with an illumined soul, then we will carry that attitude into the spiritual and do the wrong thing. Therefore complete faith and surrender are most important.

## November 2, 1978

Three most important things: (1) Be alert. (2) Never be light-minded. Keep the mind serious, introspective, purposeful. Mirth is good but not light-mindedness. (3) Be positive. Toward others, always look only to merits, never faults. Be like the bee that picks up only honey, not like the fly that sits on filth. Toward yourself, never identify with the negative.

Even if something is there, it will go away. Cultivate only positive thoughts.

**November 8, 1978**

The only way to deal with negative thoughts and old impressions is complete surrender. Pray, pray, pray. If we completely surrender, then he takes over the mind. Otherwise thoughts are very dangerous; they only go away when we don't pay attention.

**November 11, 1978**

There is no such thing as a hopeless case. It just takes more time for some people and less time for others. That is not our concern. The thing is to live spiritual life—of unselfishness, love, compassion, forgiveness—and leave to him the question of when we will realize God. It is absolutely true that Thakur can untie the knots of our past impressions. He will show us that he can do it, he will hold us when we fall, but he will make us walk. Swami Vivekananda once said, "He will make you bleed." He is like a father standing before a baby with arms outstretched, saying, "Come on, walk."

**November 19, 1978**

The minute negative forces come, say no. "I know you are there—you will be dead very soon. I am calling on Sri Ramakrishna." To examine thoughts simply means to harbor good ones and say no to bad ones. Let Thakur's name be like the windshield wiper. The second they come, say no and put your whole body, mind, everything at his feet and keep it there. No matter what comes, be happy you have taken his name and don't worry about anything else. Keep the mind in a happy mood with hymns, etc. Do all work for him and move with everyone just like that.

Just be natural. Whenever negative thoughts come, just set it right immediately. Be strong—"I will not yield." Pray to Thakur, "I don't want anything except pure devotion to you." The more you try to spiritualize, the more the *samskaras* also become intense, so the more you have to say no to the mind. The more they come, just keep saying no, no, no, to the mind and gradually they become weak. A time will come when you'll feel quite relaxed and alright.

### November 23, 1978

You must separate yourself from the thoughts, say no to the thoughts. Don't even tell Thakur; *you* say no to the thoughts. Then pretty soon the mind itself will keep thoughts away, like a trained dog keeps strangers away. And look within, look within, look within; question the mind constantly.

Let no attachment to anything outside get in. Look at everyone outside as x, y and z. See Thakur in all beings, as Hanuman went on bowing down everywhere because he saw Rama in all.

Purity means you don't seek anything.

When we know the difference between the container and the contents, we have got all the wisdom in the world. Thoughts are the contents, mind is the container. We can't throw the contents out, but we can be detached. Never seek satisfaction outside. Look within, look within, look within.

### November 25, 1978

There is nothing to purify the mind like selflessness, to feel for others. Forget yourself, care for the rest. That will purify the mind. All rules and regulations are secondary to that.

## November 28, 1978

You can conquer all personal obstacles through love, expanding your heart. All miseries are due to lack of love.

All great souls are exemplars, not just instructors, because they all traveled every inch of the way of evolution and they made it. We will also make it if we follow the path they have given us.

The meaning of Mother's life in the *nahabat* was her total loss of self in the love and service of Thakur. She knew who he was, and he knew who she was.

Guru is he who has found out the Reality beyond the matter/mind complex, the Reality which alone can finally solve the problem of existence. It is he who gives us that insight, tells us our true nature, lifts us up, illumines our hearts. Therefore such a high place in Vedanta is given to the Guru.

## December 7, 1978

Through real love for God we can realize him. A devotee's love really enslaves God. God forgets everything to save his devotee. God does become "a being" for his devotees. The same God has become Christ, Krishna, Buddha, Ramakrishna. And he does save. We only have to really love him, leaving everything else, and then we get it.

For spiritual living: (1) Be selfless. (2) Cooperate with all. (3) Avoid involvement in non-essential issues by means of acceptance. With non-essentials, just accept what comes.

. . .

## December 14, 1978

Spiritual life is like paving a road. You remove all the rocks at the surface level, saying, "No, not for me," to the conscious mind. Whatever is below, you leave there and just pave the road above. That is, whatever is in the unconscious mind that has not come to surface consciousness can be resolved by pouring the concrete of Ramakrishna's name.

"Resolve them to their cause" (per Raja Yoga) means resolve through pure devotion. The more you pour his name and his thought, gradually that, entering into the subconscious mind, becomes stronger than the unconscious tendencies, until a time comes when they cannot tip you off. They are there but they are dead. Seeds may remain but they don't tip you off. After seedless samadhi they are burned completely. So pour the concrete of Thakur's name and everything gets resolved.

When things do come to surface consciousness, don't be frightened. Look at them squarely, more sharply and say no. There was a time when I liked them, but I am not a child playing like that anymore. Now I have discovered something different. Say no and put them off.

The more we become serious about spiritual life, the more problems come, but we can handle them all through complete surrender to Thakur. His name has the power to burn everything. We can overcome all obstacles. So Ramakrishna's children should never be gloomy and morose. In a happy way, put everything at his feet. Remove the ego and everything is loosened automatically. Don't worry about anything. Be happy and content. Cultivate devotion, detachment (from everything else) and dedication (be constantly active in work, study, prayer, etc). Our present condition is nothing but the outcome of habit. Now we have to create a new habit, through spiritual discipline, prayer and meditation, study, austerity (decreasing all wants to the minimum need and being satisfied with what you have).

We have to be very careful not to indulge in low thoughts even unconsciously. We have to be very strict and stern with our own minds and tell them no.

God's love for us is more than ours for him because he is all love. We should care not for *when* we will realize God but just pray that we may feel his grace so that we may continue in his path. If we do that the goal is assured.

## December 15, 1978

Holy Mother had no individuality. She was perfectly resigned to him who is the embodiment of Divinity, so why should she need austerities? Who needs austerities when you have him and are perfectly resigned to him? She was born perfect.

## December 27, 1978

Though Swami Shivananda approached the Divine as formless, still he was a slave to Thakur. He would say Thakur was with form, without form, everything, and he would prostrate flat before him, getting up with tears. He never became petty or worldly even in the least. His mind was always on a high spiritual level.

- Don't . . . resent, resist or react.
- Do . . . reflect, reconcile and resolve.
- Don't . . . accuse, demand or complain.
- Do . . . love, respect and cooperate.

By simply hearing or reading, ideas remain dormant.

By hearing or reading, thinking and contemplating, ideas are assimilated.

Do not identify with and imitate negative thoughts.

Do identify with and imitate positive thoughts.

Thoughts become powerful by taking interest in and paying attention to them.

Evolution to higher stages is possible through devotion, detachment and dedication.

Identify with the loving Consciousness and not with the psycho-physical complex which is constantly changing from birth to death, while the former remains the same throughout.

Evil is that which separates you from the rest, which you have to hide from others.

Good is that which makes you wholesome and unites you with the rest.

In God there is no evil, as there is no darkness in the sun.

Godward is good. Away from God is evil.

God is the ground of our dwelling.

# 1979

## January 1, 1979

Whatever spiritual wish we have will be fulfilled if we only surrender to God. To deserve the grace of God we need: (1) surrender—complete surrender of body, mind, everything. (2) austerity—"I don't want anything else" (3) one-pointed devotion.

In the beginning, for a devotee, meditation just means to think of Thakur, whether through japa, prayer, meditation, hymns, reading his teachings even. If there is a little devotion to him, we need not do anything. We need not struggle to purify the thoughts. When any thought comes, think of him immediately and he will do the rest. Just as a child runs to mother when he soils his cloth, so also we must go to him with everything, constantly. It's just like a windshield wiper; the thought of him keeps away all other thoughts. Going to the shrine is like a spiritual shower. The thought of him makes us clean. All worst thoughts will come up, but if we put everything before Thakur, he will give us strength and he will purify us. The presence of bad thoughts doesn't make us unclean unless we get attached to them. Don't identify with them or pamper them; just think of Thakur. He is the only purifying element. The farther you go towards the east, the more you move away from the west. Remember the distinction between the container and the contents, and don't be frightened by the contents.

When you have to go to work, just think of all work as Thakur's. "I am Thakur's and Thakur is mine." Keep that feeling always. Whether working at the office or the temple or anywhere, just feel, "It is Thakur's work." Then where is the problem? It's just a matter of shifting the focus from me to him. If you feel everything is his, then you never feel unwilling or tired or attached or egoistic, etc. Don't get attached to anything at work. Be responsible, be friendly, but see everyone as x, y, z. Hold toward everyone the attitude of a mother—"How can I help?" And keep always an atmosphere of seriousness. Never allow light-mindedness. Learn to make work a continuation of the spiritual thought which we intensify in the shrine.

## January 3, 1979

[For resolution of all thoughts, conscious and unconscious:] If you know consciously what is disturbing you, then put it off through discrimination and meditation ("medi" means to measure). If you feel disturbed but don't know why, then make a resolve not to brood, and then put the mind on God. Put the spiritual thought consciously and that gets in and purifies the mind.

. . .

## January 8, 1979

Monastic life means not harboring any negative feelings. Hatred and jealousy must never be kept in the mind. One negative feeling like that can hold us back for lifetimes. There is no way we can move spiritually. We don't know God and he doesn't know us if we hate, because God is in that person whom we hate.

## January 12, 1979

[Talking to a group of young people:] At a certain age lust is very strong. But anyone who has got a little devotion to God can spiritualize it. Hold on to that devotion and intensify it. Turn the mind toward God and gradually the mind takes that color. Avoid all laziness. The more you indulge sensate urges, the worse it becomes.

## January 16, 1979

Self-surrender is the most important thing in spiritual life because when you admit, "I don't know anything," "I don't understand," you thereby acknowledge your doubts and limitations. You open yourself up and then Divine grace, guidance and blessings flow in. At times we feel we can't move; at every step there is an obstacle, but through surrender we open the door to grace. Girish said that through grace his mind was lifted completely above the psychophysical complex.

## January 17, 1979

The more you love God, the closer you will be to the Guru and to all. Consciously and deliberately cultivate the attitude, "I don't know," because then we open up and can receive knowledge. That is what Thakur was doing when he always said, "Mother, I don't know anything." He was thereby removing his individuality, denying his individuality, and then the Divine flowed through. We must do likewise. Whenever we have any problem with anybody, square it up by turning to Thakur. Learn to see the whole world and everything through him. Then the whole world will look different. And do everything as his work. "Thakur, this is your work." Always.

We don't see anything in the world. We only want to see Thakur. If you see anything negative, say, "I don't know." The eye sees but "I don't know, I may be wrong." Our only purpose and concern is to know Thakur. If we know him, we know all the gods in the world.

## January 22, 1979

If we seek only to understand Thakur, Ma and Swamiji and to live just as they would want us to be, then everything will work out well. Think always, "What would they advise me if they were here?" Put the mind consciously and only on why you are leading a spiritual life and deliberately keep away from all other nonsense.

## January 23, 1979

When you meditate on Thakur, think of that Divine consciousness shining through him and think that you are also that. That is really my true nature; all other things are superimposed.

## January 24, 1979

Incarnations come but they do not go away. They are eternal and are ever present and all-pervasive. But through our devotion we have to tune our minds to Thakur. He is always present, whether we know it or not. He hears our conversation, our heartbeat. We need not pray to him from the standpoint of making our needs known, but because we need to know that he knows. He knows what we need. He only wants our complete surrender to him. When we do that, harboring no other thought, then he preserves what we have and carries what we need.

Our faith in him is based on the experience of those who have witnessed his divine glory. His direct disciples really saw him in all beings. That is why they loved all and could never hate or hurt anybody. Thakur is the witness of our every thought and deed and if we remember that we will never harbor any evil.

It is good to try to understand Thakur in every way but most important is devotion. Understand as much as you can but don't worry about the rest. Really we cannot understand him. There is no doubt about his all-pervasiveness. If I feel I exist, then he exists too.

The sadhana of Incarnations is like a mountain climbing guide. He climbs with us and goes through all the same things, same suffering, but he has been through it and reached the goal before, so he knows the process and his suffering is not in that darkness of ignorance like that of others.

Thakur's message for this age is that (1) God is—he is real, (2) God can be realized, and (3) there is only one God, the same God of all religions.

Those who have come into Thakur's orbit are unbelievably fortunate. [The swami said he would not trade that position for anything.] Nowhere else can you find such a perfect ideal as that shown by the trinity of Thakur/Ma/Swamiji. Due to past experiences, the mind will tempt us and look at worldly life and say it's not so bad, so-and-so is happy, etc. But we have to say, "No, I know what this world is," and not give up our ideal. It's not that marriage is bad, but we can only know God in reality if we give the whole mind. We don't leave the world out of failure or denial, but out of a positive seeking something higher, a higher joy, a lasting peace, the highest truth.

## January 28, 1979

Three things are necessary in any field to gain intuition: (1) austerity, (2) study—we need to reason to the fullest extent, and (3) surrender to a higher power.

Then you need patience and perseverance. Intuition never contradicts reason, but it comes from a realm beyond reason. When seeking intuition in the spiritual realm, we don't know how much is in the subconscious mind and how long it will take to purify.

## February 5, 1979

Yes, we want to be happy. We want to enjoy life. But we want lasting joy, the peace that passeth all understanding. So we must always ask whether anything can give us that lasting joy, permanent satisfaction. We gain that only through being our own true Self—this is the intellectual conviction that comes through study. We can't try to straighten things outside; rather look within. Close the eyes to everything external; look within and open the eyes. Then with the conviction that this is it, struggle. Struggle must be there, but we can make it through his grace.

. . .

## February 6, 1979

The ideal of Thakur/Ma/Swamiji is one of universal acceptance and to help people in whatever way we can. The goal is to see the same in all, so the means must be that too. Therefore, being firm on our own Ground, we should be kind, affectionate and concerned for all. A man of realization feels the whole world to be his own—nothing separate from him. Witness the life of Holy Mother.

## February 7, 1979

A child of Thakur must accept everyone just as they are and make it a spiritual discipline never to complain about anybody. No matter what anybody believes or accepts, no matter what anybody thinks of us, no matter what anybody thinks of what we do, still we must love them. That is the specialty of Thakur and Mother—universal acceptance, all-inclusive love.

## February 15, 1979

Non-injury comes even before truth. Most important is never to hurt anybody. We have to swallow our opinions at times, whether right or wrong, but it is more important to gain a heart than to gain a point or to be right. When you consciously forego your opinion, you gain a lot.

Thoughts are not you; we mustn't pay any attention to them. Even with recurring thoughts, whenever they come, put Thakur there and, through strong, sustained effort, the old thoughts will die down. Just pray to him immediately and constantly. The thought of him burns the *samskaras*. Even if we have a million tons in the subconscious mind, we should not be frightened, but be glad we have started burning them. We may have to struggle for years, but have the determination to finish the job and burn the whole thing. Don't be frightened, because everything has to come up, whether in dream or conscious mind. Just don't identify with them. Be glad you have been born when you can have this ideal. We don't know Thakur's power, the fire of his name. He really can transform us, just as he did Girish. Girish still had bad thoughts come up after giving the power of attorney, but then Thakur's thought always came too and that purified his mind.

Simply don't think of anything except Thakur. Don't put the mind on anything petty or negative or the mind will always be miserable. Just try to see him in all, do all work in his name, and surrender to him completely. We can't manage everything, but give the responsibility to him and be happy in the faith that when we surrender to him, he will do everything.

Don't compare yourself with others but move toward Thakur in your own way. There are only three things we want to know: who he is, who I am, who are all these.

When we are 3, he is the 4th, as the Ground of us all. We think of the Ground as Thakur, because we are set in him, our existence is in no way separate from him, whether we know it or not. Being aware of his presence like that is like being aware that someone is downstairs overhearing your talk. Only you can never talk so low that he doesn't hear.

Be like Hanuman who thought of nothing but Rama. Say, "I have no time to think of anything except Thakur." Try to see him in all beings because the divinity of man is a fact. A gold coin may be covered with dirt but you don't throw it away. Rather you try to clean it. So never condemn anybody; it's just that people are ignorant of their true nature.

"Surrender" is the whole thing. Put everything at his feet and he will swallow it.

## February 17, 1979

Emotions are also thoughts. Thoughts means impressions, anything arising out of the subconscious mind. From all these we must be detached—anything which is not relevant to the truth we are seeking.

## February 21, 1979

Never complain about anybody. Never argue. Just put the whole mind on Thakur and don't even think of anything else. Anything that comes to the mind, put him there. Solve any argument by putting him at the center. Think of everything in terms of him. Put everything at his feet; surrender completely. Always identify only with him, with the positive. Be happy in his name. Never on any account make the mind miserable. Just beg him for pure devotion and he will grant it.

## February 22, 1979

Love for God is the secret. The Ramakrishna Order is founded on love and held together by love. Swami Virajananda used to say to the new monks, "Why have you renounced everything to be here? In order to convert the whole energy into loving service." You can work out the whole karma through loving service.

## March 3, 1979

To keep the mind straight, be like a toll gate—keep negative thoughts out. Pray to Thakur, "I don't know *anything*," and put everything on him because we are not responsible for anything, honestly.

## March 5, 1979

Don't worry about trying to purify things one by one. Just put the whole bundle at Thakur's feet. When you vacuum a carpet, you don't pick up things one by one; you suck up the whole thing. We have to create a spiritual vacuum cleaner by putting the whole bundle at his feet. "I don't know anything. It is too much for me. Therefore I take refuge at your feet." Then you can avoid being caught in the mesh of the world or your own thoughts. Do everything with his thought.

Be proud and at the same time humble—proud that I am his child, and humble in wishing the same for all. The thought of him makes you wholesome within and without.

## March 8, 1979

[Reading Swamiji's poem, "To a Friend," translated from Bengali, "For the sake of love, even as one insane, / I have often clutched at shadows lifeless."] Swami Vivekananda was such a great lover. He really wanted to love and be loved. After Thakur died, Gangadhar Maharaj (Swami Akhandananda) one day noticed Swamiji somewhat pensive and asked him about it. Swamiji replied that since Thakur's death nobody loved him the way he did. He asked Swami Akhandananda, "Don't you feel so too?" Gangadhar Maharaj said, no. When Swamiji asked him, "Do you find anybody who loves you like he did?" Swami Akhandananda replied, "Yes, you!" Embracing him Swamiji said, "Oh Ganga, I can never catch you! You are always above me."

Love is the truth of life. It is everything. Look at Buddha, look at Holy Mother. There are so many rocks from so many lives piled up on top of the unselfish love that is there in us. But once the stream starts to flow, it widens more and more automatically.

Overcome jealousy by feeling we are all one and all are my own. We are all branches on the same vine—the same divine sap flowing through all. Always identify, never separate. Pray for unselfish love, for pure devotion.

## March 11, 1979

For the path of devotion you need prayer, detachment, dedication, contemplation.

## March 20, 1979

Burning *samskaras* means not to be frightened when they show up. Don't hold anything; put all before him. When you are tested, that is the time to hold on. The night is passing! If we have devotion there is a dynamic pull. Even if a car is damaged, if it is hooked on to another big car, it is pulled along. It is just like that if we hold onto him. That is the time to be more prayerful, inward, strict with yourself, positive. That is the time to strengthen your will.

Never condemn anybody—not nature, not yourself. It will make the mind more peaceful now and help very much later on when you are trying to purify the mind completely. We simply have no time for negative thoughts. Remain as his slave.

## March 22, 1979

No matter what we read or think or say about God, the one truth of all religions about which there is no doubt is to love God and to love all. To love and serve is the gist of all religions.

**March 26, 1979**

Don't allow the mind to drag you away from the object of devotion.

Always question the mind. That way you avoid 99% of problems.

Be serious and sincere.

**March 28, 1979**

When we go to meditation, we are trying to purify and uplift our mind. Therefore at that time we must not allow the mind to wander here and there. We must try to keep off every other thought except God. Now we are accumulating positive things and those will gradually untie the knots of accumulated negative things. Surrender, as Raja Yoga says, is the best way to handle the unconscious thoughts. If the mind is not concentrated, open your eyes and look at his picture. That picture is living to us. Imagine you are at Dakshineswar and he is sitting there on that cot and just talk to him. If problem thoughts come, pray. Don't imitate anybody—everyone has their own level and their own attitude.

Music can be a great help—take any song you like most and establish a relationship through that song. [The swami said sometimes he goes on for half an hour with one song, repeating the lines most meaningful to him.]

**April 4, 1979**

Never identify with any negative thought. Mind is just like a crystal. When negative thoughts are put near it, it appears to be impure. But put spiritual thoughts there and it takes that color. Look at him, not at your mind. We all have the freedom and the equipment to turn the mind; it just takes will. We have to arouse that will.

## April 13, 1979

Two things are most important in working. First, work as a master, not as a slave. Someone else may tell you what is to be done, but once accepted it becomes *my* work. That is, I assume full responsibility for seeing that it is done. I don't offer any excuses to anybody. I don't do it to please anybody. Second, I do it for Thakur. It is my work, but *for* him. For him alone I work, to him I offer everything.

## April 18, 1979

The key to gaining humility is to feel, "How much do I really know?" When you admit your ignorance and really seek light from illumined persons, then true humility comes. Light-mindedness makes us think we know, but if we are more silent, more still, more observant, then we gain depth and realize how much we do *not* know.

"Be silent and know that I am God." Always have readiness to learn. And know that truth always lies far beneath surface appearances. Don't judge anything by what you see on the surface. As Thakur said, we want to know the owner of the garden; we want to know what is behind this maya.

Consciousness is *loving* Consciousness. Thakur's life so clearly shows it. He is the embodiment of love and all we have to do to feel it and open our heart to him. If we open even a little bit, we feel it ten times more because he is love itself. His disciples said you could see the light in him. When he paced the room at night it was like seeing a lighted lamp move across the room, or when he walked from the Ganges you could see that he was a luminous personality. Swami

Vivekananda said his body was pure *sattva*; they could only press it ever so gently. Mother was also very careful what food she gave to him.

**April 20, 1979**

[Regarding someone not telling him when they felt sick:] One must live in tune with the fact of things. Be yourself, be honest with yourself. Also, it is very important to take care of your health.

**April 26, 1979**

When things happen, reflect on them calmly, never get upset. Never carry any negative feeling about anything. That is an absolute.

Thakur seldom, if ever, said, "I am God." He would say, "He is manifesting here," or things like that. Even though God is all-pervasive, the Incarnation is like a special dwelling of God. Even Mother looked on Thakur as Divine Mother. It is true that he is our mother, more so than father, because he is more close. We go to him for everything. The direct disciples always used to say, "Go to Thakur," because they were so conscious of what he was and what he could do.

**May 1, 1979**

Just put everything on Thakur. Forget about discrimination because we have got him—Thakur—and put your head at his feet. Prayer to him is the only thing. Just put your whole soul at his feet. No matter how much you are tossed, never give up that hold. Prayer is the way to get his grace. Prayer is nothing but opening your heart to him and receiving thereby his light. So pray to him, "Guide me, bless me, I don't want anything except pure devotion to You."

## May 3, 1979

[Reading in *Sri Ramakrishna the Great Master* about Thakur's dependence on Divine Mother and freedom through her grace from all evil thoughts:] We must learn to depend on Thakur like that. Any unwanted thought, just put at his feet immediately. It's just like putting a wet cloth in fire; it dries up immediately. If we really do this, we will see wonderful effect in the mind. When man goes to the moon, he protects himself with a spacesuit, enclosing himself in earth-atmosphere. We must make the thought of Ramakrishna just like a spacesuit. Then nothing can touch us, just as not even a torch can penetrate or burn that spacesuit. What is needed in spiritual life is will-power and we get that will from Thakur.

## May 5, 1979

To be spiritual means to live in that which is neither body nor mind—to shift our consciousness from the feelings of the body and the thoughts of the mind to the awareness of the spirit.

## May 8, 1979

If there is "theft in the heart," God keeps quiet. We must enliven our self-conscious principle, be aware of what we want and live like that. We have to follow what God/Guru tells us or else they cannot help us. But if we earnestly struggle, then we get his grace.

If Thakur could straighten Girish, he can certainly straighten us. Put everything at his feet: "I have none but you, I have surrendered to you, you are my only refuge." Then relax and be joyful because we have no problem, the problem is his.

## May 9, 1979

When mind is filled with dark thoughts, tendencies, etc., it is *tamasic*; kundalini power is held down by the presence of those thoughts. But if you detach yourself from the thoughts, you are not burdened down by those *tamasic* tendencies. When you surrender to God, the mind becomes light and moves up, or the kundalini power rises. Thoughts may be there but whether you move up or down depends totally upon relationship and identification. Don't identify with them, be detached from them and turn the mind toward God. Don't worry about *tamas* / *rajas* / *sattva*. Turn to Thakur. All that talk of *gunas* in Gita is mere baby talk compared to Krishna's message at the end about complete surrender to him. That is the real message. Be like Hanuman who said, "I don't know the day of the week, etc., I know only Rama."

## May 15, 1979

Renunciation is necessary because if you want to see the Kingdom of God within you, you have to remove everything, all the impressions and identifications which are covering it. Therefore you must say no to all thoughts, push them aside and keep them off.

When once we have decided we want spiritual life, then we have to strongly exercise our will when temptations arise. If you don't exercise the will and rather keep temptations alive, they become strong. But if you exercise the will and say, "No, I don't want it," then they are cut down. But you have to say "no" again and again. It's like cutting down a tree; every time you say no, you give a blow with the axe and finally you sever the whole thing and it falls down.

. . .

## May 22, 1979

Samadhi is realization of cosmic consciousness.

Real spirituality is to feel for others. In a realized person there are two modes of identification. One is like mother with child; if she sees child being hurt, she feels it. The other is like if a finger on the hand is hurt; more complete identification.

## May 23, 1979

[To a group of monastics:] Never forget why we have sacrificed material and worldly prosperity, etc. As we have sacrificed materially, so we must be spiritually. It doesn't matter whether we color the cloth, but once we have decided to color the mind, we must keep that attitude in every situation. Remember that, move like that, speak like that, relate ourselves with others like that. We have to give the whole mind to God, not merely a part of it. It is when we give the whole mind that God's grace works, that we can demand and charge him. But if we give only a part, we can get tipped off and we cannot blame him. He wants 100% of our mind.

## June 6, 1979

If we can strengthen our love for God, it becomes easy to conquer all negative tendencies. That spiritual power makes other things fall off. We must seek only to get that deep devotion. And we must give the whole mind to God. There is only one mind, so you really can't give it to God *and* mammon. "My kingdom is not of this world."

Real love is extremely rare in this world. Real love means complete selflessness, but it is nature's way that we think of self first.

## June 7, 1979

We don't know our own minds. If we can straighten something, well and good. But if not, put it at his feet. It's like a child with a torn cloth. He tries to fix it; if he finds he cannot he runs to mother and throws it on her to fix it. It is not given to many to have such an ideal and to seek to follow it.

## June 12, 1979

We have to give the whole mind if we want to understand Thakur or Swamiji.

## August 1, 1979

In the *Gospel of Sri Ramakrishna,* Thakur says, "Whoever has sincerely called on God will certainly come here." It is because when an Incarnation comes, the pull is irresistible. It's like if you are seeking a certain commodity and you hear there is a big sale on it somewhere, you rush there to get it. It's like that with an Incarnation for those who are seeking the Divine, even unconsciously. Even when their body dissolves, they remain in their spiritual form and we can experience them if we tune our mind to them. They are like broadcasting stations whose radio waves are all pervasive. No matter where we are, if we perfect our receiving instrument—the mind—we can tune in to their presence and receive their grace.

It is really the grace of God if we get three things: human birth (because then self-consciousness is present); desire for liberation (our devotion); and refuge with a realized soul (that is the ultimate, to be in their company—realization is assured). It's like getting into a boat (great souls are the boats); our struggle becomes minimized very much if we have the company of such a great soul.

## August 2, 1979

Spiritual discipline means to discipline the body and mind so that we can lift our minds to the spiritual realm. The goal, the real meaning of spiritual, is to see the same Self equally existing in all. That is the highest.

Similarly, the way to overcome jealousy is through love and identification. You can't fight it with logic—you can only fight it with love. Love is the universal element of spirituality. As there is the same blood flowing in all the fingers, so the same Spirit is present in all beings. If you hate or hurt anyone, you hurt God. That is why Jesus said, "Love thy neighbor as thyself." That commandment is greater than the first because you can't love God unless you fulfill that one first. We have to feel, "Not I, but we," and that "we" is actually God.

All problems and tensions are to be solved by putting everything on Thakur.

## August 7, 1979

[Talking about Thakur saying that after the death of his body he would remain in the subtle body, eating through millions of mouths, to which Baburam Maharaj (Swami Premananda) replied that he wanted to see him in his gross form eating through only one mouth.] That is true. Like the gopis we want the relative rather than the Absolute. But there is more fulfillment if we can learn to love and serve him in all beings. "As you have done unto the least of these you have done unto me." As Thakur told Naren, we have to learn to think of him with eyes open, in all beings.

## August 27, 1979

[After reading some incidents in *The Mother As I Saw Her*

written by Swami Saradeshananda, Swami continued to talk about her with tears in his eyes.] Sometimes people would go to Mother at Jayrambati when she was taking rest and someone would tell the visitor she was resting. But she would overhear it and go out the back of the house to meet the visitor by the time he turned to go. Again, one boy who later became a monk went to see her. He had walked in the rain and arrived soaking wet when all were resting. Mother heard him out on the veranda and she came out and with her own cloth dried his head. He protested, but she persisted and hushed him so that others would not be disturbed.

### September 10, 1979

Keep the mind away from all mundane problems and keep it turned to the spiritual, the divine side. Do everything for Thakur and keep his thought. See everything in that light. Remember Thakur's saying to keep the knowledge of nonduality in the corner of your cloth and then do whatever you like. There is only One and that means all are mine. Even if someone contradicts or opposes or misunderstands me, still he or she is mine. That must be the thought. We have to be spiritual, and being spiritual simply means to think of God.

### September 11, 1979

The first step in spiritual life is not to harbor any negative thought. Negative thoughts will destroy us, because they prevent us from meditating on or thinking of God. Most important is never to impute any motive to anybody, because right away it prejudices and poisons your mind. Even if you see something negative, don't attribute a motive to it. Rather say, "I don't know," even if there seems to be 100% proof. Everyone is evolving and moving up but *your* mind gets stuck if you put a negative motive on somebody. They may have changed but *you* are stuck with a negative prejudice. Therefore hate the sin but not the sinner. Make everybody your own.

## September 14, 1979

Anytime a negative force comes up, surrender it to Thakur right away. If you ever feel a limitation or feel you have acted wrongly, put it at his feet right away and say, "Forgive me." Then everything goes away.

Never feel depressed, because we have taken Thakur's name. Get the mind on a positive track by thinking of his blissful face in the samadhi picture and knowing that is our nature. The significance of that picture is not just what Thakur attained, but it is a revelation of our own true nature. So think of that face and say, "That is my real nature." Through ignorance I identify with this and that, but in reality that Loving Consciousness is my nature.

## September 19, 1979

When a person realizes God, he sees the same light in all, all the time. He is never away from that awareness. That seeing is with a spiritual eye. It is a kind of spiritual perception, not with these eyes. That seeing the same light in all is like when a boat enters from the river into the ocean; then you can see all the other rivers entering into the same ocean. One gains that awareness when one transcends the body/mind complex, the little individuality, when the individual consciousness becomes one with the supreme consciousness. In reality they are always one, but it is a question of identification.

"Shakti" means the power of God. The way Samkhya uses it, it is merely unconscious activity. But the way Thakur used it, it means both consciousness and energy. It is what we call

Divine Mother or Heavenly Father. Whenever we bring God into relationship, we are in the realm of the relative. But God absolute and God relative are non-different. Brahman and Shakti are one, like a snake coiled up and a snake wriggling along—inactive and active.

It is so true that if we take one step, God takes nine. If we have the determination to live a spiritual life and take one step in that direction, we get so much divine help. But we have to take that step, have that determination with no loose ends, or no help comes. All we have to do is turn towards him and he does the rest. He is our very own. He is our father and mother, where else can we go? Go to him and tell him, "I am like this. You make me something." When the mind feels damp, just put it in the fire of Thakur's thought.

**September 29, 1979**

[Regarding Thakur's standing samadhi picture:] It demands absolute purity of heart to be able to go to that state and stay there. Saints have purity of heart, but they retain some ego of a teacher etc. They touch that state and come away. But to stay there and still keep the body is very rare. It was because of that child-attitude of Thakur's. From the very beginning he said, "Mother, I don't know anything"—complete surrender to her. Therefore he had such purity and egolessness.

**October 4, 1979**

Samesightedness is like how a child sees everyone with no distinction of male/female, good/bad, etc. We can regain that childlike state through spirituality. That child's mind gathers all impressions and becomes impure, but by denying all those *samskaras* we gradually uncover that original pure child mind. We must become like a child to enter the kingdom of heaven. In the struggle to regain purity we have to try to change the view. There is a monastic vow not to see people in a sensate way but as manifestations of the Divine. We have to struggle hard to superimpose a spiritual thought like that. We have to make a strong effort and tell the mind again and again to change the view and not allow it to project a sensate view. While we are in the struggling process we have to be extremely cautious, but after some years it becomes our nature, a new habit. We de-hypnotize the mind and create a new psyche. We have the freedom to make the mind however we want it.

As we see multiplicity and have to imagine God, so the man of samadhi sees God first and everything else in God. Nothing, no object even [Swami held up a knife as he said this] is opaque to him. It's like if there are a bunch of clear plastic figures in a room with a huge light behind. When you look at them you see that light shining through with just the skeleton of the forms. You see that light in and through. Then if you bring the mind down in order to exist on a level where you can help people, you see objects, but you never lose the awareness of that higher experience. Most people, if they attain the highest, simply merge in that and the body goes after 21 days. But as Thakur could retain his individuality and come down to help people, so also his children who have that ideal. It is a divine mystery. For a *vijnani,* who has known the truth of both the absolute and the relative, there is no negation. He sees the Divine everywhere. When he looks outside he sees a continuation of the Divine—pure consciousness on one side, and on the other, a multi-colored light as it shines through the world of objects. His ego is like a thin line between sunlight and rainbow. He feels himself to be a part of the whole, a branch on the vine when he comes down to that little bit of I-consciousness.

### October 18, 1979

Just as an X-ray enables us to see more than surface things, so also the spiritual eye of a person of illumination enables him to see more than what we see. He sees the Spirit everywhere, in everything.

### October 19, 1979

Two main points: Surrender to Thakur and don't harbor any negative thought. Anything you put on him, he will attend to it. But if you don't turn and you carry a negative thought, you scar your mind.

### October 21, 1979

Never identify with spiritual failures. Look only to those who made it, like Latu who had no other qualification than his absolute obedience and surrender. Surrendering to God is the whole key. If we do that, God becomes our slave. Even if a part of the mind is on the worldly side, pray to him like that. "Thakur, my mind is not good. You straighten it, you purify me. I am not fit. You make me fit. I have nowhere else to go, I have taken refuge in you. Now you guide me, you set my mind." It is natural that the mind oscillates toward the worldly side, but we have to make the resolve, "I shall make it!" Then if we surrender to him, he is our slave. It's only a question of our love and surrender to him. Then we will succeed.

The secret of spiritual discipline is dispassion, which means to lift the ego from the mire, from all other things except the spiritual. The mind may run toward the world but we have to lift it up. Just surrender to him; we have to come out of ourselves completely.

**November 6, 1979**

Let us "waste" just this one life for Thakur. Dedicate this one life to Thakur/Ma/Swamiji. Don't care for results, but if you put yourself at their feet, everything will work out wonderfully well. Give them this one life and see what happens. Our struggle is to deserve their grace.

**November 7, 1979**

Keep Thakur's thought, the thought of his presence. Don't dwell on anything negative; don't worry about other things.

Pray to Thakur to hold your mind steady, to hold you. Due to past *samskaras* the mind jumps here and there. But when a horse is tied to a post, it is only when he tries to move that he feels the pull. It is Godward movement that makes us feel the pull. The mind looks back longingly at times but you have to tell it firmly, there is no going back. Use all spiritual ammunition to move the mind towards him and not backwards. Worldly people have so many problems, but our only problem is how to keep the mind on God and away from the world. If you don't pay attention to worldly thoughts, and keep the mind on Thakur, they gradually die. So don't worry about them or dwell on them; just turn to him constantly.

The best thing is to surrender completely. We can't solve anything. Just surrender everything completely to him and don't worry about other things.

**November 8, 1979**

[Question: A baby naturally surrenders to its mother because it knows for certain that the mother is its own. So in trying to surrender to Thakur, how do we get the conviction that he is our own?] Every relationship in the world comes from God. And it is true that Thakur is our own. Even Holy Mother called Thakur "Mother." That is the best feeling to have toward him. We come to God with love, never with fear. He is really our own, our father and mother. We can tell him anything; we can appeal to him; we can even demand from him.

## November 12, 1979

To imagine the one Spirit in all, think of a vast glass dome, painted black, full of holes. Inside the dome is a huge light, shining out through all the holes. We are all so many holes, but there is only one Light shining through all. Each hole thinks he is the whole story, and as long as anyone remains separate from the rest, he is miserable. The secret of life and spirituality is wholesomeness, because there is only that one Light in all.

## November 20, 1979

No matter what obstacle comes—thought, feeling, question, doubt, confusion, pressure, anything—all is to be solved only from the point of Thakur. No matter what it is, say, "I don't know," and put it at his feet.

Once we have taken up spiritual life, we must struggle to think of him constantly. It is not just to get away from the world and live an easy life. No, we must think of him constantly. When we work we must keep up his thought, particularly the mantra.

No one ever said the road would be smooth. Spiritual life is very difficult, but not impossible. The more we struggle, the stronger the *samskaras* become. The only solution for everything is to surrender to him, everything.

Blessed are those who have got his name. When an Incarnation comes, those who feel his pull should not waste this opportunity. Keep the mind strong through joy and contentment. Never yield to depression. The worst things come, but I have got his name. Hold onto that because all things come, but they all pass too. "They come, they go, they are impermanent in their nature" (Gita). So just hold onto him.

## November 29, 1979

The most important thing in spiritual life is never to hurt *anybody*. *Ahimsa* (non-injury) comes even before truth.

## December 27, 1979

[Referring to Thakur's experience of completely transcending name and form, and being fully merged in the transcendental realm:] Only Incarnations can go to that state and remain there or be, as Thakur was, always on the threshold. But through the Incarnation's grace, his disciples can also reach that state and still retain the body. Ordinary souls attaining it, the body falls off in 21 days. But Incarnations and Iśvarakoṭis (i.e his disciples) can retain it. It is like a red hot iron ball into which pins are stuck, and other pins into those pins. They all then become red hot but it is all from the central red hot iron ball (i.e. Incarnation). Even now the swamis who really understand Thakur do so because they have had those experiences. But the disciples stay only briefly in that state and then come down. Through his grace they retain the body and always retain that consciousness. That is, a part of the mind is always there and they can go to that state whenever they want, usually when they are alone or lying down on the bed.

[Referring to Sri Ramakrishna's saying that he saw all men and women as mere masks:] That is an experience, not imagination. After attaining Nirvikalpa Samadhi when you come down, you see that all people are mere masks over that one Loving Consciousness. You always see that after that experience.

## December 30, 1979

[Talking about the greatness of Swami Vivekananda and what he has brought to us in terms of his message of truth and universality:] Behind Swamiji is Thakur, a luminous spiritual giant, filling the whole universe, a luminous spiritual giant filling all space.

# 1980

## January 2, 1980

[Talking about Kalpataru Day:] When Girish expressed his faith in Sri Ramakrishna's spiritual greatness, Thakur's mind soared up and in that high state everything around him was burned, as it were. It was like a spiritual flood whereby everything around was filled up, whether big or small. According to their evolution all were filled according to their capacity. What they experienced was according to their own mental framework. Whether they would be able to retain it depended on their own struggle.

Thakur was always aware. But the bestowal of that grace depended upon the occasion, upon need and fulfillment. There was therefore no knowing when that occasion would come. He illumined everything around—a very special blessing.

He had no "I." After Nirvikalpa Samadhi, "I" was gone. Only that huge cosmic vastness on one side and a little body-mind on the other. That little remaining "I" is only a part of that One. And he also sees that the same is true of all others.

## January 7, 1980

Spiritual life is when you try to lift the mind to the level where you look to the One and not to the variety and the differences. There you really love all and serve all, looking upon all as Spirit, not as matter and mind. You don't look to the temporal differences; you try to look to the very core of every individual, which is Spirit—in yourself and in all.

## January 9, 1980

Overcome your fear complex by thinking of Thakur's disciples and how they all made it through his grace. Even if it is true that they were more advanced, still they struggled intensely. As for us, Thakur can purify anybody, no matter what material we are to start with. He can burn everything; he can work miracles. Honestly, the only thing required is our complete surrender to him. Just have the thought, "I want to lead a spiritual life," and leave the rest to him. Just live the life and surrender to him.

## January 25, 1980

Put off all worry and tension by having no other thought except, "You are my refuge, do guide me." Look at what he did for others, how he straightened Latu, Girish and all. It is easy for him to straighten us!

## February 28, 1980

Gita (18. 65-66) and *Jananīm Sāradāṁ devīṁ, Rāmakṛṣṇaṁ jagad-guruṁ / pāda-padme tayoḥ śritvā, praṇamāmi muhur-muhuḥ* ("O Mother Sarada Devi and Ramakrishna the universal teacher, taking shelter at your feet, I salute you both again and again")—these are the only three verses we need. Forget about everything else. Everything is in these three verses. "Relinquishing all dharmas" doesn't mean abstinence from duty or action, but complete surrender to God. "I am his instrument." You have no other motive, no planning, no axes to grind, no self-seeking. You become natural, spontaneous, "Not I, but Thou." You do everything with his thought. You feel it is all his work. Actually he alone is doing everything; I am only his instrument. Individuality is dead. Girish and Latu are the prime examples, having given the power of attorney to Thakur.

## March 12, 1980

A true devotee doesn't need any other yogas. As Sridhara said, a devotee of Krishna attains Brahmajnana without any effort. That devotion is very hard to get. God doesn't grant it easily because once he does, he is caught. The functioning of the relationship between Bhagavan and Bhakta is very mysterious, but it does work. A true devotee's every prayer is answered if it is from the point of purity of mind or for the welfare of others. A devotee doesn't care for abstruse questions like whether Brahman is 1, 2, or 4. He is like Hanuman who didn't care for the day of the week or the phase of the moon; he only contemplated Rama. Once at Baranagore, Sashi Maharaj was doing work in the shrine, worship, etc. Latu stood there like a statue for hours looking at Thakur's picture in the shrine.

## March 27, 1980

The constant thought of Thakur's presence is most important, no matter where we are. Then everything will work out very well.

When Swami Kalyanananda received the telegram telling him of Swami Akhandananda's passing, he wrote on the back of the telegram: "The light of the Order is gone. The whole world is in darkness."

Swami Premeshanandaji said that it is Thakur's love that holds the whole brotherhood together. That love is the whole thing. It is love that makes saints, not law. Love is the essence of spirituality—straight, pure love, not passing through levels.

## April 23, 1980

The mind of the man of illumination is always in *saṁyama* (referencing *Yoga Sutras*). That is why he always knows the minds of others. His mind, like an x-ray, penetrates name and form. For ordinary people, the mind with all its contents stands, as it were, between spirit and matter. In reality the mind is only a shadow of the spirit. But when it is purified and no thought or image stands there, it becomes no-mind. Then nothing stands between the spirit and matter; ; the spirit then pours into the whole thing. The illumined soul sees everything spiritualized. He sees the spirit in everything. Like an x-ray, his vision penetrates the whole world of matter and he sees the spirit everywhere.

## May 6, 1980

You should never allow a gap in the active learning process between the ages of 20 and 30. It can continue after that, but that is when the mind is active and formative and can learn, not just know things. It can learn and assimilate. If the mind gets out of that spirit of learning and seeking knowledge, it forms complexes based on the idea of utility and what one can get out of things. But if you can keep that spirit of learning, then you are willing and eager to learn from any source and you don't seek comforts and what you can get out of it. You want rather to learn, to gain knowledge and that is the sole concern.

## May 11, 1980

Keep your mind on Thakur. Forget about world turmoil, whether internal or external, don't pay attention. Just keep your mind on Thakur. Like for a navigator, Thakur is our polestar. Keep your mind on him as on a polestar.

Faith is the key to illumination, not what we know or book knowledge. Thakur told Swami Adbhutananda one thing— keep your mind on God— and he followed it literally.

## May 15, 1980

Thakur is love and love and love, and nothing but love. He is the highest manifestation of divine love, of the Loving Consciousness. Yes, he was unique from the point of renunciation and harmony of religions, but even more was that highest Loving Consciousness.

[Referring to Swami Brahmananda saying that Thakur had such great power and how he removed lust forever with one touch:] We can get that touch even now by thinking of him. He is dead physically but he is alive spiritually, present in all as Spirit, and we can get his touch if we close our eyes to everything else and open our eyes to him. If we think of him, say, "I don't know," and surrender completely to him that will purify our consciousness without any doubt.

## May 22, 1980

[The swami was asked if it is true that Thakur helps us and guides us from within.] Certainly! Thakur's disciples were not always with him but look what guidance they got from him. He is guiding us whether we know it or not. It is like a mother taking care of a sleeping baby. She is doing it whether the baby is conscious of it or not. We just have to keep his thought. Other things come but don't mind them; keep your mind on him.

We must always care more for people than for work and achievement. We must sincerely respect everyone and never lose heart. If we lose respect for someone, it is our unconscious that is polluted. It is self-disrespect. These things are all in our own minds.

## May 27, 1980

Many know Holy Mother's nature, her compassion and kindness, etc., but very few people are aware of her spiritual content and spiritual height. Aside from the externals which we can see, the real thing, the uniqueness, is her perfect purity. Kindness and sympathy many people can have, but there is always some motivation. But in Mother's purity there is no motivation. She was perfectly unconcerned. Her message to make everybody your own, no one is a stranger to you—is one of the signs of purity. Purity means there is no foreign element, just pure Being. Others perform austerities to become pure, but for her there was no need. In Mother there was absolutely no blemish. The very thought of her purifies the mind.

We can experience Mother's presence, or the presence of any Incarnation, through one-pointedness and devotion. If we make *saṁyama* on Mother, we can experience her presence.

When Mother and Thakur took the bad karma of others on themselves, or when Christ is said to have died for our sins, the real meaning or fact is that when we take their name, their light absorbs, or destroys, our limitations. When we open up to them, their light flows in and straightens all our limitations.

## June 11, 1980

The golden rule for making it in this life is to deny the past. When old impressions come up and try to project in the present, we have to use strong will to deny them. Otherwise we create new *samskaras* and the process goes on ad infinitum. Therefore we have to strongly deny the past through detachment and on the other hand pray to Thakur only for pure devotion. In the early stages it is a big struggle to fight past impressions but we have to be completely detached or else it is like rowing the boat without lifting the anchor; we don't go anywhere.

The mind has no existence of its own. It is only a shadow of the Self. As the moon only reflects the sun's light and then illumines things, so also mind has no light of its own. It only reflects the light of the Self and then functions in perception, etc. It then gathers impressions and, if we are attached, those impressions stick to the mirror. But if we don't identify, they don't stick at all.

## June 16, 1980

[The swami was speaking about things that Swami Kalyanananda taught him at Kankhal.] It is good to be strict within but don't put it outside on others. Always be very generous with others. Accuse yourself but excuse others. Only thus can you make everybody your own. Always think and speak in terms of "we," not "I."

. . .

## June 18, 1980

In the highest realization, when the river enters into the ocean, its river-ness is lost completely. The highest advaita is the truth. But Thakur/Swamiji's ideal is the welfare of all. Therefore individual freedom is there to keep that desire to help others. When one reaches the highest, that desire is there so that he retains just a little ego so he can come back to the relative realm to help people. He can even take another birth to do so.

## June 25, 1980

[Having read that Mother said Thakur's best ornament was his renunciation, Swami said we should think of him like that.] We become what we contemplate, so we should think of him as an embodiment of complete renunciation and complete love. Then our renunciation won't become hatred of the world. We will still feel that everyone is our own. When we see someone very worldly, we should look deep within and think of the Divine presence there. When we keep the thought of Thakur, nothing will go wrong. The most important thing to mind in leading a spiritual life is to constantly remember his presence with us. We must be *Ramakrishna-maya* ("filled with Ramakrishna"). When we come out of the shrine, we must bring his thought with us and keep it always. As Mohammed was always mindful of Allah, as Thakur was ever in the thought of Divine Mother, so we must always keep his thought in our minds. Then we will never go wrong. Strongly imagine his presence always.

The first most important thing in spiritual life is to keep the mind positive. We must not carry any negative thought because it is a very destructive element in the mind—for meditation, prayer and even our positive thinking. It always disturbs us. Just as we keep dirt out of the house, we must keep negative thoughts out of the mind.

## June 26, 1980

The one big problem is that people don't learn. Learning is a great art. We have to be able to learn and thereby evolve. Opinions are the obstacle. The secret of God-realization is to lift the anchor. To lift the anchor means to deny the ego. Not I, but Thou. I am nobody. I don't know anything. Not I. You have to completely deny your own mind and the ego.

Even if our faith and devotion and surrender are imperfect, Thakur accepts them. He knows we are trying. He takes our responsibility and burden, and he himself will make them perfect.

## July 4, 1980

What we previously did consciously is now the unconscious and that causes the trouble. But our present conscious desire and struggle is now making a new unconscious. Slowly, slowly that becomes stronger and the old one is suppressed. So now we have to go forward with courage and strength and not let the past drag us down. Through Thakur's grace and power and blessings we can make it.

Now we have to consciously make a new unconscious and a time will come when that will naturally carry us in the spiritual trend. But we have to have strong will and be alert. Don't look at or carry or hold any negative thought. Try to keep Thakur's thought constantly. We have got a strong hold [pointing to Thakur's picture]. We should work like servant maids, as he taught, with complete detachment.

Spiritual laws transcend human reasoning. That is why God's grace is not subject to our concept of law and reasoning. But the one true law is that you can definitely get God's grace by denying your ego, by coming out of yourself, by opening your heart. Self-denial is the key to spiritual life and to obtaining God's grace.

**July 14, 1980**

[About Sri Ramakrishna's saying that we can see and touch and talk to God:] That is true and real. What is required is purity, one-pointedness and devotion. Once you attain that realm, you can have that experience whenever you want, but you don't seek or ask anything because you are desireless. It is not a physical seeing and talking; it is a spiritual realm, a spiritual contact. In dream you see and touch and talk, but there it is not real and it does not transform your personality. But in the spiritual realm it is real and it totally transforms us.

**August 9, 1980**

[About Gita 14.19: "When the seer does not see any agent other than the three *gunas*..."] Gunas (tendencies) are nothing but the coloring of our own mind, based on our knowledge and experience. Every work we do has a motive, and that motive is based on that knowledge/experience coloring. It determines what we do and in that sense there is no agent other than the *gunas*. That is, we are slaves to that coloring of our minds. Now what we have to do is objectify the *gunas,* that coloring, and be detached. We have to say no to the motivations that come from that coloring and work with a new spiritual motivation, untainted by all those unconscious urges. It is human nature to seek the 3 P's—power, prosperity, pleasure. But we have to renounce those motivations and act as free souls.

An advanced soul sees the *gunas* but pushes them aside and keeps them under control. But a fully illumined soul has no tendencies at all. They are all completely burned. He has the spiritual vision that sees the Spirit in every being. He sees the existential limitations—nothing is hidden from him—but he also sees the Ground and knows that the limitations are only temporal. Therefore he pays no attention. That is what is meant by not finding fault—don't identify the person with the limitation. That is why Jesus could tell that woman, "Go thy way, sin no more." Because he did not identify himself with anything except the Spirit, he also did not identify anyone else with their limitations. But because we identify with our body-mind complex and all limitations, we look at others in the same way. We have to stop that and give up all prejudices and negative feelings.

Work itself is rest if we don't resist but just accept the process and do it with spiritual feeling, just as Holy Mother never tired of cooking and serving people. It was her feeling that all were her own and it was her joy to make them happy.

## August 11, 1980

All prayer, japa, hymns, karma yoga, etc. are for the one purpose of completely remaking the unconscious. We make our own unconscious. To remake it now, we have to purify and spiritualize the mind. Purity means no foreign element. Therefore we have to completely fill the mind, drop by drop, with Divine thoughts. Two things we have to do:

(1) *Be constant.* Somehow or other we have to figure out how to keep the mind in the spiritual realm. That is how we build a spiritual unconscious and how we keep out new negative thoughts. Either pray or sing or repeat the mantra and while

working do everything in his name. Keep a prayerful attitude always.

(2) *Don't pick up anything negative.* That means absolutely avoid paying any attention to anything negative or sensate. One second of attention, and you pick it up! But if you keep your mind occupied with prayer and spiritual thought, then you won't pick things up.

Simply forget about the world and keep the mind on Thakur. Except for the purpose of helping when you can, don't pay any attention to what is going on outside. Just mind your own business. And absolutely avoid all laziness. If the mind slips out of the track due to laziness or non-alertness, you are gone. We must keep the mind always active and alert with study or work. When working, keep up the prayerful attitude.

## August 19, 1980

Renunciation doesn't just mean coming away from home—that is easy. It means to identify with all, and that is difficult. We must feel that the joy and happiness of others is our own joy and happiness. We have to really avoid the "six enemies" or else the mind is stuck there. Spiritual discipline means to straighten the mind, not to just sit doing japa. Nothing helps at all unless we straighten the mind and exert strong will to curb it from every negative twist. Only then can it enter into the spiritual realm. Never let the mind get into jealousy because it is disastrous for spiritual life. Never lose heart, because the more we struggle, the more the dirt comes out. We don't see change right away. We have to struggle and wait.

Introspection means to be aware of how things affect my mind, what I say and what I do. If you are introspective, you will never go wrong.

### September 10, 1980

Develop a humble, prayerful attitude. Avoid stubborn ego. "I don't know."

Never react, but reflect. If you are humble you never react. Reaction has a very bad effect on the subconscious mind.

Never harbor any negative thought. Make a strong commitment to that.

Never be light-minded. Consciously, deliberately, avoid it.

"What can I learn from this?" should be the attitude toward everything.

### September 27, 1980

As you move in spiritual life negative forces become stronger along with the positive. Some people fall prey to them and go back to worldly life and suffer. But if you intensify your spiritual life and go forward with a strong spirit of renunciation and detachment—and don't pay interest and attention to negative thoughts and feelings—then the negative slowly loses its power and you can get through it.

### October 2, 1980

Just keep your eyes on the shore—that is the secret—never take your eyes away from the shore. [The swami told the story of when he saved a boy who was being carried away by the ocean tide from drowning. The swami himself did not know how to swim but he told the boy to hold onto his neck. He was swallowing water and struggling but he made it because he kept his eyes on the shore.]

## October 23, 1980

We have to develop strength and will in spiritual life. No matter what trouble or temptation comes, be strong and don't yield. Never yield to any lower pressure. Never yield to any kind of weakness. If you make a mistake, don't give outward expression or cry over it. Rather turn deeply within and pray to Thakur. Otherwise mind becomes light and it all goes out and you gain nothing.

The Guru takes the responsibility of his disciple with full spiritual awareness. He turns the course of the disciple's mind to the spiritual. At the same time he makes the disciple struggle hard for realization.

If you have a positive spiritual attitude towards others and you do not look to their faults, that very attitude lifts them up.

## November 3, 1980

We have to humble ourselves totally before Thakur, admit our limitation and deeply feel that we don't know anything. We must develop egolessness and complete surrender. Then illumination comes.

## November 13, 1980

Absolutely nothing is in our hands. At the same time we have to take full responsibility to follow him. Here self-effort and complete surrender are not contradictory but must go together.

[About Holy Mother's teachings where she says she dwells also in the cat:] The consciousness of an illumined soul can freely go up and down to many different levels, unlike an ordinary human being whose consciousness is fixed at the human level and can understand neither illumined souls nor animals. When illumined souls meditate, their consciousness goes high up, but when they come down, there is a level where they identify with whatever they see. Consciousness is linked to the eye and where the eye falls, there they feel identified and even feel physically the pain of others. Only illumined souls have that freedom of consciousness.

**November 17, 1980**

[The swami spoke of a mystery devotee occasionally leaving a flower outside the Providence center.] You may not see it; I may not see it; but somebody sees it. *Somebody* sees it.

The same one Consciousness is present at every point, just as when the President gives a speech, all channels broadcast the same thing. As radio waves are all-pervading in a linear way, so Consciousness is all-pervading in a wholesome way. With radio waves all channels are present at any given point; you only have to tune your instrument to catch whichever one you want. With Consciousness, we have to tune our minds to catch it; it is a spiritual tuning. And as that Consciousness is fully conscious, so also those who become in tune with it become fully aware. It is literally true that God hears even the footfall of an ant. He knows the thought before we say it.

**November 26, 1980**

[Reading the *Gospel* where M. first saw Thakur enter into higher moods:] Thakur was fully one with the highest supreme divine Consciousness. He could come and go from there spontaneously, like a turtle going in and out of its shell. When he talked, people didn't feel like it was someone talking about God; rather they felt like it was God talking. Like Krishna, Thakur had that consciousness, but he called himself the child of the Mother.

## November 28, 1980

When Swami Vivekananda said that Sri Ramakrishna could raise thousands of Vivekanandas from a handful of dust, it is absolutely true. Because we fail to realize the truth of it, often we fail to remember that it is our privilege if he is using our body as his instrument.

If we are humble and surrender to God, his name will purify us and remove all our limitations. We can definitely be changed and purified if our prayer is sincere and we really feel it. We must be alert and careful about how we act. His name is like a huge fire that purifies everything. Anything coming, put it in that "dryer;" it dries up all wetness. Both Sri Krishna and Thakur gave that promise: surrender everything to me and I will free you from all limitations.

## December 9, 1980

If you want to spiritualize your life the *best* way is to love your enemies, bless them that curse you. Remove all knots in the mind by loving and accepting all.

## December 17, 1980

The key to being a karma yogi is not to be moved by anything external.

The key to spiritual life in general is to be absolutely detached. Let the world burn.

You can't help anybody; you can only help yourself—to get out of this mess. You can only help others to help themselves.

Never react, but reflect. As soon as you react, you become a slave.

Be strong. We have the blessings of Thakur, Mother and

Swamiji and should always feel that we can face any situation. Never complain or react or speak negatively of anyone to others. Be active and concerned, but don't expect anything from anybody. Forbear, forbear, forbear. Live the life, accept whatever comes and never become miserable under any circumstances.

There is a period in spiritual life when we must constantly struggle hard. Faith and devotion may be there but the thing is to be very strong on the point not to harbor any negative thought. Don't accept any obstacle. I am not the thoughts. I don't know; I don't even want to know. We have to gain momentum and keep up a constant mental process, no matter what we are doing. We have to struggle to keep the mind pure by completely denying all negative thoughts. The thing is, if we completely surrender to him, suddenly we may get Light. St. Augustine said he deserved eternal damnation, but Christ deified him; he had completely surrendered to Christ. Same thing with Girish and Thakur.

## December 26, 1980

[Comments on some teachings of Christ:] "My Kingdom is not of this world." If we seek it in the material world we get nothing. We have to realize it within and then we see it everywhere. That is how we reconcile this teaching with Thakur saying he saw God everywhere.

"The Kingdom of God is within you." We have to realize it within first. It is only true realization when that spiritual perception remains when you open your eyes and see the world. Then you see the multiplicity but you see it filled with his Consciousness—not with the physical eye, but it is a kind of spiritual perception. If you tune a radio to a certain station and then go around the room and get that station on the radio no matter where you go, you conclude that the station is all-pervasive—you have that firm conviction. God is like that, only he is not confined to any particular meter or wavelength. He is absolutely all-pervasive. After realization you have that absolute conviction and never forget his presence even for a moment. What Thakur gave Naren was to lift his consciousness to the level where he experienced the transcendental Reality beyond all names and forms in which everything melts down into one wholesome Consciousness. But it is another experience to be able to see with open eyes the world of multiplicity filled with that Consciousness. Again, if you want to see God with form you tune your mind to that wavelength and you can see Christ or Thakur, etc. But you don't get even that, unless you get it within first.

"Seek ye first the Kingdom of God." Realize him within and then you see him everywhere. How to seek, how to realize? By completely purifying the mind through complete detachment and denying all negative, by following his commandments—love God, love your neighbor, love your enemy.

Pray to Thakur for pure devotion, then everything else follows. Keep his thought in all your work; always feel it is his. Then, by feeling "Not I, but Thou," your ego doesn't swell. If you remember him, all goes well, but if ego swells, all problems come. See him in all beings. Think of Thakur's presence in everyone. If you put a drop of poison in a vat of milk, it poisons the whole thing; everywhere you pour, the poison goes. Similarly, since Thakur became one with Brahman, he is all-pervasive just like Brahman. So think of him in everyone and do all work in his name; then everything will go well and nothing will go wrong.

· · ·

## December 29, 1980

[From an inspired talk on Holy Mother:] Unlike other great saints who appear to be other-worldly, Mother swallowed that transcendental experience and manifested it in a very simple, highly spiritualized life in the thick of the world. We don't even understand the meaning of words like "Mother of the Universe" and it is meaningless to compare her to mythological goddesses. But she occupies a pedestal of her own—as a real universal Mother and as a perfect human being of the highest spiritual quality. She had the unique capacity to truly make everybody her own. She *felt* that motherliness toward *all*. In her there was no discrimination. She accepted all as her own. Her life teaches us that the important thing is not what you *do,* but what you *are.* Being is most important.

What must be the purity of that lady if Sri Ramakrishna, who had the highest spiritual illumination, worshiped her as the Divine Mother and surrendered everything to her, even down to his rosary?

It is the first time in the history of monasticism that a lady has become the head of a great monastic order. She gave certain unwritten laws that are the foundation of the monk's life in terms of how to *be*. In one hymn of salutation she receives the first bow, even before Sri Ramakrishna.

There was one boy who felt frustrated in his attempt to live a pure life. When he went to take leave of Mother, saying he was unfit to come there anymore, she put her hands on his shoulders and looking him straight in the eyes, said, "When you are disturbed, my child, think of me." From that moment he couldn't think of anything but those eyes and those words and the next day he renounced and joined the Order and became a great monk. That experience with Mother purified him completely and is still purifying people today who think of her.

One great thing Mother gave us was her last message about attaining peace of mind—to make everybody our own, know that no one is a stranger to us, and not to find fault with anybody. We will really have peace in this world if we make a resolve not to see the defects of anybody. We will be happy everywhere. When we see defects outside, it is because the devil is within. So cast out the defects, but don't look to the defects of anybody else. Our problems in life are at the human, psychophysical level. If we follow this precept, we not only get peace with others, but that very attitude helps us to evolve and move up. There is a *brahmacharya* vow that says the fly sits on filth picking up dirt and the bee sits on flowers picking up honey, so let me follow the path of the bee and not of the fly—let me look at the good in all and imbibe it, and never look at the defects of anybody. Everybody should know this vow.

Swami Kalyanananda had an apparently blank cardboard on his wall in Kankhal which had been there for 35 years. Even though what had been a photo of Mother had completely faded away so that anyone else saw nothing there, in that he vividly saw the form of Mother which was so brightly imprinted on his own mind. He was lost in her.

Like Sri Ramakrishna, Holy Mother is a real Kalpataru (wish-fulfilling tree), but she is hidden.

# 1981

## January 8, 1981

We have to be masters of nature and that means having a strong control over oneself. Many times there is a leak somewhere and we waste much energy. So we have to control everything with intense strength and will, and not waste our energy through a leaky self-control.

## January 29, 1981

An Incarnation is one who has merged completely in the Absolute. Swami Vivekananda says that only Avataras can reach the highest and then come down to do good to the world. Avataras include also those who come with him. Through his grace and power, others get that power. It's like a magnetic pin cushion. All the pins stick to that magnetic ground and as you pile them up, the upper ones stick to the bottom ones, but the magnetic attraction is still coming from the magnetic ground. We just have to tune our minds to him and we also get the power of that illumination. We need purity, one-pointedness and devotion, and then we can get that Light.

And that Light resides equally in all. Those who realize clearly experience it. For us, to practice that equanimous love is the means to the end. As we love God, so we have to love all, because the truth is that he is in all.

The truth is that the Light is everything. Einstein said that matter is frozen energy, so the man of illumination sees it as frozen consciousness. It is just like if you freeze water into molds of different shapes and you get an ice-dog, an ice-cat, an ice-house, etc. If you then put those forms into a bucket of water, slowly they all melt into that one water. Then it evaporates and becomes vapor. All names and forms are flimsy. When one's consciousness is raised beyond the psychophysical complex, all names and forms melt away into one Consciousness, one Light, pure loving Consciousness; and we are that Light, that loving Consciousness. Therefore we should not identify with things and persons outside or with thoughts inside.

**February 3, 1981**

Brahman means vast, infinite, expansive. Whenever you hear the word "Brahman" or "God," think of that vast, all-pervasive Consciousness. Bhagavan means one who has become one with That. That is why we call Thakur "Bhagavan" or "God."

Thakur and Mother are like the hub of a wheel. The direct disciples are the spokes. Swami Vivekananda is the rim holding them all together. The others all understood a part, but Swamiji understood the whole picture.

. . .

## February 8, 1981

Only two things are needed: prayer and struggle. You don't see change right away, but just keep your mind on him and pray for purity and unselfishness.

## February 12, 1981

"Knowledge sacrifice" (Gita ch. 4) means anything you do with wisdom.

[Reading from the *Gospel of Sri Ramakrishna* about ego and renunciation of ego:] We make the end the means by meditating on the fact that we are that Light, we are in truth that loving Consciousness. Ego is immediately attenuated because we thereby deny all other identifications and identify only as a spark of God. The wall of ego goes down and all limitations go with it.

In practical life we subdue the ego by first cultivating the feeling of "we"—everyone is a child of God, everyone is just like me, I am part of the whole. Later on that evolves into, "Not I but Thou." We come to see God behind that "we." At the human level the "I" is dead.

[About the seven planes of consciousness:] The sixth plane is psycho-spiritual. You care only for God, feeling the desire for union with God. But the individual psyche is still there. In the seventh, the individual psyche is completely gone, never to return—what Raja Yoga calls seedless samadhi. From that state you never come down, in the sense of losing that awareness. Those who have no urge to help mankind give up the body after 21 days. Those who have the urge to help others, externalize their consciousness. But they never, even for a second, forget that experience or lose awareness of the Divine Presence. When their consciousness is completely internalized, the sense of "I" is gone totally. When they externalize it for the good of others, they retain their individuality—what Sri Ramakrishna calls the "appearance of ego"—but they don't lose that awareness ever.

**February 19, 1981**

Spiritual life is like swimming with a crocodile chasing you. If you stop swimming, it swallows you, so keep swimming.

**February 24, 1981**

Religiosity is easy but spirituality is very difficult. To jump to spiritual life means you are on the other side of the fence and that means keeping yourself in a different realm altogether. It means you have to rise above all mundane differences and see things from the spiritual standpoint.

Being spiritual means to see the same Spirit equally in all. It means to equate yourself with the rest. We have to keep it up through prayer and alertness.

Monk or nun means constant alertness. That is the obligation that comes with the declaration to lead an exclusive spiritual life. We have to keep the spiritual thought constantly. The three musts are chastity (control all sense-craving); poverty (no sense of "mine"); obedience (makes us humble, which is the way to overcome ego, the last rock to go). Obedience means to obey Swamiji's dictums to be positive, positive, positive. It is most important to keep the mind absolutely away from all negative thoughts. Don't dwell on them even for a second. Have love and concern and serve people without any selfishness. No light-mindedness. Think before speaking, be reserved, avoid unconscious indulgence. Beware of even innocent attachments. Always be alert about your own motives. Repeat Thakur's name constantly and that will be the way to overcome all obstacles. Don't dwell on anything negative.

**February 25, 1981**

The reason we have to be constantly alert is that, if we don't guard and guide the mind with our will, then it is guided by *samskaras* and then we get into unconscious indulgence, and then all troubles come.

**March 5, 1981**

[Studying the idea of "sat" or pure Being in the *Chandogya Upanishad*:] Our true nature is pure loving Consciousness. A baby is just like that. But psychic limitations then begin to pile up due to all negative experiences. When we spiritualize our lives, we resolve to return to our true nature and regain that unobstructed loving consciousness. As we struggle, our limitations slowly go down and then things like jealousy, comparison, competition melt away.

When the scriptures say that the illumined never come back, what it really means is that they never return to the same ignorant condition. When such a soul comes to another birth in order to help others, it is a matter of mental and physical development until that previous state comes to fruition in the present life. Even while that process is happening, they are in the world but not trapped by it. In their youth they are different and you can see they are rebels against orthodox traditions and customs. Then as they develop and fall into the hands of a proper master, that fruition takes place. Even before that a different awareness is there in them and they are constantly seeking something beyond the mundane existence.

An illumined soul doesn't go to deep sleep, i.e. unconscious condition. Sleep is only physical rest. For them the mind is always at rest. That awareness of pure Consciousness is always there. They *identify* with it.

**March 9, 1981**

At times in spiritual life we are seemingly going in circles. Spiritual life is never in a straight line. At times we seem to go down and then we come up. But there is upward movement. Even if you feel like a baby at the foot of Mt. Everest and are being told to climb it, the man at the top is holding a rope for you. We have to climb but if we hold on to the rope we will make it. God's name is how to hold onto the rope. Don't give up that hold.

Thakur's name, his thought, is the only way to purify the mind. Any bad thought coming, picture his face immediately. Every day before going to sleep, intensely picture his face, have no other thought. You need not even say anything; just picture his face. And don't pick up any negative thought. Never dwell on the negative or look for it, either in yourself or in others. Be like the bee and never like the fly.

**March 16, 1981**

Every unselfish act purifies us. Unselfishness means not to expect anything. You serve because of need and fulfillment. Tell yourself, "I don't expect anything." No seeking name and fame or anything—no expectation. That purifies the mind because it keeps the ego down. When you break the line of egoism and selfishness, so much light gets in.

## March 24, 1981

If one can level up at the human level, then God is in our hands. [The swami said that is his own experience.] If you can harmonize your human relationship, then the mind becomes clear and God is easily attained. Love thy neighbor, love thy enemy, bless them that curse you—then love God. If you can do the first part, the second part comes easily. What is required is just a positive outlook, a simple turn of the mind to look only to the good and not to pick up any negative. Even if it is there, don't pick it up. Just like a bee in a garden—so much dirt is there, but the bee goes straight for the flower and picks up the honey. It doesn't touch anything else. We have to make a vow to be like that.

All our problems are at the human level, not the spiritual level. When we can square up the former, the spiritual is in our hands. In former ages, for realization people had to leave society and cry a lot, and pray and pray, and it was extremely difficult. But Swami Vivekananda has given us a new ideal of completely spiritualizing our life in the world. Then we are there in the midst of everything, but it is not in us. If we can practice his ideal of spiritualizing our life here, then realization becomes easy. God is really in our hands.

## March 25, 1981

[Swami said in Raja Yoga class to always remember two things:] (1) I am not the thoughts. (2) My mind belongs to me. I am the master of my mind.

## April 1, 1981

By brooding don't bring the past to the present. By worry don't bring the future to the present—in both cases losing the present. Live in the present by taking his name.

## April 14, 1981

Until the sixth stage of samadhi the *samskaras* are still alive. And thoughts are very, very powerful. If we are not constantly alert and struggling, we never know when they may tip us off and get us into something from which we cannot extricate ourselves and end in terrible suffering. That is why we must be always alert and struggle, struggle, struggle. We are never safe until all the thoughts are totally resolved and silenced. That means the sixth stage of *samadhi*, not before that.

## April 22, 1981

[Reading from Swami Gambhirananda's *Holy Mother Sri Sarada Devi,* about Guru and disciple:] It is true that the Guru really does take the disciple's burden. That is why we should never worry about the past. Our only concern is to follow the Guru's teachings now; he will take care of the entire past. Because of his spiritual power he can take on the responsibility for the disciple's past; but to him it is not suffering.

What Holy Mother said is true. If we surrender to the Guru, he holds us—not that only we have to hold to him. When we really surrender, he holds us and he takes care of the past. Our part is simply to be detached and not identify with the past. Our trouble comes when we see those thoughts and identify with them. But if we don't identify and rather follow him in the present, then we have less fear. Not only Mother but all the disciples have that attitude of putting their disciples at Thakur's feet. To them Thakur is everything and that is why they tell their disciples, "He is your Guru."

When Mother says the Master will take all her disciples by the hand, it means those who have truly surrendered. If one has surrendered truly, then one will automatically follow their teachings and morally and spiritually one will not go wrong, regardless of what actions one performs at the worldly level.

"At the last moment" doesn't mean death. It means the end of the struggle. When you struggle and struggle to overcome your limitations and impressions and you fail and feel really helpless, then if you admit your helplessness and surrender completely that illumination can come. That surrender acts as the magic to completely purify the subconscious mind.

[Regarding Holy Mother saying it wasn't necessary to do japa and meditation in her place:] There is nothing like the purifying power of their company. If we have the opportunity to be with them and serve them, with full awareness, or even without awareness, that is enough. Unconsciously their company lifts us up, keeps our minds up, draws us to something higher. Austerities are for when they are absent, but when we are with them we can relax. Swami Akhilananda felt it when he was cooking and serving Maharaj (Swami Brahmananda). He never studied or even meditated much. That company itself kept him so well. [Similarly, when Swami Kalyanananda died, Swami Sarvagatananda realized what that company had meant in terms of example and lifting up.] Unconsciously you imbibe so much.

## April 29, 1981

Someone asked Latu Maharaj something about philosophical questions. He replied that Thakur was his only answer for everything, that whenever he had any doubt about anything, he just looked at him. That was it.

Beware of innocent, unconscious indulgence. Otherwise you build up *samskaras* unknowingly and they ruin you later on. Instead we have to struggle to build new spiritual *samskaras*.

Karma is not absolute. If you decide you want to make it, you are absolutely free to deny your *samskaras*. Once you choose your path, be firm, because *samskaras* do come up and try to tip you off, but at that time you have to say no.

Saint Francis said that when you pray, you must pray as if everything depends upon God; when you work and struggle, do it as if everything depends on you.

Don't look back, look forward. Put everything on him but at the same time struggle yourself.

## May 13, 1981

Be like a kitten who is content no matter where the mother puts it. Our idea should be only to put our mind on God, not to have any will of our own with regard to externals. Desire only his will. Fear of the future comes from a feeling of isolation or separation from God, but we are not separate from him and therefore should not be afraid.

## May 19, 1981

Holy Mother stands above all as an exemplar for personal behavior. If we think of her whenever we have to make a choice of behavior, we will never go wrong, [the Swami said smiling] with all apologies to Thakur. We may get illumination from him, but with regard to behavior, we look to Mother. In her there was absolutely no discrimination.

When we are at the Vedanta center, or in a temple, we shouldn't look upon it as the Vedanta Society. No, it is the abode of Thakur, Mother and Swamiji and we should always be aware of it. Narrow-minded people may not approve of all we do, but if we think of God and then act, we will never go wrong.

Holy Mother is really the Divine Mother.

## May 21, 1981

There is no such thing as a guarantee in this world. But if we are true to him, then there is guarantee, as Sri Krishna says in Gita 9. 22.

Constantly be mindful that all work is his and offer every action to him.

Make everybody your own and don't see the defects of others. Love everyone that comes, overcome hatred with love, accept and try to help.

Be more unselfish, concerned, compassionate, and detached. Keep an attitude of dedication. Then no worldly feeling can get into the mind. Be strong, be cheerful, be Thakur's completely.

## May 27, 1981

Always feel, "I am nobody. He will save me." We know what he is, because his son has told us. He told me and I am telling you.

Don't worry about anything else for beginning spiritual life if you have the desire to live a pure life and devotion to Thakur. The urge to realize will come later on. Just put all difficulties at Thakur's feet. Imprint the stamp of his thought on the mind and don't worry about anything. And don't be deceived by false appearances outside. It is all slavery and misery.

. . .

## June 4, 1981

[Reading reminiscences of Latu Maharaj in *Vedanta Kesari*. The next day Swami Sarvagatananda said he had had a very clear vision in the middle of the night of Thakur and Latu—alone in Thakur's room—Latu a little teenage boy, very serious and sincere and guileless—and Thakur bent down as to a little son, telling him, "Latu, life is very difficult, this is what you should do..."—and giving him instructions.]

[Regarding Rakhal's limitations (as mentioned in the above reminiscences):] In very highly evolved souls, until the sixth stage of *samadhi, samskaras* are still there. Some become victims, some don't; it's all a process of human evolution. In these Isvarakotis, souls who are very close to the shore, there is still a little bit of human imperfection but it is burned off immediately when they come into the light of a great soul. A little dampness in the corner dries up very fast. An illumined soul understands that this little human limitation is nothing.

[Regarding incidents of miraculous healing (Girish's son and Ram Babu):] It is true about the power of faith, but it is also true that Thakur's grace was there. Thakur could do anything, but he didn't, except under extraordinary circumstances. But the working of his grace is a fact. If we pray for that grace with respect to pure devotion rather than worldly matters, it is even more true; we will definitely get it. Follow what the guru says and leave the rest to him because his grace does work.

As illustrated by Latu, along with the grace of God and guru, our mind must be there. We have to have that firmness and determination that, "I shall make it!" The great danger is unconscious indulgence. We must be very alert and careful or we will be caught. And never dwell on negative thoughts.

When they come, turn the mind immediately to Thakur. As he told Latu, "Remember me." If you ignore the negative thoughts, don't look at or worry about them, and turn the mind immediately to something positive, then they all go away.

## June 15, 1981

Tapasya means self-discipline. Self-discipline is the very essence of spiritual life. One who is really self-disciplined can easily gain depth and light.

## June 25, 1981

"Purity is to will one thing" (quoting Kierkegaard). Remember this: to will him is purity. Don't worry. The more you struggle, the more the dirt comes out. When it comes, be strong. But in the shrine before Thakur, be absolutely humble, and cry for devotion.

## July 30, 1981

[Still discussing Latu Maharaj's reminiscences, where he said not to think that a sadhaka who experiences Nirvikalpa Samadhi can have it any number of times or whenever he wants it.] That is true for a person who has had just a glimpse of it. But when once you experience complete identity with the Ground/God, that experience is yours forever. You become one with it. You are that. I and my Father are one. Then you are never away from that awareness, even in sleep. It is like standing on the threshold of a house and looking out. You see everything passing by outside the house, but you are standing firmly grounded and unmoving inside the immovable, unchanging house. Those who are absolutely desireless merge in that and leave the body soon. Those who, through some grace, have the desire to help people, can retain their individuality for that purpose. But they are never away from their identity with the Ground.

Innocent indulgence is the greatest danger because it is like going unnoticeably down a small incline until it is too late and you can't stop it. The way to avoid it is constant alertness.

Sri Krishna is the supreme manifestation of one who could move with perfect naturalness at the human level while at the same time being established in the highest supreme divine Consciousness; that is, identifying as that. He didn't lose external consciousness and go to that state. He kept his external consciousness and human functioning while in that highest state of divine identification.

## August 13, 1981

[To young women aspirants:] Never look at the face of a man, except when you must greet or talk to them, and then do so with a very spiritual attitude. Our own attitude can convert the whole world.

## August 15, 1981

Nothing is absolute except the truth that the Kingdom of God is within you. Nothing is absolute except the purity of your soul. That is why I say, it is never too late and no case is hopeless.

## September 25, 1981

It isn't what God knows—it is what *we* know that he knows. That is the significance of our prayer. It is a process of opening up to the Divine. He knows everything even before we say it. He is the very ground of our thought. He never winks, he is always awake, always alert.

## September 29, 1981

[Yesterday was Swami Akhandananda's birthday.] There is no death for me. Only death to this body. If the mind is linked to God/Guru, then life and death make no difference, either in his presence or in the functioning of his grace. In order to really feel that way, the mind must be ripened through keeping the constant thought of Thakur. Then the death of the body makes no difference.

## September 30, 1981

No spiritual life will be thwarted.

## October 8, 1981

Sannyasa/renunciation means to be detached from everything.

## October 22, 1981

Monastic life means no individuality. I am nobody; God is everything.

When we are close to the Vedanta center / temple, we are representing Sri Ramakrishna. Whatever we do reflects on him. We are nobody but his slaves. We should always be very, very careful in thought, word and deed.

Never speak a harsh word to anybody. On the other hand, if anybody speaks harshly to you, forgive. And never jump to negative conclusions about anybody.

Austerity means restraint and self-control of mind, speech and actions. That means you have to be alert and conscious every moment.

In the highest spiritual experience, in that state where you completely transcend the psycho-physical complex and "the salt doll melts in the ocean," there all names and forms melt away. There is only is-ness. You experience that oneness—not that you see it with these eyes—no, there is a spiritual eye and you feel it. Then when you are coming down from that state to the individual psychic consciousness, there is an intermediate stage where you see the names and forms but in a sort of semi-fluid state in which you see them all pulsating with that same Consciousness. It is that state which made Jesus say, "I am the Truth, I am the Life," or Buddha to say, "The light of Truth is in all."

Don't accept anything apparent. Don't let the mind run after the flimsy, apparent things of the world, like husband, wife and children. They are very flimsy things when compared to knowing the Truth. They have no substance.

Will is nothing but the power of love. Only if you love a thing do you will it. Will is love transformed into power.

## October 26, 1981

As you intensify the will in spiritual life, all other things become stronger too. They are always there staring at you, ready to pounce, but if you are alert and mindful they are tied up and can't get out of the cage. Even if the mind is disturbed 99% of the time, just keep the hold on him and struggle. Even if you have 1% devotion and 99% disturbance, that 1% devotion is more important than all the rest put together.

At the center / temple, do all work as God's work. Serve people as if they are all part of him. If you work outside, see all people just as shadows; see his presence in all.

. . .

## November 18, 1981

The most important thing is to struggle. If we struggle he will take care of the rest. The struggle alone is our part. But we have to be honest with ourselves. We (monastics) have cheated our parents and relatives out of their normal expectations, so we must be fully honest in leading the spiritual life.

Most important is always to question yourself, why you are doing a thing or why you are avoiding a thing. If you avoid a thing, you create a psychic limitation (suppression or repression) which creates a tendency to indulge innocently, unconsciously. Therefore resolve things, don't avoid them. Resolve by thinking of him and find a way to sublimate or substitute. Always question your motives—be alert and mindful.

In the beginning the *samskaras* do come up and give a lot of trouble, but if you are firm and determined they do go away, or rather become powerless to tip you off and make you suffer.

## November 19, 1981

[Explaining the salutation to the Guru in the first verse of the *Vivekachudamani*:] When a man realizes God, he takes on the attributes of God. It is like placing an absolutely clean glass in front of a picture. You see only the picture. It's like that with an illumined soul. There is nothing in that absolutely pure mind to obstruct the divine Light. That is why it is true that your Guru is Satchidananda. It is the pure light of God coming through the Guru; he is a channel.

## November 27, 1981

Swami Virajanandaji once said that the best gift is the gift of a devoted heart given to God.

When we surrender to Thakur, that means we become heirs to his spiritual treasure. Because of what he attained, we know what the goal is, but to get that inheritance requires complete surrender to him.

Through constant prayer and surrender, avoid the danger of unconscious indulgence. Be alert and mindful.

Pray to Mother when jealousy and envy come up. These things are like a block to the mind and in spiritual life we must be very careful about them. Differences will be there but in God's eyes we are all equal. Always feel that we are all one.

[Regarding Latu Maharaj's dependence on God:] There are two things involved in "getting orders" from God. In Latu's case, whenever he was in doubt, he would think of similar cases when he was with Thakur and what Thakur had told him to do, and he would follow that. But if there is no precedent, you have to wait to get inspiration from within and that Voice does come. But to hear the Divine Voice you have to absolutely silence your speech, mind and ego. Only in that pure and egoless heart does inspiration come.

### December 2, 1981

Only after *samadhi* is there absolute desirelessness, as in the case of the man at Kankhal who passed away after 21 days. Until then you keep breathing because you desire to live to realize. The man of illumination is always conscious. His sleep is not one of self-forgetfulness like ours. It is like Swami Turiyananda at Kankhal, who could warn others when a wild bull was approaching the Ashrama in the middle of the night. When Swami Kalyanananda said, "Maharaj, don't you sleep?" he replied, "Not like you all."

## December 10, 1981

God doesn't change events—nature functions—but miracles do happen. Saints can and do work miracles, but in general they do not change events. [At one point Swami said, "I can change your mind."]

Mother greatly encouraged people who came to her wanting to lead a monastic life. When at times people felt discouraged and thought of leaving, she would not only encourage them to stay on but bless them without their knowing. Later on they would realize that it was her blessings that were at work in their lives.

[Regarding Mother's teaching that the injunctions of destiny are overcome if one takes refuge in God:] What it means is that karma stands on ego alone and, if you truly surrender to God, all karma goes down with the ego—completely—even the worst karma is gone. If you really say, "Not I, but Thou," and keep it up, then no karma can touch you. You feel you are not doing anything; you are only his instrument.

[Regarding Mother's teaching: "He who is able to renounce all for his sake is a living God":] If you surrender, you become like whatever you surrender to. You become that. If you surrender to Hitler, you become like Hitler. If you surrender to God, you become like God. There is no difference.

[Regarding Mother's teaching that the ochre robe of a sadhu is like the collar of a dog:] As a dog's collar says, "He belongs to so-and-so," so also the ochre robe says, "He belongs to God."

The one person who had absolute detachment from money was Swami Ranganathananda. He raised so much money for others and never spent a cent on himself. When the Karachi

Center was destroyed, Swami Ranganathananda (who was the head of the center and had not been present when it happened) came after a couple of weeks. He looked around and said to Swami Sarvagatananda, "Narayan, just imagine if you had to move from here and you had to pack everything. Just see now how fast they have done it and what a good job. They took *everything*!"

When you go to the shrine make a firm decision not to think of anything but God. Then wonderful things happen there.

## December 14, 1981

[From a talk on "The Compassionate Holy Mother":] "Holy" is with reference to her transcendental experience—we don't know what height she reached. "Mother" is with reference to her behavior at the human level. The love and acceptance —*kshama* (forgiveness) and *daya* (compassion)—that she manifested were unparalleled. She was beyond even Sri Ramakrishna in her all-inclusive love and acceptance. She even defied him in the name of that all-comprehensive motherliness. She met the needs of all at whatever stage they were —whether they were in distress, or seeking something, or inquiring after knowledge. Those, like Swami Vivekananda and Swami Brahmananda, who understood who she was, trembled in her presence.

Those who gain that transcendental experience and then come down to help others are very rare, and their position is very mysterious. They are never away from the awareness of the Ground—they never lose that experience—but at the same time they come down to our very level to help us and they really live at the human level. The key to their infinite forgiveness and compassion is that they know what is meant by human suffering at every level. No one evolves without going through. So they know what is meant by suffering. They know, actually, not just imagine or have an idea. Therefore Mother met the needs of everyone who came to her. Once she asked Swami Saradananda to purchase some things that were obviously not for use in her household, so he objected. But she insisted and so he did purchase those things. To whom she gave them nobody knew. Another time somebody came to the door at Udbodhan in the middle of the night. The monks told the person it was no time to come there, but Mother heard it and came down and talked with the girl who was there and then proceeded to go with her in the middle of the night to her house in the slums near Udbodhan. Two swamis followed behind and stood outside while Mother went inside. After some time she came out and all was calm and quiet within, and no one knew what transpired.

## December 18, 1981

[Talking about Holy Mother's teachings on herself, when she says that whatever she has to give is given at the time of initiation; those who struggle get peace now, those who don't, get it when the body falls:] That is really true. If one has received initiation from a truly liberated soul, it is also true. One does get that liberation; evolution is complete; *samskaras* are burned; karma is neutralized completely. It happens because at the time of death there is no physical limitation, no outside temptation and at that time the seed given at the time of initiation comes out. It is like a bomb that hadn't exploded yet and now it goes off. Even if a person has committed the worst sins, it happens like that. Because the mantra is not given unsought. It is given because at some point that person was seeking it. It may be that strong *samskaras* prevent its immediate effect and keep the person from struggling for a while, but it is bound to work. It is like if a person opens the mouth and you quickly pop a pill in, the medicine is bound to take effect because it has gotten in. Mantra is like that. It is alive. Because of *samskaras* it may be submerged for a time, but it is bound to work its effect sooner or later, at least when the body falls. But if received from a liberated soul, liberation is assured. If you struggle now, you get that blessedness very soon and enjoy it while alive. It doesn't take long to undo old *samskaras*. Just follow the teacher's instructions. But even if you can't do that, you will get it in the end. What is depicted in Raja Yoga as all the stages you go through before the *samskaras* are burned is not applicable to those who are initiated by a liberated soul. The worst sinner can get it in the end because the Ground is pure. The mantra has come from Thakur as its source and, as Mother said, "is of proved efficacy."

Even though salvation is assured, the reason the Guru wants his disciples to struggle is so they can enjoy that blessedness now, while alive. Then the question of life and death doesn't bother you at all. Therefore be alert and mindful, serve in a selfless spirit, and be positive toward all people.

[The Swami answered further questioning about getting liberation "when the body falls":] The truth is, whatever you haven't gotten while alive, you don't get after the body falls. But the effect of the mantra remains with you after death. Nothing is lost. You don't get liberation until you struggle and purify your consciousness. If you fool around while alive, you don't get it at death. You do have to come back and struggle again. But liberation is assured in the sense that the effect of what has been given, by one who has the power to give it, is never lost. If you don't fool around and you struggle hard now, you can get it in this very life.

Thakur is really the source of the mantra. The disciples got it from him. He gave different mantras to them but they all ended with him as their ideal. Once one of them told him that he was using the mantra given by Thakur, but Thakur himself came to his mind. Thakur replied, "They are non-separate" (i.e., he and the chosen deity). At Baranagore, Naren asked his fellow disciples what mantras Thakur had given them and it came out that they were all ending up thinking only of Thakur.

What happens psychologically when you surrender to God is that your own individual ego is for the time being submerged in your own pure consciousness and you thereby get so much light. Psychologically and spiritually it is a fact.

**December 26, 1981**

Evolution begins when you turn within and question your own motives.

# 1982

## January 23, 1982

Don't worry about karma. One who takes refuge in God need not worry about karma. But don't assert your ego or you have got the problem again. Thakur can definitely illumine us; there is no doubt about it.

[Regarding Mother's teaching about the disciple's sins affecting the Guru:] The truth behind Mother's way of putting it is the collective unconscious which functions very intensely between Guru and disciples, even among co-disciples. There is really only one psyche. The Guru deliberately, consciously, willingly participates in the karma of the disciple. He actually thereby minimizes the burden of the disciple, even at times neutralizing things. But he does not suffer. He does pay but, because he does it willingly, he does not suffer. It is like throwing something in fire. Yes, fire is affected in the sense that it receives what goes in; yet it is not affected —rather it burns up what it receives.

. . .

## February 1, 1982

Say, "I shall not carry any negative thought because it is not good for my subconscious mind." Be devoted to God, detached from everything outside, accept whatever comes and you will be at peace.

## February 2, 1982

It is true that you can experience Incarnations. Just as planets and other smaller bodies come out from the sun and some with greater mass retain their form and continue orbiting around, so also Thakur, Krishna, Jesus and Buddha reached such a spiritual height—their spiritual mass is so great—that they retain their name and form in the cosmic Divine realm and one can experience them. You experience the name and form according to your own mental concept, but you get true vision in the sense of their inner substance. You get true revelation of their true substance, spiritual substance. That experience is not like a dream or a vision. With the Incarnations it is a *revelation* of a very direct and intimate nature. You can talk to them, as Thakur said. That talking is different from what we know. It is a kind of spiritual contact, spiritual communication, and it is very real—no fantasy. What is required for that experience is purity (no desire, urge, ambition), one-pointedness, and devotion. It is like pointing a telescope to see a planet. You need a clean lens (purity); point it toward the planet (devotion); focus (one-pointedness). If you gain experience of one of them, you can gain it of others too, because purity is already there so you need only focus in a different direction.

. . .

## February 3, 1982

[Regarding Mother's teaching on reverence for the Guru:] Thakur said, "Satchidananda is your Guru." Yes, that is ultimately the Source, but he through whom that grace comes is the Guru. The source is the Incarnation or revelation, and the grace comes from him through a line—to his sons and to their sons, etc. Guru is the faucet, as it were, through whom the water of Divine grace comes. Guru is one who has attained to that state through his own realization; he has understood the meaning of it; he has become one with it.

## February 10, 1982

[Regarding *Vivekachudamani*, verse 30:] Intense renunciation means a complete turning away from everything external. It means an inner turning. At the same time it means turning *toward* something spiritual, something which is very real and tangible. The very existence of mind means it holds thoughts. So if you don't feed it some spiritual thought, it will be influenced by all the subconscious contents—old urges, tendencies, *samskaras*. That is exactly how the mind works—it holds the thoughts that are there, so you have to constantly feed it something spiritual or else it is automatically influenced by the *samskaras* and urges that are already there inside waiting to come up.

To gain something spiritual you must have intense renunciation: "I don't want anything else." Keep the mind detached from everything. And beware of indulgence, conscious or unconscious. Struggle to have renunciation. Objectify your whole life. Stand as a witness and be keenly observant of how the mind is working. Use your will. Force the mind to hold the spiritual thought. In meditation keep the mind under your control and don't allow it to wander away to other things.

**February 17, 1982**

Intimate closeness between Guru and disciple is very important. It is even more than the closeness between mother and child, or any other relation. In other relationships there will be parting someday, but here there is no parting. Until illumination the Guru-disciple relationship continues. Even after illumination that contact continues. The only thing that matters is surrender to him. It doesn't even matter if you know what you are seeking or what is to be done. Just be like a kitten, as Thakur said, and surrender to him. He will do the rest.

**March 4, 1982**

We put our whole burden on Thakur. "If I am impure, you make me pure. If I am not holy, you make me holy." In millions of years and lives we don't get an opportunity like coming into the orbit of Thakur. Very rare is such a spiritual manifestation. That is why someone like Swami Vivekananda, who had such a scientific approach to religion, couldn't help calling Thakur the Incarnation Supreme. So let the world go in its own way—we go in *his* way.

**March 25, 1982**

Responsibility means cooperation, never competition or possession.

[Reading about Girish in the *Gospel of Sri Ramakrishna,* where Thakur tells Girish he was purified because he had faith:] We must have the same faith that Thakur can do the same to us. The only thing required is our sincere surrender. "I am no good. You make me something!"

## April 8, 1982

When offering food to God, the idea for us is not whether he "eats" it. We offer it with the idea that nothing is ours, everything is his, and we are seeking his blessings. Then only we take it and share it with others.

Tyaga means to give up. Sannyasa means to get out of it completely. In practical spiritual terms, where there is real *tyaga*—real detachment—then there is also *sannyasa*. There are two types of *sannyasa*—*sannyasa* as a discipline and *sannyasa* as realization. That is why in the Ramakrishna Order, there are those who are in the field of action and there are some who have reached a level where they can follow a life of exclusive contemplation. Again, there are some, like Swami Kalyanananda, who followed karma yoga throughout and were *paramahamsas*. That is the highest ideal.

Those who do not practice karma yoga don't evolve because the *samskaras* are crystallized rather than resolved. In the field of action they come out and then you can resolve them and evolve. That is why we shouldn't worry when bad thoughts come up, either consciously due to outside suggestion, or unconsciously in dream, because the fact that they are coming out means the crystal is breaking. Just like when you do laundry the dirt comes out. If you don't pay attention, they go away. If you pray, that is even better!

## April 14, 1982

For a man of God-consciousness, the world does not vanish except when he is in samadhi. But he clearly sees what is real behind the appearances. As Sri Ramakrishna said, he saw

God first and then all other multiple perceptions. It is like seeing all transparent glass vessels immersed in water. There is water above and below, inside and outside. To an illumined soul, physical forms are not opaque. He sees God or Pure Consciousness everywhere.

## April 22, 1982

Both Jesus and Sri Ramakrishna said that the pure in heart will see God ("Blessed are the pure in heart for they shall see God"). How do we get that purity of heart? By following Mother's teaching on not finding fault and making everyone our own. If we can follow that one teaching, we will have no problems. Purity of heart comes when we don't see evil outside. Be like the bee and pick up only the good. Don't pick up any dirt.

## April 28, 1982

Sadhu means soft. "Holy man" is a more accurate rendering than "monk."

The rising of spiritual consciousness (*kundalini*) is compared to the movement of a serpent because spiritual growth is like that. You go straight and then curve, straight and then curve. As long as *samskaras* are there, the bends and curves come. You are going up and then *samskaras* come and make you bend. You don't go down. It's just that the movement is curved. Then you go up again. It is upward movement but not straight up. However, an illumined soul can give it a straight upward lift, like Holy Mother did to many of her disciples. When we struggle hard but can't do it, their grace can help us do it and lift our consciousness.

. . .

## June 25, 1982

Mindstuff (*chitta*) is like a videotape. Everything is recorded there. Thoughts gain depth depending on interest and attention. Now we are stuck with the *samskaras* we accumulated in the ignorant condition and some we cannot get rid of even though we want to. The way is to create a new, very powerful spiritual *samskara*. That is why we regularly go to the shrine and with love and surrender try to deepen the thought of Thakur. Gradually that spiritual *samskara* becomes so powerful that it interpenetrates all other *samskaras*. Any other thought coming, the spiritual thought comes with it. It's like frying things and soaking them in syrup. The syrup gets in and penetrates everything. That is what is meant by creating a new spiritual psyche. Then old *samskaras* slowly become powerless. A time comes when you cannot do anything wrong even unconsciously. Now, in the struggling process, at times old *samskaras* draw us out, we are tempted, influenced, but the spiritual thought comes and saves us. Slowly it will take over completely.

## July 10, 1982

Life here is a lease from the Divine and we are to deliver it back to God in the end. Samadhi is delivering it back. In the struggling process, purity of mind means not to resent, resist, or react.

## July 15, 1982

Regarding externals, we must always understand and adjust. It is a very high spiritual quality to accept whatever comes. In the morning we are to set our minds well in the spiritual thought and then from the moment we come out of the shrine, leave the rest to nature. That means complete detachment from externals. There is no other way to become really spiritual.

No matter what happens in life, hold on to Thakur and adjust to whatever comes. Just hold on to Thakur, let everything else come, leave the rest to nature.

## July 20, 1982

In social life we compete, show ourselves, etc. But not in spiritual life. "When shall we be free? When the 'I' ceases to be." Here we must deny ourselves—bear, bear, forbear, not I, not I.

## July 27, 1982

What people usually think of as freedom is just freedom to do this and that. But true freedom comes only when you touch the Ground and become free from the psychophysical complex. No matter can touch you. But there you also realize that your freedom is in the freedom of all, your happiness is in the happiness of all.

## August 18, 1982

Two things are necessary when once you have decided to lead a spiritual life, whether as a monastic or not: (1) Adjust with all people; harmony; no complaints. (2) Intense inner struggle must be kept up. Otherwise you may think you are doing well but then slowly, unconsciously, old *samskaras* slow you down because your mind is not alert and awake. Therefore keep up the struggle and remain alert.

In spiritual life, remain true to the ideal, and pray sincerely to Mother, things will work out. When you pray sincerely, somehow things work out.

The blessings of illumined souls never go to waste. They definitely have an effect on our minds. This is something of the spiritual realm and therefore we don't see it. But it does have an effect and helps us in our struggle for illumination.

Never see evil outside. Always look for the good in people. That will purify the subconscious mind and you will *have* peace and you will *give* peace to all.

## August 19, 1982

When we surrender to him we get his grace. But there must be no reservation. One must feel absolutely that "I don't know anything. Thy will be done." But how do we know his will? We have to be always conscious: "If Thakur or Mother were to be here, what would they want me to do?" To keep that consciousness constantly is to surrender to their will. Then you become free, you are like a child, there is no responsibility on you, all is his. There is freedom in that surrender and also self-denial.

## August 20, 1982

The function of the Guru is to link the disciple with God, like a branch linked to a tree. The Guru's unseen blessings are always there. The Guru is always with you but *you* have to struggle. It is like a father teaching his child to walk. The father is there behind, holding the hand, guiding and catching the child if he takes a false step or is in danger, but the child has to do the walking.

The Guru lives in his teachings. Therefore follow what he says. Pay no attention to what others say. Just follow what he told you because every person is different and gets instructions accordingly. Just struggle in your own way, constantly, and follow exactly what the Guru has told you. Keep God-consciousness always and don't worry about the world or what others say. Develop conscious deafness to what goes on around you.

When the Guru scolds you, don't think it is out of distance but rather out of intense closeness.

## August 25, 1982

As a match is a medium of fire, so Incarnations are spiritual mediums.

## August 26, 1982

[Swami said, remarking on his own illness at the time:] Sri Ramakrishna said you have to take the whole orange because juice cannot hang from the trees. So also, we have to accept everything, the whole orange. The only thing is we take only the juice and leave the rest off.

## August 27, 1982

[Swami answered a question about where self-effort leaves off and Divine grace lifts us up when we feel helpless to overcome our limitations.] Illumination is a sure thing if you follow the disciplines properly. But the time factor is also there. It is just like if you start on the road to a distant place at 55 mph, it will take some time but you are sure to reach it if you follow the road. At the same time, there are laws of grace which we do not know and cannot understand. The only thing necessary is our serious and sincere effort to follow. If we do that, if we surrender to God and follow him, even with all our limitations the divine grace can function to give us illumination. To deserve that grace, our part is to knock and seek and blindly follow what the illumined ones have told us. Our *acceptance* of others—not just toleration—and compassionate attitude towards all, lift us up and draw the grace of God.

Life is a big problem, a big mystery. We can know the Truth, but we cannot solve the problem of life. We just have to accept it. That is why contentment is a great spiritual quality. We just have to accept life as it is, and that also means to accept all people as they are. That is a very noble quality and draws the grace of God to us.

## August 28, 1982

Never compare. Never care what people say or what people think. The only thing that matters is that I am directly accountable to Thakur in my own heart. God sees the heart direct; nothing else counts. What matters is how we live, what we are, how our mind and heart are. Many householders are just like monks and nuns in that respect. God sees the heart, not the stamp.

Imagine a glass jar immersed in water. The glass is porous so that water is not only inside and outside but actually interpenetrating the glass itself. God is that substance which is within and without and interpenetrating everything. And it is that which gives us consciousness, which is the foundation of all our feelings, the power behind all our actions. The man of realization sees that God alone *is*, everything else is temporal. He sees God everywhere.

## August 29, 1982

[Regarding Sri Ramakrishna's teaching on the steps of sadhana:] Only Incarnations get *mahābhāva*. Bhāva is intense spiritual feeling which all saints get, but *mahābhāva* is a depth of spiritual experience known only to a few. [Upon further questioning:] Sri Ramakrishna's disciples also got it, though not to the same degree. But they got it because they had merged in him completely. His disciples were not ordinary saints. Their disciples can also get it if they maintain the same attitude toward Sri Ramakrishna as his disciples did. That attitude means complete merging in him—"I am nobody"—then his power functions. Whereas some people keep a little separation, a little individuality—"I am a teacher, I am teaching people"—they do not get it. But those who completely lose their individuality in him can alone get what he experienced. We know what he *said*, but to know what he *experienced* one has to lose oneself completely in him.

Detachment from negative thoughts is like letting mud settle at the bottom of a pool of water. If you stir it up, the whole thing becomes muddy. But if you let it settle to the bottom undisturbed, then you get clear water at the top, which you can drink.

## September 1, 1982

Incarnations retain their individuality (name and form) in the cosmic Divine realm. Therefore we can experience them even now. [Swami was asked how that applies to saints who have merged in him, and what it means when someone like Swami Akhandananda says, "I will always be with you."] It is impossible to generalize about saints and there is much flexibility in these things. What is between a Guru and a disciple is an individual spiritual relationship. Disciples do experience the Guru's presence in his spiritual form, and we are very close to him in our prayer and meditation. But this is something the disciple alone experiences, whereas the state reached by Incarnations is a cosmic occurrence. Any devotee can experience them. Incarnation is a cosmic occurrence, whereas Guru and disciple is a spiritual relationship at the individual level.

### September 7, 1982

Most important for spiritual life is not only japa and meditation but to level up our human behavior. Never dwell on anything negative, either something happening or someone's limitations. Either say, "I don't know" or "What can I learn from this?" But never condemn or judge or complain. Spiritual life means to lift ourselves above the psychophysical complex. If you point the finger outside and condemn others, you can never be spiritual.

The mind is always hungry so you have to constantly give it good food consciously or it will dig the unconscious and you automatically become a victim of past *samskaras*. Therefore be alert and conscious always. This is the use of mantra—to give the mind spiritual direction constantly and consciously.

In the spiritual realm we are moving in the dark and may not know that we are progressing. Therefore (quoting Swami Vivekananda), "Hold on my brave boys, the night is passing."

At the same time one way of measuring progress is to ask: (1) am I unselfish? (2) do I love people? If you have any selfishness or hatefulness, be careful. Unselfishness and all-lovingness are the automatic results of realization and they are also the means.

### September 13, 1982

We can't change the thoughts in the mind but we can be detached from them. Then they become powerless. When they come, pray immediately to Thakur, "Bless me!" That is why Krishna and Patanjali ask us to practice and develop dispassion (detachment). There is no shortcut.

If a little child is at home and a suspicious person comes to the door, the child immediately calls the parents. In the same way, when thoughts show up, immediately call, "Oh Mother!" Thakur and Mother are more powerful than all bad thoughts. Only we have to bring their thought into the mind. They look like mere flesh and blood human beings, but who is dwelling inside the human covering?

Illumination and his grace are not two different things. He is the Light of all lights, beyond all darkness. When that comes, all other spiritual treasures—devotion, faith, renunciation, unselfishness, etc.—are there in that. When any limitation comes, think of Thakur and Mother immediately, and pray to them for the spiritual treasures you want.

## September 14, 1982

Once when Swami Akhandanandaji came to Belur Math from Sargacchi, Swami Vivekananda embraced him and said with great emotion, "Ganges! You are the man! You are the only one who is doing Thakur's work."

In dreams there is no time, space or causation—no logic, no structure. Dreams simply let you know what you have got in your mind. If you get disturbing dreams, simply know you have got those thoughts and therefore be alert and careful.

## September 20, 1982

A person can realize God through worship and surrender to either an Incarnation or a mythological deity—it depends on faith. The essence of spirituality and gaining Light is purity. If faith in a deity enables you to gain that, you will get Light.

But when you realize, you understand that that deity is a symbol of something behind and therefore you are not dogmatic about it. Experience of an Incarnation is different. It is something very tangible, not a mere symbol. They are not symbols. They are real.

**September 30, 1982**

Our whole struggle is simply to clean the heart. Then God is waiting there to open the door.

Two things kill the soul: jealousy and hatred. We have to completely overcome these two.

No one who cares for satisfaction can ever be spiritual.

**October 5, 1982**

Our prayer should be for pure devotion. Devotion is a very rare thing and, once you get it, you are hooked. It holds you. You may make mistakes, but you will be saved. Pray to Thakur, "Please give me pure devotion. Draw my mind to your feet and don't let it go anywhere. Keep it under your toe!"

**October 14, 1982**

When one realizes God, one's view of the world changes completely. This is a sudden experience. In the process of spiritual struggle, your character gradually changes and your imagination of the Reality continually deepens. But when you get the actual experience of Reality or Truth or God, it transforms your vision completely. That experience is not unexpected, but it comes suddenly, as if in the twinkling of an eye. Until then you imagine, you imagine God in all, etc. But with realization, you *see* everything differently. That seeing God is most important. It is like actually seeing water after only imagining it, or actually going over the edge of a mountain when you have been moving towards it.

Thakur's illumination was so high that even his whole body was illumined because consciousness pervades the whole body. Therefore it shone everywhere, just like putting a light inside a clear plastic form. This happens only with Incarnations, not others.

Not all saints get the experience of seeing God everywhere. Some may get a vision of their Ishta (Chosen Deity) and that's it. Thakur's disciples all got a higher type of experience because they had surrendered to him completely. That vision is like a spiritual X-ray; it penetrates everything. That is why Thakur sometimes couldn't walk properly, because he didn't see difference at all, like between a gate and a wall. He saw only the One everywhere. If anyone were to touch him in that state, prostrating before him, they were sure to be purified completely. The experience of others, when compared to that of Thakur, is like a firefly next to the sun.

## October 15, 1982

It is very rare to have the desire to realize the Truth and even more rare to have an ideal like that of Thakur, Mother and Swamiji. Keep the mind turned to Thakur and don't turn away. At times we turn to him and then turn away, so keep the mind turned constantly to him. Pray to him to make you his instrument. Be humble, be devoted to his cause. In Thakur everything is there, all gods and goddesses.

## October 20, 1982

Those who have attained *nirvikalpa samadhi* can go to that state any time they want. There is no question of "how many times" they have had it. Once it is attained, a part of the mind is always in that awareness and identified with it. But these illumined ones have no big desire to go often to that state because, once they reach it, they are more concerned to help people, to remove their misery in whatever way possible, whether physical, mental or spiritual. There is no need for isolation or exclusion. But when they are alone with no external demands, the mind jumps there. You will be surprised to know that many times, just sitting in the shrine before the picture of Sri Ramakrishna, they go to that mood. If you ask them if they have attained *nirvikalpa samadhi* they will just laugh. Yet how many times they go nobody knows. And the funny part is that they act just like ordinary people, expressing great concern even over a cut in their finger.

## October 22, 1982

Never look to the negative side of anything, nor to the sensate side. If you work in a worldly environment, if you are alert and prayerful you will gain tremendous will and strength. If you are earnest, Sri Ramakrishna's grace will function. Anyone who really turns to him will definitely get the Light.

## October 28, 1982

The need for too much rest shows you need to try harder for good meditation because that itself gives so much rest. In the shrine, be more alert and mindful. Try to keep the mind there 100% and don't allow it to stray away. Be careful and intent on the preparation, including pranayama. Pay attention to the whole thing. Don't bring other thoughts there and don't allow the mind to wander. Remember Thakur slapping the Rani when her mind wandered. Meanwhile, how we behave in daily life affects our meditation.

Brooding unconsciously on negative thoughts takes away much of our energy.

Unconscious indulgence is the worst enemy. The worst part is that we say we don't want a thing but then we look at it. Then we get all the problems.

We must keep the mind calm.

We must be aware of our motives, in whatever we do, say and even think. We must gain introspection and keep the mind straight by always questioning ourselves. We have to pay deep attention to what is going on internally. The problem is failure to pay enough attention to the internal state of affairs.

With one firm sweep, keep the negative thoughts off the road. Say no to the mind. It is like driving on a narrow road with ditches on either side. Go straight and carefully. Even if dogs are pulling from behind, the more they pull, the more you must put him there. Doing like that again and again you will get the effect of it later on, even though you may not feel it right away.

Keep an attitude of dedication to Thakur in all work. Once we have decided on exclusive spiritual life, the attitude of dedication must always be kept, in whatever work we do anywhere.

## October 30, 1982

What must be done in order to be spiritual is to perfect ourselves at the level of human relationship. Like a mother with a baby, there must be identification—"mine." That is why Mother's teaching about not finding fault and making the world your own is so important. Like the Gita (5.19) verse about being even and stainless.

## November 3, 1982

The mind is nothing but the link between spirit and matter. The mind has no existence of its own. It is but the reflection or shadow of spirit falling on matter.

The secret of mind control is nothing but detachment, detachment, detachment.

## November 9, 1982

[Talking about what mind is in a talk on "Ways of Controlling the Mind":] Mind is very, very fine matter. It is the link between consciousness and matter, spirit and body. It is very fine and transparent. It is but the reflection of consciousness falling on matter, like the reflection of the sun on a lake. When consciousness is separated from matter, mind is gone. Subtle tendencies form a psychic residue which is like a seed that goes to the next birth. Mind is by its nature pure and clear. It is really like a crystal. It is only thoughts that give it a coloring, like the way a crystal takes blue color when you put a blue flower before it. You don't actually control the mind; you control the thoughts, either psychologically (refuse to identify), philosophically, devotionally or practically (develop unselfishness and identify with all). If you have devotion and put the mind on him, you don't need anything else. That draws you because in reality the mind is very close to the spirit and therefore likes that pure thought.

Again, the mind is like a screen on which the movie of life is projected. The pictures fall on the screen. But switch off the movie (that is, practice detachment) and the screen becomes absolutely pure and unmarred.

. . .

## November 10, 1982

Once you have devotion you are safe. Until you get devotion, you are holding onto him like a child holding the father's hand, as Sri Ramakrishna said. But once you get devotion, then he is holding you.

## November 18, 1982

Actually, mind is a very fine point, like a searchlight, which moves very, very fast. "I" am nothing but the consciousness and I can direct that searchlight any way I want. "Mind" (in the sense of awareness) and "me" (as I feel it in the ignorant condition) are the same. To turn me toward God or to turn mind toward God simply means to turn the attention, to turn that searchlight from worldly thoughts to the Divine. That means I am the master. I can turn toward any thought I want. If I don't understand that, then worldly thoughts which I used to like may cheat me. That is what is meant by, "Mind will cheat you." But if I understand the secret that I am not the thoughts, then I can turn to whatever I want. Then I can put the whole mind on Thakur because I am the master. Mind, as opposed to thoughts, is nothing but consciousness and that is me. Mind or me is absolutely pure but thoughts give a coloring. Therefore control the thoughts by detachment and you are the master, pure and free.

The reason we surrender to Thakur is so that we can open up and receive his grace. *Samskaras* are nothing but clouds and, when we open up to his light, they fly away. It doesn't take even a minute to be purified completely if we totally surrender.

Feeling close to Sri Ramakrishna is the best meditation. Keep that feeling, intensify it.

## November 23, 1982

The more you surrender to Sri Ramakrishna, the more you understand that you have to bear everything and just do the right thing in his name. Don't worry about what other people think. Accept them and never be rude or impertinent.

## November 26, 1982

From the point of Pure Being and their experience, Holy Mother and Thakur are the same. But from the point of manifestation, she was superior. She converted that transcendental experience into the power of love and compassion. Her power of acceptance and the power of her grace are unparalleled. Thakur loved all because of the transcendental experience and seeing the same in all, from the Vedantic standpoint. But the position Mother took of actually being a mother to all—saying even Amjad and Sarat "are the same to me"—it is beyond compare in the history of spiritual luminaries. She accepted everything. She granted everything to those who asked, even worldly things.

Never pick up negative things. "Picking up" means reacting to it or putting a label on a person saying, "You are like that." When we see things we should just say, "I don't know," and don't react or condemn or judge. Otherwise we get that mental impression ourselves.

In spiritual life there is a tremendous struggle with *samskaras* within, and with what comes from outside. But if you can just keep your head above water, the time will come when a wave will throw you ashore and you will say, "I'm glad I went through it. I'm glad I made it."

. . .

## December 10, 1982

If you yield to one negative thought, you are exploited by other negative thoughts. Assert, "I do not want to be exploited by the thoughts." Therefore pray the moment they show up. Otherwise they become very powerful and ruin one's spiritual life.

## December 30, 1982

The way to overcome all negative feelings is to pray, "I don't know," to Thakur and pray only for pure devotion.

The highest realization is like a cosmic X-ray that penetrates all matter completely. In the highest awareness you don't see matter at all. In that experience you feel only, "I and my Father are one." "I am the Life." That is the state of no-mind or pure mind. You see everything filled with That. Swami Jagadanandaji told the younger monks that it is like putting a piece of tissue in water. You see water above, water below, and water in and through the tissue itself.

Ordinary saints just touch the highest absolute consciousness and come down, without exception. But the Incarnations (Krishna, Christ, Buddha, Ramakrishna) merge in it, retain it, and continue like that. No one else can do that.

The minute you separate anybody from yourself, you are gone. We have to use spiritual reasoning and take everyone as our own, no matter what. "Even if you curse me, I love you; even if you are bitter against me, I love you."

Desirelessness is purity.

Being a monk or a nun means completely renouncing the ego.

# 1983

### January 14, 1983

The question of whether spiritual progress is fast or slow is to be left to Thakur. Leave that to him!

### January 31, 1983

Behavior is most important in gaining spirituality. The spiritual realm is closed unless the lid is lifted—psychophysical lid. That means, be very, very careful about human behavior.

The heat of the sun's rays cannot be felt unless and until the rays hit some surface. Only when it is reflected is the heat felt. Similarly, God-consciousness must touch a person to be reflected as love. But to reflect that Light, the heart of the person must be pure. The sun, hitting a surface, is reflected as heat. God, reflected on a pure heart, is felt as love.

### February 1, 1983

Two forces are at work in the world and in all beings: love and freedom. In matter, love is expressed as adhesive force or gravitation. Freedom is expressed as the outward force. In beings, love misunderstood causes misery and people seek freedom to get away and then become isolated and unhappy. Love and freedom combined, in the context of unselfishness, is the highest. Only he who is free can love all beings.

**February 8, 1983**

Mind is nothing but thoughts. Our job is not to identify with the thoughts, to control the thoughts. Also not to think about them, because interest and attention make the thoughts powerful and they will tip you off later on and cause great regret.

Mantra—"that which protects the mind"—is very helpful in this struggle. If the mind is set in that thought, it is protected from other thoughts.

The other struggle is when the intellect says one thing but unconscious tendencies say another, and the heart is still attracted by something outside which is supported by the unconscious and you are torn by all these conflicting ideas. If you are not careful, you become neurotic. The solution is to be introspective and contemplative, and ask yourself what is to be done, taking the help of all the great teachings we have got. We see all these things going on and we have to decide what to "mind." Even when psychic residue is there, you can deny the whole thing when, through the grace of somebody, you decide you want nothing but to know your true nature. Then when thoughts come up, you resolve them by saying, "No, I don't want it." The will to do that comes through love of the ideal.

Man is a combination of three things: body, inner organ or mind, and Pure Consciousness. (Don't call it Brahman because that has no place when speaking of the individual.) Mind (or inner organ) in turn has four functions. Manas cognizes. Buddhi decides or determines. Chitta is the storehouse, the unconscious. Ego identifies. All of our struggles take place in this inner organ. It is the Pure Consciousness reflecting on it that makes the inner organ lively. Everything is due to that Pure Consciousness.

Forget about things being composed of the *gunas*. Gunas are not outside. Nature knows no evil and no *guna*. Gunas are within and simply refer to the mind of the beholder according to the thoughts one has got. We see through those thoughts and view the world or nature accordingly.

To get rid of the "garlic smell" we have to struggle again and again. That is why we must be alert. And cry constantly. And don't take life lightly. "Tendencies" means the *vrittis* or urges or modifications which we feel as effect, but we do not know the unconscious cause. These are to be controlled. When such struggles come, just strongly intensify the spiritual thought.

## February 17, 1983

Mind is like the sky. As the sky is the upper atmosphere, so mind is an inner atmosphere. Thoughts are like clouds. If there are no clouds, where is sky? You directly see the sun. Sky, as it were, becomes one with the sun. In the same way, pure mind and pure Self are the same. When thoughts are silenced through detachment the Sun of Pure Consciousness shines without any obstruction. Our job is to control the thoughts, not the mind. "Mind control" means controlling the thoughts.

Mind is the meeting point between spirit and matter. Pure Consciousness falling on this *antahkarana* or inner instrument reflects as me, the individual. First we realize the Atman within, as our own true Self. When mind is completely purified, the Atman realizes its identity with the Paramātman or Brahman. The realized soul becomes very powerful. That is the power of love, the power to make everybody your own and silently work in their lives.

Our job is to realize our true nature as that pure loving consciousness. It appears to be like a finite spark but really it is neither a spark nor finite.

## March 23, 1983

[Gita 15.7 begins with, "An eternal portion of myself having become a living soul...."] That eternal portion is the real "me" in everyone. That is the Atman. But on that Atman we pile up so many thoughts and then proceed to identify with them. Now we have to deny all other identifications except the spiritual. There must be no trace of anything else. Then realization comes. When you really become nobody, then you become somebody.

## April 8, 1983

We have to accept everything. If the wise cannot adjust to the unwise, then what is the good of that wisdom? That is where Mother's greatness was revealed, in her capacity to accept everything and adjust herself.

[The swami said at first he read Swami Vivekananda and was lost in that wonderful spiritual trend. Then slowly he came to understand that Thakur was the huge spiritual giant behind him, the greatest Light the world has ever seen. But then he read Mother and there was something else.] *Nowhere* have we seen that complete lack of discrimination. It is the *only* case where we have seen that kind of all-inclusive feeling manifested. We are her children and must be like her. If we can do that, God is in our pocket.

Don't run after people, but when different types come, accept it. Be yourself, don't change your own ideal. When negative types come, just do the right thing and be yourself according to your own ideal.

## April 14, 1983

[The swami said the two ideas that move him most in Swami Vivekananda's teachings are "freedom" and "divinity of man."] Swamiji is the culmination of 5000 years of world culture, including Thakur. Wherever Thakur is, there is Mother too. And they are eternal. The only thing we have to do is cry for them constantly.

Surrender to Guru or God means shifting the ego from me to him. Where there is true and complete surrender, you are freed immediately and completely.

## April 21, 1983

- DO: love, accept, respect, and cooperate.
- DON'T: accuse, demand, compete, complain.

In the case of a mentally imbalanced person something happens in life and thick clouds of karma pile up. But behind it is the same spark of divinity, spark of pure loving consciousness, in every soul. Gold may be covered with mud but gold is still there. The diamond is still there. You love and respect them for that. It's not what is there externally. It is what you know to be there essentially.

The sin of selfishness is the worst and hardest to purify. But if unselfishness is there, all other sins are easily purified. All other sins we commit out of ignorance, but selfishness is rooted deep in the ego.

Self-purification is the only thing that matters. Don't pay attention to anything external, but struggle hard to take care of the internal. If you make that big turn within, your whole view of the world changes. You experience a whole new motive power within. Pray hard for that inward turning. Also pray that one's own pure attitude may not be affected by the attitude of others: "From me no danger be to aught that lives."

Knowledge and smartness are meaningless. What are needed are wisdom and understanding. We may read many things, but what's the point if we don't follow them?

## May 31, 1983

[Talking about the "psychology of acceptance":] Ninety percent of a problem is over if you *accept* it. If you take any problem as *our* problem, accept it through identification, instead of reacting or resisting, then you can easily handle it.

## June 1, 1983

More important than vows is to try to deserve Thakur's grace.

Never eavesdrop. Never put any judgement on what you hear. Always feel, "I do not know the whole story," and never allow your mind to be polluted by any judgement or prejudice or any type of negative feeling.

To purify the mind we have to be absolutely firm in the determination never to harbor any negative thought. Otherwise the pure consciousness will always remain covered by clouds. Whenever such things come from the unconscious to the conscious, we must resolve them right away, or if we can't resolve them, then pray. But never allow any negative thought to remain (he was speaking particularly of bitterness against others). If these things are allowed to remain unresolved in the unconscious, we never gain Light or peace of mind. We are held back and we don't know why. Therefore when they come, resolve or sublimate them right away. Otherwise they are like strings that tie the mind down or like clouds blocking the sun.

## June 3, 1983

Keep up the mantra because it protects the mind and it also leads us to the Reality. The element of Supreme Reality is in the mantra. As Thakur said, Satchidananda Brahma, Satchidananda Atma, Satchidananda Bhagavan are one and the same. Bhagavan is one who has become one with Brahman and that same Reality is also within us. So by repeating his name, we are led to the him.

## June 7, 1983

A baby is between two worlds of past and present. The past is in the unconscious in a subtle form. As the present begins to fill the mind with new thoughts, the past goes to the deep unconscious. Our job now is to fill the mind with spiritual thought so that all other things go to the deep unconscious where they become ineffective because they are covered, as it were, by three layers of spiritual thought—conscious, preconscious, and even unconscious. But to do that requires consciously keeping up the spiritual thought constantly, either through japa or a song or repetition of something, and study. It is like painting a black table white. You put one coat, still it is dark. So you put another and another—three layers and now it looks pure white. So also with the mind. If you fill all the top layers with the thought of God, then nothing else can come. They are all in the deep unconscious, ineffective.

It's like if you want to cross a mountain. You build a path which is many feet across. On either side are ravines and cliffs and rivers and forests, but the path is clear. Like that, all thoughts can be there on the sides, but keep the conscious mind clear through detachment. To do that we have to struggle to imagine the Reality behind all these layers of thoughts. That we can do by keeping the thought of Bhagavan who is one with that Reality. Keep the mind on his thought and then other thoughts cannot come and clutter the path.

## June 8, 1983

[Gita 3.30.] "Adhyātma" means "with spiritual consciousness." "Renouncing all actions to Me, with spiritual consciousness, getting rid of egoism and selfishness, fight...." Without egoism means no feeling of "what can I get out of it."

When realization comes, it isn't actually that individual consciousness "enters into" Divine Consciousness. It doesn't "enter." It becomes one with it, like when you remove the walls of a house, the space within automatically becomes one with the space outside. So if you remove all the thoughts, the individual consciousness automatically becomes one with the Divine.

. . .

## June 15, 1983

It is only after the highest realization that you see the reality in all beings. Until you experience that, know that you are still only on the way.

Many aspirants who are dependent on an Incarnation, stop with the realization of "God with form." But because of Thakur's experience and his teachings, we know that God is both with form and without form. If we keep that in mind in our meditation on him, then we not only realize him with form, but he takes us beyond form as well.

## June 22, 1983

To see the truth in ourselves we have to realize the Self, which is beyond time, space and causation. The "I" is unaffected by time—this means the truth within us which doesn't change with time. The body changes according to the food we take. The mind changes according to the thoughts we breathe in. Therefore the truth is neither the body nor the mind.

Beyond space means beyond form. Again, all forms are constantly changing. Food affects the body; thoughts affect the mind. What is it that is unaffected by these things? Therefore, that in us which is beyond time/space/causation means that in us which is beyond the body-mind complex, non-material and non-mental. That we call Spirit. That is beyond the psycho-physical complex, beyond change. That is Pure Loving Consciousness. Awareness and love have remained unchanged throughout. The objects of love may change, but love itself does not. Love was born with me.

Jnana yoga cannot prove anything through reason alone. Only realization can prove it. But intellectual faith means to put together all the sayings of all the great souls, whose lives prove their greatness. And see for oneself that they are all saying the same thing; there is no contradiction. Particularly if someone close tells us in close quarters the same truth—these things give intellectual faith and conviction. Then our struggle and realization give true faith.

In our behavior, make Mother the exemplar. When trying to decide what to do in any situation, she is the Supreme Court, not even Thakur, because she never discriminated. Never lose heart; always make more hearts your own. Our true wealth here is not in possessions or security or anything material. It is in how many people we love.

[Kena Upanishad 2 .4.] *Pratibodha viditam* means "with every pulsation of thought." Swami Premeshanandaji said, *Bodhe bodhe viditam* (Bengali)—"known between thought and thought." In the millionth of a second between one thought and another, the truth shines. Thoughts are like a moving train. If they move slowly, you can see the space between the cars. If they are moving too fast, you don't see the space. Pratyāhāra means, don't allow the train of thoughts to move. We want to see that which is eternally present behind, and hold onto it. We want to catch that which is seen between thought and thought, and hold onto it. On the other hand, if the train is moving extremely fast, you don't see it at all. Like with a fast moving fan, you don't see the blades but you see that which is behind. The train moving so fast that you don't see it is like detachment. Thoughts move but you don't pay any attention, so your view of what is behind is unobstructed.

## June 29, 1983

Swami means *swa-ami*, "I am myself." Or "I am that I am." Actually the word was first used for God. Then it came to be applied to a monk who had realized God. Brahmachari means God-living. Therefore it means one who is devoted to God or one who lives in God.

Visions are good. At times the picture becomes lively and that is good. Or at times you are walking and then think and get visions and that is good. But the best thing is to see him in your own heart. Then you move closer and closer to him, you touch his feet and then finally merge in that Light.

## June 30, 1983

The secret of spiritual life is expansion of heart. We must love and accept everyone. Life will be blessed here and everywhere if we have love and concern for everyone. We must always be ready to serve and to share, and never try to hold or possess. If we open up our heart, the light of God shines there. And you say, "What did I do?" You didn't do anything except open up your heart. Just as a mother loves anyone who loves, and takes care of her children, so God is just like that. If you love and serve his children, he comes to you unasked. If you serve one person, you really are worshiping God.

## July 5, 1983

[The swami was talking about the value of unselfish work. He once jokingly said to another swami who used to sit five or six hours for meditation, that he had to meditate 'til fire came out of his head.] Swami Vivekananda's disciple Swami Achalanandaji once commented that those who came to Thakur at young age needed no *tapasya*. Those who practiced such *tapasya* had done terrible things for which they were doing penance. But these young people needed to do only one thing: be concerned for others. Do Swamiji's unselfish work, and no other tapasya is necessary. That kind of unselfish work does the job of purifying. Swami Turiyananda said the same thing. He said he had failed to follow Swamiji in that respect and had suffered for it. He had had trouble with anger, losing his temper. But when he gave himself over to Swamiji's ideal, it came under control. Later on he could inspire young boys to follow that ideal. He said there is no easy way to purify the *samskaras* except through unselfish work.

You need not work in a hospital or school to practice unselfish work. It is an attitude that can be practiced anywhere. It is a feeling of, "What can I do to help others?" To do that requires tremendous self-discipline. You have to overcome your own limitations. You have to overlook the limitations of others and not say one word when they accuse you of the worst things, even when you have done good to them. In the process you have to be alert and question yourself and your motives and reactions constantly. Obstacles come from without and within, and you have to reflect. In this big struggle, the knots of the past are undone. You can renounce everything materially and gain nothing. What is required is surrender of the ego. That means to have no feeling of, "What can I get out of it?" That is the real renunciation. This is Swami Vivekananda's unique message to the modern age and this is what is needed to truly be the child of Thakur, Mother and Swamiji.

[Talking to some young people who had gotten exhausted doing heavy work:] Health is most important and Thakur will not curse you for sleeping one more hour. We have no organization, no stipulation, we have only one thing: total dedication to Thakur and his work. We have to keep up meditative awareness throughout. There should be no reservation or limitation in that dedication, such as, "Oh, I don't have enough time to meditate," etc. Rather keep his thought throughout.

## July 6, 1983

It was the specialty of Thakur that with a touch, or even a mere wish, he could illumine others. Not only then, even now. As we are talking, he is present here hearing our talk. As he said to Mother when she was removing her bangles after he left his body, "What are you doing? I have only gone from one room to another." For any sincere aspirant, his grace is still here.

## July 7, 1983

Thakur is still with spiritual name and form in the cosmic spiritual realm. In *Jnana Yoga* Swami Vivekananda says there can be no form without matter. At the material level that is true. Name and form are material. But God does play dice. At the spiritual level there is no determinism. God can do anything. And these Incarnations *do* retain name and form beyond the material level. It is a Divine mystery, but it is true. Christ did appear to his disciples. So also Thakur.

Negative thoughts are like black clouds; positive thoughts are like white clouds. But Thakur's thought is not a cloud at all. It is the purifier. It has got a purifying element in it and washes away everything else. When you use detergent, it doesn't get into the fabric itself. It just washes out everything else. So Thakur's name purifies the mind. But you have to feel it.

## July 15, 1983

The key to feeling spiritual consciousness even in a big group, full of many uncertainties and even negative elements, is to have an attitude of total acceptance of everyone and everything. The secret is to take everyone as your own, looking only to the spiritual element in all and overlooking all relative factors. Feel that no one is a stranger, as Mother said, and don't find fault, don't look to the negative in anybody. Look for the positive element, for what you can learn from anyone and completely accept everything, without any feeling of trying to get rid of anything or anyone. If you do that, the mind becomes calm and you need not struggle much—this attitude has such a great effect. If there is any negative element, take it as a lesson: "I need this friction for learning something." Or "Thakur has kept me in this situation for my own learning."

Develop the habit of repeating his name constantly and think of all work as his, not mine. Then let all relative things come and go. The only solution to life is God-consciousness. Keep his consciousness and accept everything, just as Mother did. As she accepted all, so we have to develop the spiritual strength to do the same thing.

With regard to purification, when any negative feeling comes, even if you don't understand its nature or source, don't examine it or dig to understand it. Just turn to Thakur and that immediately puts a wall against the negative unconscious and purifies the mind. Never examine any negative; just pray. Otherwise examining it, reinforces it.

## July 18, 1983

The only thing is to be concerned for others. All other things are indirect methods, but love and concern for all is the direct way to get experience of real spiritual Light. There must be no exclusion, only all-inclusive feeling—but with divine consciousness. Otherwise you become attached if you take it as yours. But if you take everything as God's work and all as God's children, then you love and include all without any attachment. Then the ego does go down and the mind becomes pure.

You have to struggle. It takes time. Just pray to him, "I have come to you. I have nowhere else to go!" Keep Mother's thought and always a positive attitude. God-consciousness and acceptance.

## July 31, 1983

In the Guru's absence one must keep up spiritual contact through the mantra. Initiation is not a simple thing. Through that a relationship and a contact are established which are eternal. By creating a constant mental vibration of that, non-separation is established. Then you always feel that contact and it protects you from everything else. We have to generate that vibration through practice. Sri Ramakrishna is present to us in his name. This constancy also helps us to keep up the attitude of, "What would he want me to do," whenever there is any doubt about what is to be done.

In relief camps they had no time even for meditation, but the mantra was what they could hang on to, to keep up the spiritual trend. At Kankhal during cholera relief, Swami Kalyanananda told all the *brahmacharis* to compulsorily go to the shrine because he was concerned about their spiritual life (they were young and new). One of them said, "What about him?" (meaning Swami Sarvagatananda because he had also been working all day.) Swami Kalyanananda said, "Don't worry about him."

One of the most important ways to create a spiritual psyche is to take all work as his work. Nothing is my work, all is his work. That is literally true because we can't do anything without that Consciousness. Jesus and Krishna both made it very clear that, "Whatever you do, you do unto me."

When circumstances are difficult, the solution is to make greater effort.

## August 2, 1983

Mantra is eternal in the sense that it is the sound-symbol of that which is eternal, immortal, infinite, and all-pervasive. That Light in Thakur is what we are to think of in the mantra. We don't know Satchidananda, but Satchidananda Bhagavan we have in Thakur. He is everything to us.

It is absolutely true that surrender to God burns all karma. Karma stands on ego alone. When you deny the ego by surrendering to God, karma literally has nothing to stand on. Otherwise you have to work out the karma. But if you have devotion to God, in the sense of genuine surrender of the ego, then karma is loosened completely. The way to surrender the ego is to remember him constantly with real feeling as you repeat the mantra. When you do that, you are protected from things outside and *samskaras* also have no hold on you. First they are silenced and go down, and later they are burned completely. What happened between Girish and Thakur is one proof of this, but even there it took a little time. Angulimāla is the best example. Buddha said, "Follow me," and Aṅgulimāla literally followed then and there, and was thereby freed immediately and completely from all karma and bondage.

**September 4, 1983**

Think of the Light within as pure loving Consciousness: "I am a spark of that Light of pure loving Consciousness." Then meditate on Thakur *in* that Light and *as* that Light, and keep every other thought away. Keep other thoughts away by feeding mind with *his* thought. Try to concentrate on his form while repeating his name. If you can't do that, use hymns and prayer. As you gain concentration and then meditation, a time comes when the whole consciousness is illumined by that Light. If we are not alert, the conscious mind fills with thoughts from the pre-conscious and unconscious, and they whirl about there, and we get no meditation. We have to use strong will and say "not now" at the time of meditation and keep the whole mind on Thakur.

The same alertness must always be kept outside the shrine too, in order to catch and say no to the tendencies and *samskaras* that come up. Otherwise in a split second you may become a victim.

**September 5, 1983**

Always try to keep the body healthy. For monks and nuns, healthy body and mind are a must. It is our responsibility to keep it that way.

The only goal of life is to realize our true Self. Pure mind and pure Self are the same. Pratyāhāra means to hold all thoughts off. This requires strong will and strong detachment. "I am not the thoughts." Then you concentrate only on that pure mind, or on Thakur as the embodiment of that Light. "You are the Light. You are the Self. You are the Bliss. You are God." Then you make the mind totally one-pointed, like putting a lens before the sun in order to burn an object. You focus it and keep it one-pointed. Then you have to exercise strong will to hold that concentration and continue it. Then it becomes meditation and, when you continue to hold thus, it becomes samadhi.

**September 9, 1983**

Anyone who says he "had" *nirvikalpa samadhi* is still a struggling soul. Once you have fully attained that state, that awareness is never away from you. Thakur didn't say, "I *saw* God." He said, "I *see* God, more clearly than I see you." So also, not that Thakur *was,* Thakur *is.* And those who have attained that spiritual height experience it. To others they take it on faith; to us it is a spiritual fact. Both with that form and without.

Renunciation means not to possess anything. It is for the sake of total freedom. The means is complete detachment. Non-possession and detachment are with reference to persons and things outside and thoughts inside. We have to be totally detached from all these three.

**October 26, 1983**

The first step to spirituality is expansion of heart. And the best formula is Mother's teaching not to find fault and to make everybody your own. Accept all without any complaint.

Pray only this: "I don't know anything. I don't want anything. Please give me pure devotion."

**November 1, 1983**

One of the great dangers of organized monastic life is that, once you feel secure, you cease to be sufficiently introspective and struggling. Then old *samskaras* come up, the ego comes up, comparison and competition come up, and you completely lose the spiritual touch. Organization gives protection, but it works against realization by making you "comfortable." The struggle is up to the individual. If you keep up Swamiji's ideal, then no work will hurt you. That means work with love, with detachment, with wisdom.

**November 17, 1983**

[On doing Thakur's work:] Life is a process. When you jump to spiritual life, everything you do ("work" means all of it) is spiritual work. Everything is his work—I am only an instrument.

No likes and dislikes. Keep the "I" down. Likes and dislikes are what bind you. As it comes, so you fulfill it.

Because you take life as a process, there is no distinction between work and meditation and devotion. You take everything as his, and then everything is harmonized in that attitude.

Don't expect anything.

Avoid patterns. Take things as they come. Otherwise you get into patterns, and then resent and resist anything outside of the pattern. You become just a network of patterns and you are bound in that. Don't get into patterns.

**November 23, 1983**

The thing is to shift the center from here ("I") to outside of ourselves. Think, "What is to be done?" instead of, "How does this affect me, what am I going to get out of it?" Then you accept things as they come in a spiritual way and nothing disturbs you.

**November 28, 1983**

God or Spirit is Light, spiritual Light. And our true nature is a spark of that Light.

In monastic life the important thing is not how much or what we *do*, but how we *are*. We must always have a positive and harmonious attitude toward everything and everybody. Then whatever little we do will shine. But if we don't have that attitude, no matter how much we do, there is always a limitation. Why have we become monks and nuns? To feel for others, to make everybody our own. Be concerned.

The best way to deal with evil is to realize that we are all prone to temptations and limitations, and therefore never to judge or condemn but always to feel, "how can I help?"

**December 2, 1983**

All doubts are resolved, all contradictions are harmonized, in complete surrender to him.

**December 21, 1983**

The ideal of monastic life is to renounce and serve. Complete renunciation means complete dedication to service. To lead a completely dedicated monastic life there must be no reservation.

Our monastic ideal is not a dry routine of meditation, study, bath, and bread. It is a life full of love.

The worst thing that can happen in spiritual life is to keep away consciously and indulge unconsciously. The minute any unwanted thought comes, repeat God's name. Otherwise interest and attention make the thought very powerful and literally no God can help us. No God can give you *mukti* if you bind yourself through unconscious indulgence.

There is no guarantee anywhere. You have to make it.

# 1984

### January 28, 1984

When we surrender to Thakur, the ego goes down. "I am zero, he is the One." Zero becomes powerful in proximity to the One. Being is more important than doing. You may not accomplish much. Our only prayer should be, "Make me what you want me to be."

### February 13, 1984

Monk or nun means I am nobody. Meekness—"Blessed are the meek"—is the first condition of the life of renunciation. One must be absolutely humble and egoless. No pride, no vanity. For renunciation of ego Swami Vivekananda has given us the prescription: Love and serve. Not to "help" but to serve. The ideal is no individuality.

Simply turn the mind to Thakur as soon as any negative thought arises. Don't analyze or evaluate—just turn the mind and look at him. Don't look at the dirt, rather apply detergent. He is the spiritual detergent.

For those who look at Thakur, no scriptures are needed. We get everything by looking at him. These Incarnations are standing on the shore to give a hand to those who are struggling in the current and are near the shore. At times they even jump in to rescue us. That means they come to our level. For those who are weak and helpless but are looking at God and struggling, he even reaches down to pull them up, as in the case of Girish and St. Augustine.

The three greatest virtues are poverty, chastity and obedience. Poverty means no sense of possession. Chastity means not to look at anyone as something separate. No "I belong to one group and someone else to another." Rather, "The sexless Self, whose father he, whose child?" Obedience is not in the slavish sense but obedience to the spiritual.

## March 20, 1984

Our task in spiritual life is to clear the mind of all thoughts—clouds (negative thoughts are thick dark clouds)—and then to surrender that purified ego at Thakur's feet. But if there is either attraction or aversion, we cannot surrender.

## April 24, 1984

The only way to be spiritual is complete surrender to the Spirit. The meaning of monk or nun is to lift the mind to the spiritual. For us Thakur is the Spirit. No big prayer is necessary, only complete surrender to him. We have to simply feel, "I don't know anything, you are everything," and deny our individuality completely. That is the only way to truly spiritualize the mind. You have to deny your own intellect. When you do that and surrender to him, then the intellect becomes very broad. You enter into a wonderful new consciousness altogether.

He is the vine, we are the branches. The way to keep the connection is through constant remembrance. Separation and non-separation are in consciousness.

We must do all work as his. Simply surrender to him and take whatever comes. No matter where you are or what you are asked to do—simply do it for his sake. Do everything in the spirit of complete dedication to him. "I shall do Thy bidding" is the highest surrendering attitude.

When you surrender and resign to him like that, then life's problem is over. You don't condemn or criticize anybody. You can live with any problem. Problems and difficulties may be there but you can live with them through that surrendering attitude.

We are Thakur's and he is ours. The only thing necessary in spiritual life is complete surrender to him. He is omnipresent, omniscient. Believe it. Have faith in it. Akhandananda Maharaj told me and I am telling you. When you surrender like that, illumination is not far off. We don't know his power but his disciples have told us. He can re-mold our brains. If you don't have that kind of devotion, pray for it, that through his grace we may surrender to him. Keep your soul at his feet.

This surrender is the key to not feeling separation from the Guru in his physical absence. The way to feel non-separate is to follow his teachings. Concentrate on the spiritual aspect, not the physical. Look to the spiritual, not just the immediate.

## April 25, 1984

It doesn't end with Sri Ramakrishna's acceptance of you. We must follow exactly what he said and always feel, "What would he want me to do if he were here?" The love that comes from him must be permitted to flow to others through us. Otherwise movement of the sap stops and the branch itself withers. We must constantly keep ourselves in tune with him. If we do that, then his love becomes pure will in us—not *our* will, but *his*. Will is love converted into power.

We must feel not that "I am working for him," but that he is working through us. In the former, the "I" remains. In the latter, the "I" is removed.

## April 26, 1984

Buddha said that all life is spiritual. With our very limited vision, we see only body and mind, but the spiritual is the main factor in life. And prayer works. An honest, sincere, selfless prayer touches the Ground, and it does work. We don't know how or when—it is a Divine mystery. We should never pray for the survival of anybody, only for their peace of mind.

## May 1, 1984

Everything depends on only one thing—surrendering to him. Then nothing can go wrong. See Gita 9. 22: "I preserve what they have and procure what they need."

Everything will be wonderful if you keep your head at his feet—no "I"; and make everybody your own.

Have no identity, no ego, except, "I am Ramakrishna's child."

## May 2, 1984

The only solution to all problems—interpersonal, institutional, and personal—is surrender to Thakur.

The key to interpersonal harmony is acceptance. Don't find fault with anybody; make everybody your own. Consider every work as *our* work. This is *our* place.

**May 8, 1984**

When you completely surrender to him, just like a little baby who knows absolutely nothing, then miracles do happen (miracles in a spiritual sense). We don't understand it, but there is an unknown spiritual power at work. There is an unseen divine hand.

**May 9, 1984**

In Christ, Krishna and Ramakrishna we have the wonderful combination of God Impersonal and Personal. And in that we have a special closeness to the Divine. It is like a father holding his child's hand. Our part is only to extend our hand to him. That is our surrender. And when we do that, he takes the responsibility.

The key to beginning life in a monastic setting is, "As I have loved you, love one another; as I have served you, serve one another." That is, make everybody your own.

**May 10, 1984**

Relax completely in the shrine. When one man was meditating with eyes closed in Thakur's presence, Thakur asked why he did like that when he was in the very presence of him on whom he was meditating. Be just like a little baby in the lap of the mother. When you feel cold, you go and sit before a hot fire and bask in the warmth. So also, just be in his presence and relax completely. You need not even pray or have a big meditation on him. Just simply relax in his presence like a little baby. Keep in the mind the image of a newborn baby.

## May 19, 1984

Thakur *is* the Light. We need not cut him in two in order to see the true Light. He *is* the Light.

## May 31, 1984

Thakur is one with the Absolute Ground, but he is also present with name and form in the cosmic realm. These Incarnations retain name and form due to their huge spiritual mass. Like when planets come out from the sun, little ones burn out but big ones continue orbiting around the sun. They are like 24 hour high-power broadcasting stations which anyone can catch with a properly tuned instrument (mind). Thakur, like Krishna, Christ and Buddha, can be experienced if we have purity, one-pointedness and devotion. Even if we don't have purity, if we have one-pointed devotion to him, he will do the miracle, as he did for Girish.

Holy Mother is a great Divine mystery. We can only pray to her to reveal herself.

Always remember that after Thakur's physical passing, he appeared to Mother and told her that he had only gone from one room to another. The direct disciples also experienced it. Swami Akhandananda would pray to Thakur while wandering in the Himalayas and he used to experience his presence.

Thakur is not a symbol or an image. He is one with the Absolute Ground. He *is*.

The key to life is acceptance, inclusion, identification. Reflect, don't react. Never be unwilling. Never react. Accept everything.

The *jiva* is a pure ray of consciousness. If we keep all thoughts out of the conscious mind, we are nothing but that pure ray of consciousness. When you move up, you become one with cosmic consciousness. A river merges into the ocean; the salt doll melts into the ocean.

The pre-conscious is thoughts pertinent to the subject you are thinking about. Sub-conscious is all other accessible thoughts which you bring to the pre-conscious as needed. The deep unconscious includes even thoughts from past lives. They come only if an outside suggestion draws them out. We can bury them under spiritual *samskaras*. Eventually they come out with *sadhana,* but by then you can handle them.

The ray of consciousness is *loving* consciousness. Let it flow unobstructed to all.

In monastic life we must identify and take everything as *our* work.

## June 4, 1984

Spiritual life is not an easy thing. Success depends on our complete surrender to Thakur. Spiritually it works. Keep in mind the image of a newborn baby and be just like that. When you go to the shrine, individuality should melt away. Just relax completely like a little baby. Then everything works out well. We must surrender to a higher spiritual power like Thakur, Krishna, Buddha, or Christ, who can bear our burden, and who is of the nature of our own Self.

## June 6, 1984

Thakur is really real, not just in the Vedantic sense, and not as a mere symbol. Holy Mother said he is "still living." He is both with and without form, and he can be seen and felt. We don't "see" God because we *are* That. But when we see, we see Thakur as the embodiment of That. He is always present with us, hearing every conversation of ours. If I just lift my mind to that Pure Consciousness, I can see it. When we think of him and pray to him, he knows every bit of it—and not just in the Vedantic sense but in a personal sense. Because of the curtain of our mind we don't know it, like when Thakur held a towel in front of his face. We get his response—that is, we know and feel it—when we purify our own consciousness. The curtain is only for us, not for him. When we pray, he knows it. When we think of him and repeat his name, he knows it. He is eternally real, present in the cosmic realm with name and form due to his tremendous spiritual mass.

[In a *Vivekachudamani* class, about mental purification:] Remembering Thakur is our means of purification. There is nothing like devotion to his name that can do that job. When we go to the shrine, what we are to do is fill our consciousness with his name, his thought, and not allow any other thought to come. If we can do that for even ten minutes a day, it will work a wonderful transformation in our minds. If we can keep it up, even while working, then all the more it will work.

## June 10, 1984

Always hammer on the mind the idea, "Not I, but Thou; not I, but Thou." We have to keep away from egoism.

Spiritual struggle must never be relaxed. It's like riding a bicycle. Keep on pedaling or the bike will fall down. If you don't keep up your struggle, you are sure to fall.

You can never love God if you hate even one person, because God is also in that very person. We have to learn to make everybody our own.

## June 11, 1984

God is the chooser. We choose him in one sense. But when it comes to living an exclusive spiritual life, ours is only to struggle; but *he* must choose us. When we cry, something happens. From above. Even though it is from deep inside ourselves, it is from the Ground. That is his grace, his choosing. All depends on his grace.

## June 13, 1984

One can renounce everything in the world but not Thakur and Mother. They are the very embodiments of the Supreme Divine Ground. It is very difficult to be detached from all thoughts. For that we need their grace and blessings.

## June 19, 1984

Realization is in the heart. You *feel* it. In our being, there are only two things: consciousness and love. Consciousness is an unobstructed flow, but love can be obstructed and distorted through negative experiences. Therefore our struggle is there —to purify our love and open up the heart. That is where service purifies our heart. We have to gain identification with others. Then we rise to a higher level. The heart must be opened up.

There is nothing called mind—only consciousness and thoughts. There is only one consciousness. Depending on the function it performs we call it mind (cognizes), *buddhi* (decides), *chitta* (storehouse), ego (identifies). When it doesn't "mind" anything, then there is no-mind, pure consciousness.

It is only when consciousness minds a thought that we call it mind. "Mind" is only a concept. It is a verb rather than a noun.

## July 1, 1984

There is no perfection in the external world. That is why we must accept and not find fault.

Keys to monastic life: (1) Keep up spiritual practice. (2) Accept and identify with everything and don't look to the faults of anyone. (3) Love, respect, and cooperate. (4) Keep your head at Thakur's feet. (5) Keep an inward outlook. (6) Don't identify with anything except, "I am his child." (7) No egoism. Not I, but Thou. (8) No comparison or jealousy.

## July 4, 1984

The profound uniqueness of Mother is that she showed the link between illumination and living. Tota Puri was illumined but he was not perfect because he didn't know that link. But Thakur and Mother knew.

## July 5, 1984

Spiritual life is never in a straight line. For a while it may seem to be at a low ebb and then it goes up again.

Don't worry about understanding things. Just leave it to Thakur and Mother. Think only of living the life, leaving everything to Them.

## August 4, 1984

Feel in the shrine just like a little baby in the lap of the Mother. Relax completely. You need not do anything except be aware of Thakur and Mother's presence. Eyes open or closed, it doesn't matter. Simply feel, "I am Thine, and Thou are mine." Nothing else.

When you go to the shrine there should be no individuality. Forget the whole world there.

Those who have got devotion can *change*.

**August 9, 1984**

[Someone asked if Thakur's grace is passive like the sun shining, or active like the Guru's grace, like the Incarnation standing on the shore to help pull people out of the current.] It is a combination of both. Two things are needed. Complete unconditional surrender and complete self-denial—"I don't know *anything*." His grace is like the sun in the sense that when we come out of the enclosure, we get it automatically. When we take one step, he takes nine. Krishna's promise in Gita (18. 66) about liberating you from all sins is literally fulfilled in Ramakrishna.

Thakur is not outside. He is actually part of our own consciousness, and not just in the Advaitic sense. There is also dualism in him and he is there as our savior. When we pray to him with real surrender and self-denial—and we have to pray even for that attitude—he does remove our obstacles, many times unconsciously, that is without our even knowing when it happened. But when we look back, we realize that at times difficulties went away without our knowing when or how.

What Krishna says (Gita 9. 22) is literally true—he *carries* what we need. Ours is only to do the best we can according to our wisdom in any situation, in the face of any problem, and leave the rest to him.

We will surely experience his presence and his grace if we have purity, one-pointedness and devotion. Purity comes from feeling, "I don't know anything." "Purity means to will one thing" (quoting Kierkegaard). One-pointedness towards him: while working it is there unconsciously, but in meditation it must be complete—no other thought should come in. Devotion: "I am Thine, and Thou are mine."

Thakur really does pull us up by the hand. This is beyond logic; it is a great Divine mystery. But spiritually it is true. Thakur's grace is a fact. Incarnations remain in the cosmic realm, retaining their names and forms, in order to help people. And they do help. Even when you reach the state of nonduality, you don't give up your Guru or Thakur, because it is through his grace you got the Light.

Try to keep the flame alive through the day with some spiritual thought or slogan in the mind. Mantra is to protect and lead the mind. Use it to keep the flame alive, to keep up the contact with him. Then other things cannot come in.

When any trouble or doubt comes, just say, "I don't know," and put your head at his feet.

Along with devotion to him, the other main thing is to love and make everybody your own. Accept and identify with everything—it is Thakur's place (the temple or convent). Then overcoming obstacles becomes much easier. If you fail to do that, the struggle is much greater.

## August 20, 1984

The greatest renunciation is to make everybody your own. To accept and identify with all is the real renunciation—renunciation of the ego.

## August 30, 1984

Don't worry about unwanted tendencies because we are a combination of human and divine. *Samskaras* and limitations remain until the end. Even after a little light, even after a little glimpse of *nirvikalpa samadhi, samskaras* remain. They are burned completely only after total merging.

Broadening is the most important thing but it doesn't come without purity.

## September 5, 1984

When joining the convent you go with only one thought, now and forever: We have come here to live according to the spiritual ideal of Thakur, Mother and Swamiji. Our desire is to live that life. Don't be disturbed by any other thought. Always feel these three things—this is our place; we are all one; we are all his. Just turn your mind toward him, nothing else.

Never compare or compete, just like plants growing side by side in the garden.

## September 14, 1984

There is an unseen Higher Power behind the scenes, in whose hands we are.

## September 20, 1984

If the mind gains concentration through prayer or hymns, then the preparatory steps are not necessary. Otherwise they are necessary to draw the mind away from other things to meditation. One's inner struggle is the main thing. Others can only show you the way. In this, one must be very conscientious. Don't fool around and waste the time meant for meditation.

**October 5, 1984**

You cannot solve any problem outside. You only learn to live with it.

You cannot change anybody. You can only learn lessons from everything and everyone.

In monastic living: (1) Never argue. (2) Lose a point but never lose heart. (3) Always be careful what you say and never assert (this was particularly with reference to group scriptural study). Better to be silent.

**October 10, 1984**

In spiritual life there is no failure; it is a process. Leave the fruits of your struggle to Thakur and Mother. We do not know the distance we have yet to walk. Therefore just keep on walking with your eyes on them and leave it to them to guide you. Even if you were to get no Light in this life, that does not mean failure. What has been gained is never lost and the process will continue. Leave it to them and rely on them to guide you. Don't look back. Keep on struggling. Never relax it.

**October 18, 1984**

[Swami had said the disciple's relationship with him is eternal. He was asked whether it was only in the Vedantic sense or was it more than that?] It is more than that. My life is set in him and you are part of that. He is in us [pointing to himself]; we [pointing to himself] are in him; we are in you, you are in us. The statement that the relationship is eternal is not an ordinary statement. You will understand it when you realize.

Then you will know your unity with the Divine and you will understand the meaning of that statement. It is true in Reality but now you do not know. Later, what you imagine now will be realized. But you must be careful to remember that the Power is coming from him (Thakur) and the unity is in him. In order to realize it you must keep the thought of his Presence constantly in the mind. You must dedicate everything you do to him. This relationship is not temporal—it is eternal. Every other relationship in time and space is merely temporal.

**October 23, 1984**

The desire to be a human being, to love and be loved, is not contrary to the desire to know the Truth. Life is a process. Just keep the mind on him. The desire for the company of spiritual or struggling souls, the desire to do good to others, these desires are absolutely good.

Never be afraid of what comes to the mind. Just pray to Thakur for guidance and light. Even when old negative thoughts come in, at times unconsciously during meditation, don't be afraid. It is good they are being loosened, like dirt in laundry. Just take everything in a calm, quiet way. If we keep up a prayerful attitude, keep up the hold on Thakur, then nothing bad will happen. There will come a time when there will be no more worldly thoughts in the mind. But don't be frightened while they are coming out. Just say, "Once I thought like that, now I think like this." Take it with calm, quiet, prayerful attitude. Even at times you become confused and wonder, "What am I doing here?" At times like that, just pray to Thakur for guidance and light.

He is the vine. In That is the eternal sap, immortal sap. Nun means "none." We have no separate existence apart from him. We must be "Ramakrishna-maya" ("filled with Ramakrishna").

## October 29, 1984

Whenever you are in doubt in any situation, ask yourself, "What would Mother want me to do?" If you haven't the authority to follow it, at least keep that feeling in the heart. But whenever your personal priority can be exercised, let Mother be your guide.

Avoid resentment by looking only to the positive in a person of mixed character.

## November 12, 1984

[Quoting Taittiriya Upanishad (2.7.1) about how any separation causes fear and is to be overcome through reflection:] Reflection is not a process of the intellect. It is a spiritual process. You lift yourself up above cause and effect, and it is an intuitive thing. Don't resent, resist or react, but lift yourself up to that spiritual attitude of reflection.

## November 20, 1984

Our ideal:

1. To transcend everything (Thakur)
2. To accept everything (Mother)
3. To love and serve (Swamiji)

*Jagat* means "moving" (world); *janma* means "coming into" (birth). When Gita (8.16) refers to *punarjanma* (rebirth), to an enlightened person it actually means no return to the original state of ignorance. The man of illumination may take birth again out of the desire to help others, but he never returns to that same ignorant condition. In the early stages of life, due to psychophysical limitation, he appears to be just like everybody else. The brain takes time to fully develop. But with psychophysical maturity comes the unfoldment of the perfection already gained.

With your every breathing in and breathing out, surrender to Thakur. If you can manage that, it will keep you well spiritually. It will also do the Guru good, as well as your parents.

### November 25, 1984

The spiritual functioning of an illumined soul is the same whether the body is alive, sick or dead. He is completely detached and looks upon the body as a mere machine.

In convent life, always be amenable to correction and even reproach, even if you are falsely accused. Never become negative. Be positive, positive, positive, no matter what.

### November 27, 1984

[Speaking of group monastic life:] So many people say so many things, but the most important thing is to bear, bear, bear.

### December 28, 1984

What we are seeking is unselfishness, egolessness.

[Swami said that the longer he lives, the more he sees that all work is only temporary.] Therefore do all the work that comes, but the only thing that matters is to do it with Thakur's and Mother's consciousness, constantly. Mother's teachings about japa are very significant. Try to keep up the mantra while working, a part of the mind always on that thought. What is meditation? It is continued thought of the

Divine. Therefore keep that up constantly and don't worry about anything else. Don't ask for anything—just surrender to Thakur and Mother completely. "I don't know anything—just give me pure devotion to you both."

The more we struggle, the more the *samskaras* come out. So when they come, just pray to Thakur and Mother. It takes time and Thakur tests us a lot. Struggle must be there, constant struggle.

# 1985

### January 20, 1985

Madhusudan Saraswati said, "I do not know any Truth beyond Sri Krishna." So we say, "We do not know any Truth beyond Sri Ramakrishna" (*Ramakrishnāt paraṁ kim api tattvam ahaṁ na jāne*). He is Truth and he is God in entirety.

### January 24, 1985

As Holy Mother said, "Remember that you have a Mother here." Only we have to look at her. That is enough!

### February 28, 1985

Work with the feeling, "I am not doing anything, simply fulfilling." Then there is much less fatigue. Avoid the feeling of doership.

## April 17, 1985

Just feel, "I don't know *anything*." It is true. We know only a part, not the whole thing, and even the part is distorted. Therefore just put everything at Thakur's feet.

## April 29, 1985

There is no difference between praying to Thakur or to Holy Mother. Either or both—no difference. They are two sides of the same coin. Pray for pure devotion. That is the connecting link.

## August 21, 1985

If there is anything unresolved, if you say, "I don't know," and put it at Thakur's feet, things will be resolved through his grace.

Thakur can do miracles. Only we must deny ourselves and follow him.

Old *samskaras* will come up. They may even be from your past lives. They will trouble you, but just see them and say, "I know you." The thing is they must be washed off right away.

Try to be conscious always of your dependence on Thakur's grace.

## December 26, 1985

Karma is not what happens. It is how you take it, how you evaluate what happens.

# 1986

## February 12, 1986

Three things are required for real meditation:

1. Be alert.
2. The mind must be set on Light, illumination. You may meditate on a personality but the Light there is the point.
3. Real meditation is when you are alone, without time pressure. Then the mind can dive deep in search of that Reality. This must be done if you really want illumination.

## February 17, 1986

You never know when Light may come. The difficulty is that all past *samskaras* must be resolved. The best way of resolving them is surrendering—no egoism—only to feel before him, "I don't know." And surrender completely to him. We don't know how far we have to go or how many *samskaras* are left. So do your job and leave the results to him. Don't think of when Light will come, just leave it to him.

In surrendering you see everything positive, everything Divine. He who loves God must love all people because God is in all. If you have any negative feeling towards anyone, you can never see God.

**March 11, 1986**

Let the body know its pain but keep the mind always positive and cheerful. The only thing that matters is total dedication to Thakur. That is the meaning of monastic life.

**April 7, 1986**

In this life there is no guarantee of anything. The only thing that matters is to surrender the whole being to Thakur. Body, mind and soul, I am at your feet. We don't even know how we came to this world, but the day we met him is our birthday. Who cares if the body stays or goes, just be in his hands.

**April 14, 1986**

When you are in any difficulty, convert the pain you feel into pleasure by depending on Thakur. Intensify your own spiritual life while being natural and loving with all.

Pray to Thakur for pure devotion. "Where can I get it if you do not give it?" You must have patience and perseverance.

Work is good. What Swami Vivekananda said about getting salvation just by doing unselfish work is true. But if you want to intensify it and hasten it, that comes through devotion to Thakur in addition to the work.

. . .

## August 5, 1986

The desire for purity of mind and a dedicated life are enough. If that is there, everything will be taken care of.

## September 28, 1986

The only guarantee for spiritual progress is to dive deep.

## October 2, 1986

The most important thing is to remember Thakur constantly and to surrender to him completely. Everything is there in that surrender. Just pray to Thakur, "May I not forget your name," and try to repeat his name constantly.

## November 19, 1986

If you have ill health, just leave it to the doctor, and from your side lift the mind from the body and be happy in Thakur.

Just pray to Thakur, "I have come here (to monastic life) in your name. You take care of everything."

## November 30, 1986

[Swami was questioned about St. John of the Cross saying that you should live in the monastery (or convent) as if you are alone. His reply probably considered the temperament of the people he was addressing:] That is a dry approach and is not our ideal. The ideal given to us by Thakur, Ma and Swamiji is something more sublime. Even if we are not highly evolved but if we are prayerful, the loving approach will be alright. To live in a group with love and understanding makes spiritual life much smoother, tension much less. Close friendship is alright, because it is not a question of partiality but of levels.

[Regarding meditation:] To feel I am *in* him rather than looking *at* him is fine; it is very good.

## December 8, 1986

[Regarding illumination:] Not coming back means not coming back to the ignorant condition. It doesn't even mean a big light, no growing two horns. Simply you become unselfish, all-loving, and deeply concerned for all. You become free from all anguish and fear. You are not away from nature. No, you are there, but you feel you are completely untouched by it. And you feel you are just the same as everybody else.

# 1987

## January 11, 1987

Realization does not depend on long hours of meditation. It depends on selflessness, devotion, surrender, and purity. Then when the mind is calm, ego is down, consciousness is clear, it can flash at any time. You may be sitting in a room alone and suddenly it flashes. Or you may be walking and singing something and suddenly it flashes. It comes at funny times, not necessarily in meditation. Surrendering is most important—to feel I don't know anything. At times we think, "I know," but even then we must say, "I don't know."

## January 20, 1987

Keep your mind in his direction. He can do miracles.

## February 6, 1987

Spiritual life is not a big jump. It is a process. We have an ideal, we fall short, we struggle, etc. This is the process of evolution. Be cautious and be aware and just keep Thakur's thought in the mind. He is always present if you sincerely invoke him. You do not know, but he is fully aware.

**February 9, 1987**

The true religion is—do you *feel* for people? Do you care for them? Do you love them? Do you identify with souls outside of you? That is real religion.

Silent service without being seen by others is very difficult.

Be unselfish, don't seek *anything*, be motherly to one and all, think that all are your children. And you see what will happen in your life. Purity of heart is a very big thing, practically impossible in this world. You can have that purity only through these two things: unselfishness and love, as a mother loves her children. Not me, but thou.

**February 26, 1987**

You can practice Thakur's presence with an ambassador mentality, where you constantly feel that attitude unconsciously. You move in that attitude. In that way, constantly remember that you are here only for Thakur. You have left everything only for his sake. Then move in that awareness. At times say to him, "I don't know, *you* know it."

**March 26, 1987**

Learn to live in an independent way, being friendly with all but not depending upon anybody. Stand on your own feet.

Be more indrawn, more introspective. Think of him as Light. Remember his presence always.

Free yourself from 3 things: External temptation, internal thoughts, and ego.

## April 20, 1987

Whether you feel you are "working for Thakur" or you feel "Thakur is working through me," both are alright. But "working for Thakur" must be accompanied by "Not I, but Thou," because the point is that we cannot do anything without him.

If you have a health problem, you can have a mental attitude of unselfishness and still be careful.

## May 20, 1987

The will never gets tired; only the intellect gets tired. Always feel that he is watching us every moment.

The highest experience is to come down from *nirvikalpa samadhi* and see God with open eyes. Even when you come down, you see no separation. In terms of intensity, an illumined soul feels the non-separation a million times more than what a mother feels for her child. It is like when Thakur actually got welts on his back from seeing someone else beaten. It is because there is only one consciousness. If a sheet of water is disturbed and waves come up, the whole sheet of water is affected. That is why they love people so much.

## June 7, 1987

Sri Ramakrishna sees the inner growth of the person. Your social life is one thing, your personal life is another. You have to be strong in living your own personal spiritual life.

## June 14, 1987

In spiritual life patchwork is no good. With one sweep you have to say, "I don't know anything," and pray for pure devotion. If you can get that feeling, "I don't know," 90% of your problem is over.

## June 16, 1987

Have no identification except as a spiritual child, spiritual consciousness.

What we need are study, meditation, and constant awareness of Sri Ramakrishna's presence.

Sri Ramakrishna is Light, and that Light is everywhere. Because he has realized it, we take him as our Guru.

The only thing that matters is to live the life. Spiritual life is a big cleaning process. When fulfillment comes depends on the intensity of our struggle.

## August 13, 1987

Don't worry about anything in this relative world. Just pray for pure devotion. Nothing else counts. And Sri Ramakrishna is capable of giving it. All obstacles will go but you have to continue striking matches until the flame catches and burns steadily.

Accept everything. "For your sake I accept everything."

When obstacles come to the mind, immediately picture Sri Ramakrishna's face and feet. Do it when they come, immediately.

The mind is absolutely superfluous. It goes back and forth between positive, negative and neutral. What matters is what you really are and how you are set.

## August 18, 1987

[From a tape of Swami speaking on the teachings of Holy

Mother:] This is to me the greatest austerity—to serve and to feel one with others. You need not serve patients. Wherever you are—identifying with others, treating them as your own, bearing all the limitations, to me that is the greatest karma yoga. All disciplines become secondary. Unselfishness and loving concern—that is the main note of karma yoga. You need not go someplace to do karma yoga. Wherever you are, whatever you may be doing, you can practice it, with unselfishness, dedication to God, without greed, without egoism, without mental fever—to work—that is karma yoga...

This is a new discipline in monastic life. The monastic wants to realize Self or God or Truth in this very life. What is the way? The old order is to get out of the world and do it. Then the locked up *samskaras*, tendencies, psychic residues, are not resolved and life after life you have to go. But karma yoga makes the mind pure right away, quick. In action and reaction, when you are in society with people of all types, you have to bear it. One who practices karma yoga, wherever he or she is, that individual is sure to gain some spiritual depth. Karma yoga doesn't mean we have to go to some place. It is a discipline to be practiced wherever we are, under all circumstances.

That detached loving concern—that's it—detached loving concern. No, you don't accuse. You accept everything. All limitations you accept, without retaliation, without resentment, without resistance, without reaction. It is a great discipline. Mental growth, human progress are possible: the human becomes Divine by controlling one's own tendencies, particularly selfishness. Selfishness is the greatest sin and obstacle in spiritual life. In social life also—all problems you see are due to selfishness. It is selfishness that we have to conquer and that is the main theme of karma yoga.

### September 17, 1987

Some things you can straighten yourself. But whatever you cannot straighten yourself, you should surrender. "I don't know anything; you make me straight." When there is confusion inside, pray, pray, pray.

### October 9, 1987

Don't see negative in anybody. Who doesn't have negativity?

### December 10, 1987

There are stages in spiritual life, like in mountain climbing, where you feel like you are going off the mountain, or downhill, whereas you are actually about to climb to a new height. You feel like you can't go on. But these dark nights of the soul are the paths we go through on the way up.

Spiritual growth is a process and we have to go step by step.

Being upset, irritable, having negative reactions are not bad signs as long as you are *aware* of them. Just be silent and reflective. Just hold on, hold on, hold on. [Swami quoted Swami Vivekananda saying, "Hold on my brave boys, the night is passing."]

I would advise you to identify with Sri Ramakrishna completely.

For a long time it is all struggle. Where is joy? But one can be happy and contented putting the burden on Sri Ramakrishna.

❋

# 1988

## February 26, 1988

Many times we do not know what is going on. Therefore just say, "I don't know," and completely surrender to him.

Be positive towards everyone.

## June 18, 1988

Swamiji's religion is expansion, not contraction. Pray for expansion of love.

The world is not unreal. The world is real. People do not understand Thakur's religion. What is wanted is expansion of love. Have detached loving concern for all.

Never harbor any negative thought because it is poison to the mind. We don't know, so be always positive.

## August 12, 1988

Life means problem, because life is not an easy thing. Life means people—different minds, different attitudes. You can never be in harmony. It is impossible to get real harmony in the external world. Harmony is within. If there is harmony within, then you can try to bring harmony outside.

**August 13, 1988**

Whenever unwanted feelings come, immediately turn the vision to Thakur. Don't pray even. No words, nothing hard, don't struggle even. Simply look at him like a baby looking at her mother. Then the miracle will happen. You will see it. That is Thakur and Mother's grace.

In spiritual life, have no hesitation. Don't be afraid of anything. Everything will work out. Have faith! All we have to do is think of Thakur and Mother; that is their grace.

Spiritual life is steady-making.

**November 18, 1988**

Think only of developing selflessness, not how long you meditate or study. In every action, think of how you can help people. You will advance fast if you can develop that. Pray to Sri Ramakrishna and Holy Mother to make your mind selfless.

Don't accept any obstacle. Have the determination, "I shall make it." Anyone who keeps up that struggle *will* get the fruit of it.

**December 17, 1988**

Don't separate work and "being spiritual." Just cultivate unselfishness.

For those who renounce, Thakur and Mother are there behind the mind. Behind our mind they are there. We have to remember that constantly. If you bear everything in their name, miracles do happen. But you have to empty yourself and that is to be done through karma yoga—to constantly feel, "What can I do for others?" Miracles do happen. We don't know how and they cannot be explained, but they do happen.

# 1989

## September 11, 1989

See all as Thakur's children. Love him first and see all others as Thakur's children.

The prescription for any obstacle is, "Think of Me." Put your head at Thakur's feet and say, "I don't know." Try to be in tune with his grace.

"I am just Ramakrishna's child." Let that be the theme of your whole life. If you feel, "I am no one but Ramakrishna's child," that is the only qualification necessary. If you have that *one*, you can add four zeroes after it.

## September 12, 1989

Nature functions. Ours is simply to accept everything in his name. Whatever comes to you to do, fulfill with dedication to him. Never seek power or position—that kills spirituality. Only be true to Thakur. [Swami gave the example of Swami Saradeshananda, the author of *The Mother As I Saw Her*, who appeared to be just nobody when he was staying in Kankhal.]

[Swami was asked about restrictions like not eating meat:] The only restriction is to love and help people.

To get Thakur's grace and help, we have to turn to him within. Do not expect any external help. Accept everything. Forbearance! And keep your head at his feet.

## September 18, 1989

We are struggling for two things:

1. To accept everything outside
2. To get the Light from within.

## September 27, 1989

The power to feel that all are your own and to accept everyone comes through spiritualizing the mind. That is done simply by hooking up to Thakur. Just like plugging into an electrical socket, immediately you get the power; it is as simple as that. So our effort is simply to be in him. Then all limitations can be overcome. Think of Mother.

## October 26, 1989

When any negative feeling comes, pray right away even if it seems futile, because it works unconsciously.

# 1990

**March 22, 1990**

My motto is detached loving concern.

**May 2, 1990**

The essence of communication is self-abnegation. Never complain. That is the most essential factor of living together, because complaining raises a wall of separation, and all separation is suffering.

**May 30, 1990**

The main thing is to be positive. Keep nothing negative in the mind. That is the way to keep the mind clean and clear, it's even better than prayer to God.

**August 11, 1990**

Our main principle is to make everyone our own. You have to do certain things just for that purpose. Wherever you are, you have to do what is in tune with that place—willingness to do anything and everything. Then you are a part of the whole and then you rise up. Otherwise there is psychic restriction, and any psychic restriction is slavery. Unrestricted willingness makes you 100% a part of the whole. Otherwise you separate yourself, and all separation is slavery. "I will fulfill my part."

**October 11, 1990**

Be detached from everything. Detached loving concern is the key. As you want love and concern, so have love and concern for all. Strengthen the tie—"I am his and he is mine."

# 1991

## January 9, 1991

One must become like a newborn baby to enter the kingdom of God—no identification with anything. We have to struggle to become like that.

A new definition of Man: M-A-N = manifestation of Atman in nature.

## January 25, 1991

Be positive and see the best in all. Don't accept any negative thoughts.

## March 7, 1991

Spirituality is not in how much meditation and japa you do. It is in how you keep your mind, how calm it is. In that deeply calm mind, illumination comes. Be absolutely positive.

. . .

## March 26, 1991

In a convent don't depend on externals—neither the abbot nor other sisters. Depend only on God, look only to God.

You have to raise yourself up. But when you feel helpless to do so, pray, "I have not got the strength," and hold his hand.

# 1992

## April 3, 1992

Think of Thakur as the embodiment of Light. A time comes when name and form drop off— Light alone remains.

One must live the life to understand what Mother was and what she is even today. Regarding any external situation, just follow her example. Don't expect anything. No expectation, no disappointment. And be positive. "From me no danger be to aught that lives."

## October 11, 1992

Don't compare. Spiritual life is a journey of the alone to the Alone. Therefore be yourself. Slow or fast doesn't matter. You do not know the *process* of spiritual life.

The meaning of purity is unselfishness.

If you can feel, "I don't know anything," then you have no problem.

# 1993

## July 9, 1993

Accept all. Most important is willingness, unselfishness. Be helpful to all. Take the overall picture and do whatever is to be done as it comes and according to your capacity.

## September 17, 1993

No monk will look at people and evaluate grade 1, 2, 3. It is like a garden where there are small and big plants, some growing slow and some faster, but they are all just plants in the same garden. Just be yourself. "I am that I am."

## December 10, 1993

The three problems of man are senses, thoughts, ego. These must be controlled.

If you see something wrong in someone else, it doesn't mean you have it in you. But if you make an issue of it, then you have got a problem.

# 1994

## August 10, 1994

No negativity. Overcome it by feeling, "I don't know." We think we know or we know a little, but really speaking we don't know. We don't know the whole thing.

## November 26, 1994

The grace of your own mind means complete surrender to him. That surrender nullifies everything. When contrary thoughts come, don't worry about any other kind of *pratyāhāra* except thinking of him. Surrender to him completely, resign to him completely. That is the grace of your own mind. Pray to Thakur for the strength and the will.

# 1995

## June 8, 1995

[Swami was asked whether one goes to "divine worlds" after death.] Thakur is within. Pure Loving Consciousness is within. There is so much joy in that experience. There the question of "what next" never arises.

[A disciple expressed apprehension about ill health and realization.] Realization is in the heart. If that is open, you don't have to worry about other things.

The way to live above small-mindedness is to not find fault with others. Be positive and forgive, forgive, forgive, even if others speak against you. There is no other way. It is our nature to love. The way to get the strength to do this is to think of Holy Mother. She is the ideal.

Don't complain—that is the secret. Never complain against others. No accusation, no demanding.

Think of Thakur as focused light. Simply keep his thought. If you can't do anything, just surrender to him, like Girish surrendered to Thakur.

**September 1, 1995**

Climbing a mountain is never straight up. The parts when you are going down (as part of going up) feel like a dark night of the soul but they really aren't. The only thing you have to do is keep in mind where you are going. Then you will never be lost.

Forgive, forgive, forgive, because we know not what we do. Even if we *think* we know, we really don't.

**October 17, 1995**

Only those who are absolutely pure, absolutely unselfish and all-loving, can know others.

[A disciple told Swami that this day was the anniversary of the day she had met him. The swami replied that the important thing is not how we begin but how we end. That is in our hands.]

# 1996

## April 27, 1996

The main thing is to love all. Thakur is a thousand times with you if you do that.

We are in him and he is in us. That which is in him is in me and in you—exactly the same.

1997

## April 1, 1997

Do your job and be detached from everything.

## June 25, 1997

[Swami was asked about using writing as a practice to resolve problems.] It is better to put them at the feet of Sri Ramakrishna, because you should not dwell at all on any negative thought.

# 1998

## July 2, 1998

Life is fun if you accept everything. The problem comes when you create likes and dislikes.

## July 9, 1998

To be spiritual means to ignore all the little pinpricks of life. You must be strong, and rise above all these things.

God is nothing but Light. And we must love all because of that Light in them. We must never hate anybody. We ourselves must identify only with that Light.

With Holy Mother's grace we can overcome all obstacles, internal and external. Thakur and Mother are the same, so it doesn't matter who we go to.

Only *being* matters. It doesn't matter what we *do*. Therefore never compare or compete with others' achievements. It is the heart that counts.

Never complain against anyone to a third person. That separates.

The quality of the Divine is unselfish loving concern.

To be spiritual is to be natural.

Do every work as worship of Sri Ramakrishna.

God is *here* (looking at those present)—in you, in you, in me.

## July 10, 1998

You can tell a person has realized God if he is unselfish, all-loving, and deeply concerned for the welfare of all.

## July 11, 1998

Be humble but not weak.

We don't know where we are going, what the goal is, what will happen when we die. We don't know until we get the Light. But don't worry about any of it.

The bottom line is unselfish loving concern. Always feel, "How can I help?"

Accept everything. Complain about nothing.

# 1999

## April 1, 1999

There is only one mission in life: to live well. In order to live well, we have to do two things: Accept all as your own, and live with Thakur in the heart.

Swami Kalyanananda asked the boys at Kankhal what they had renounced. Father, mother, house? Did you own them that you could renounce them? No, you did not own them. Renounce selfishness and serve people with love. That is real renunciation. Live the life.

## May 19, 1999

If you say, "I don't know," and depend on Thakur, then he takes charge. But if you think you know, he doesn't do so.

## August 6, 1999

Be spiritual, be yourself, and be positive. Pray for others. Don't care who you are with or whether you feel happy. Just live your own spiritual life and be positive. Then you will have peace within.

## August 21, 1999

Life is not about what you get; it is about what you give.

Be true to yourself.

# 2000

## June 29, 2000

Sannyasa means unselfish loving service. And it means to be yourself. Pray for the happiness and peace of mind of your parents.

Both these ideas are wrong: (1) disease is the product of bad karma and that (2) a person doing spiritual practice properly will be healthy. Even great souls are bound by their times and traditional thinking (with reference to those traditional ideas).

The only thing that matters is what you *are*, not what you *do*. Do nothing, it doesn't matter. To *be*, that is what is important. And that boils down to detached loving concern. I want to see a loving face! To be positive and loving and concerned for all is to be somebody. Be detached from what anybody thinks.

People are "human units." Each unit is the product of that person's knowledge and experience. A truly spiritual person sees them all and says, "That's alright, that's alright, that's alright." Accept them all as they are and love them. Really no one cares for anybody, but "spiritual" means detached loving concern for all.

If you want to be truly spiritual, be absolutely positive. That means don't react, resist or resent but reflect. Don't allow any negative force to remain in the mind; it has a bad effect in many ways. That means no reaction to anything external. You have to have that confidence that everything is impermanent, everything comes and goes, and learn to identify with the inner peace. Take full responsibility but don't be disturbed by anything.

## July 12, 2000

Sannyasa means the time has come that you want to intensify your practice, to *experience* God. It means detachment from everything. Give up all identifications and then identify with all and love all without any discrimination.

Satchidananda = Being, Consciousness, Love. *Chidanandarupah shivo'ham* means I am that Loving Consciousness Divine.

The obstacles are sense attraction, thoughts (mental clouds, *samskaras*), and ego. Detachment is the cure—from sense objects, thoughts and identifications.

Sannyasa is something positive, it is not negation of anything. You don't give up the substance of anything, only your imaginations about it. You don't "renounce" family. You are *detached*; then you love all the more. When Thakur left Vrindavan to go to his mother, it was not out of attachment to his mother but out of pure love, all-love.

When in doubt follow Thakur, Mother, Swamiji. Mother is the best example of how to lead the life of sannyasa. She identified completely with all.

Where are love and consciousness coming from? From that sublime Light within. A little bit is leaking out. "Within" doesn't mean any location; it is all-pervasive.

Light, life and love are inseparable.

Truth must be impersonal, universal, eternal.

Religion is impersonal, universal, eternal.

Science is impersonal, universal, impermanent.

## July 16, 2000

Not only are you Brahman but everyone else is also Brahman. Live with that attitude of love and respect.

## July 17, 2000

The most important thing in group monastic life is unity. Cooperate, cooperate, cooperate. Consult everyone, even the newest *brahmacharini*.

[Swami was in San Francisco to give monastic vows. He was asked at a group meal with the convent how to deal with difficult people.] The way is to accept. Don't resist, react, or resent, but reflect.

As Swami Brahmananda said, pray and meditate first, then go out and work. When he (Swami Brahmananada) was asked why he was leading a contemplative life in Kankhal in 1904 he said, "I have been given a big estate. I have to learn how to manage it."

## July 20, 2000

It is ego, selfishness that we renounce. That is the only thing we own and which we can renounce. "Unselfish loving service" is the motto of our Order.

[Swami was asked if the power of the sannyasa ceremony would be the same if a knower of God was not present.] Even if a knower of God is not present, it only depends on our thinking. If we are invoking the presence of Thakur and Mother, if our consciousness is there, we will get that power in the same way. It is all in our thinking, even if we are not illumined.

## August 16, 2000

"Dharma" means unity. Our unity is in Brahman. Therefore dharma is to look upon all as Atman.

# 2002

## July 11, 2002

In monastic life it doesn't "happen." You have to make it happen.

In every environment, be absolutely positive. But live according to your own ideal. Don't budge on that.

About externals you must feel, "It doesn't matter."

The life of complete renunciation means unselfishness, egolessness, and to love all people without any restriction. That doesn't mean gadding about. Be yourself, but with that attitude.

Whatever comes, remain above it and be positive and happy. If you accept a thing, then there is no problem. Accept everyone as they are. Be happy and peaceful and no complaint. Get rid of ego and selfishness. Then you have wonderful perception of everything. It is ego and selfishness that ruin everything. Consciously keep "me" behind.

# 2003

## March 7, 2003

Pray to Mother. She is more powerful. Thakur would send hard cases to her. Thakur and Mother are inseparable. Think of either whenever you wish.

## November 3, 2003

When Mother said, "Think of me" that is for us, too. Any disturbing thought coming, just think of her face, "Mother." It is Mother who guided me in my life, I tell you.

It is not what you do; it is what you are.

## July 7, 2004

The way to dispel the dark night is to look at Mother's face.

## 2005

### January 5, 2005

Mother is so pure that you don't even have to pray to her. All you have to do is think of her.

### September 24, 2005

Mother came down from the transcendental plane to the relative plane to help Sri Ramakrishna. She gave him a big boost; he said so himself.

Mother was the only one who could just look you in the eye and transform you.

Vedanta is evolving and the modern Trinity is the latest such phase.

## August 26, 2006

Holiness is inside. Look inside. If you look outside, you will only see faults.

## 2007

### April 4, 2007

The only thing is to resign to Mother. Young people suffer and old people suffer. The only thing is to resign to Mother.

### September 10, 2007

Depend on Thakur, Ma and Swamiji and do what they would want you to do. That advice is forever.

Try to live up to the ideal. We are Thakur, Swamiji and Ma's children and so is everybody else. So live well with all with that idea. They are taking care of the whole world.

### September 12, 2007

[Swami said of himself (he was 94): "I am no longer in the stage of life where I do and act and get things done. I let nature function."]

# 2008

## May 3, 2008

Mother is taking care of me. As long as she is there, I am protected. I never change. Yama will not come until I call him.

(He called Swami exactly one year later.)

# ABOUT THE AUTHOR

**Footprints on the Sands of Time**

Swami Tyagananda

*Lives of great men all remind us
We can make our lives sublime,
And, departing, leave behind us
Footprints on the sands of time.*

—H. W. Longfellow (1807–1882)

It is impossible to adequately express in words anyone's life, let alone the life of an illumined and illustrious monk. Words are all that we have when we try to convey to others who Swami Sarvagatanandaji was and what his life means to those who had the privilege of being in his company and learning from him.

Born in Andhra Pradesh in southern India on November 27, 1912, he was named Narayan by his parents. His mother died when he was only 9. He often spoke of his mother as saintly. She would do her daily worship with the little Narayan in her lap. His father was a Sanskrit scholar and would narrate the Ramayana to the villagers in their language. Narayan attended these Ramayana narrations regularly and was profoundly moved by the story.

As a young man, Narayan experienced the harsh, cold reality of life when his older brother contracted tuberculosis. It was in those days a feared illness that spread contagion and claimed many lives. No one in the family, not even the brother's wife, would go anywhere near him. Narayan took it upon himself to take care of his brother and remained by his side until the brother died. Filled with dispassion and yearning to make sense of it all, he then chose to remain by himself for nearly six months in a garden house away from his family.

Probably inspired by his uncle who was an auditor, Narayan decided to be an auditor himself, seeing in that occupation the possibility for maximum independence while he continued to grapple with the meaning and purpose of life. Among his readings of various saints and teachers, it was Swami Vivekananda that captured his imagination most and nourished his inner longing for the spiritual ideal.

In 1933, while studying in Mumbai, Narayan met a man named Rao who was a disciple of Swami Shivananda (Mahapurush Maharaj). During the Christmas holidays Narayan was preparing for his exams, so he couldn't accompany Rao who went to see Mahapurush Maharaj. In early 1934 Narayan wanted to go and have Mahapurush Maharaj's darshan, but he couldn't because he didn't have enough money. He was crushed when he read in the papers a few weeks later, on February 20, about Mahapurush Maharaj's passing. It was later that year in Mumbai, in November of 1934, that he met Swami Akhandananda, who was to be his teacher, mentor and inspiration.

Just a few meetings with Swami Akhandananda were enough for Narayan to make up his mind about his future course of action, which was to lead a life dedicated to spirituality and service. Swami Akhandananda recommended that he join the Ramakrishna Order's branch in Kankhal, a suburb of Hardwar on the bank of the Ganges, as it would provide an ideal environment for Narayan's monastic life to flourish. The Kankhal branch was primarily a hospital where the monks served as a part of their spiritual practice.

It took a few days for Narayan to figure out the best way to reach Kankhal, as there was in those days no direct train to it. When Akhandanandaji found that Narayan hadn't yet left for Kankhal and the reason for the delay, he commanded Narayan to walk to Kankhal on foot, not travel by train. Akhandanandaji himself had walked hundreds of miles in the Himalayas, and he assured Narayan that it was the best way for him to prepare for his monastic vocation. He also specified three conditions: to do no sightseeing on the way, to carry no money, and to subsist on a single meal every day. With Swami Akhandananda's blessings and a firm determination animating his heart, Narayan set out on December 3, 1934.

His experiences during this long walk from Mumbai to Hardwar are the stuff of legend and are dearly cherished by his students and devotees. It was an arduous walk of nearly a thousand miles and done with bare feet. Some description of it can be found in his absorbing book, *You Will Be a Paramahamsa*. The long walk was filled with hardships. When Narayan reached Nasik, he met a monk named Nepali Baba who advised him to wear an ochre cloth in order to make his journey easier. Narayan hesitated since he hadn't yet been formally ordained. Nepali Baba told him that nobody *becomes* a monk; either you are or you are not. "In your case," he said, "you are!"

On December 14, eleven days into his walk, Narayan's endurance was severely tested. He had reached a breaking point of exhaustion and, thinking that death was near, he lay himself down under a tree with a prayerful heart and fell asleep. He was awakened by someone who, seeing his condition, lifted him up and took him on a bus to a town named Dhulia. There Narayan was taken to a house of a lawyer, in whose home he discovered a shrine dedicated to Sri Ramakrishna. It turned out that the lawyer was a disciple of Mahapurush Maharaj. Narayan spent that night before the altar, looking at Sri Ramakrishna, weeping profusely at the grace that he was being shown—what with a stranger noticing him, picking him up, and driving him to the welcoming home of a devotee!

This incident completely changed Narayan's outlook on life. He said later that he had faith, but his faith became *real* that day. Quoting the Gita (9.22), he would say that the Lord literally "carried him" that day. After this inspiring situation, his walk to Kankhal thenceforth had no major problems. He walked barefoot, slowly and steadily, with firm determination, finally reaching the Kankhal Ashrama on February 7, 1935, where he was welcomed by Swami Kalyanananda, who told him that Swami Akhandanandaji had written to him, asking him to "take care of this boy." Under Kalyanananda's loving tutelage a firm foundation was laid of Narayan's monastic life.

Pointing to the shrine, Kalyanananda once told Narayan, "This is where we offer fruits, sweets, incense for worship." Then he pointed to the hospital and said, "That is where we offer kind words, food and medicine for another kind of worship." Then he added, "The two are not intrinsically different." Years later, Narayan told his disciples that he felt no difference between cleaning a hospital spittoon and a puja vessel in the shrine. He said he learnt three fundamental principles of monastic life: (1) to accept every situation while also being true to oneself, (2) to understand and adjust with one's environment, and (3) to forget one's ego and to care for others.

Once the sweeper woman who worked at the hospital got sick and didn't come for a couple of days. Without being asked and without telling anybody, Narayan got up at 2 a.m. and cleaned all the hospital bedpans and spittoons. Kalyanananda couldn't believe it the next day when he found the work done. He told other monastics what Narayan had done, which inspired everyone in the monastery. They became a good team, sharing duties and responsibilities, and helping one another whenever needed.

In 1936 Narayan went to Sargacchi to receive initiation (*mantra-dīkṣā*) from Swami Akhandananda. On the way, he stopped in Allahabad to have the darshan of Swami Vijnananandaji. He delivered to him a packet of mangoes that Kalyanananda had specially sent for him. Vijnananandaji had a south Indian meal prepared for Narayan and the two ate together.

In Sargacchi, after he initiated Narayan, Swami Akhandanandaji told him that Thakur (Sri Ramakrishna) is "the avatar, he is the Truth, he is your Guru, your Ishta." He said, "Think of him in whatever way you like. Thakur is your everything." One day, when everyone in the Ashram had gone to a fair, Narayan stayed back to be with his guru, who taught him how to do a simple pūjā in the shrine. Through his guru's grace, he had his first experience of transcendence that day. He wanted to continue staying with his guru, but Narayan's presence was needed in Kankhal, so he had to go back. On his way, he stopped in Kolkata and had a good visit with Swami Abhedanandaji.

Back in Kankhal, he had a dream of Mahapurush Maharaj in which he asked Narayan to bring him two pieces of dhotis with red border. The dream was so vivid that Narayan couldn't stop thinking about it even after waking up. It so happened that a monk came that day with a packet containing two dhotis, exactly of the type Mahapurush Maharaj had requested in the dream. Narayan at once took the dhotis to the shrine and had the pujari make a ritual offering to Mahapurush Maharaj. He spent more than an hour in the shrine, weeping with gratitude at this miraculous turn of events. In the afternoon he called two of Mahapurush Maharaj's disciples to his room, told them about the dream, and gifted them the dhotis. That helped assuage his regret of not having met Mahapurush Maharaj in person.

When Narayan was due for sannyāsa in 1943, he did not go to Belur Math because he was engaged in relief work. After the relief was over, when he went to Belur Math, Swami Virajananda, who was the president of the Order, blessed him profusely, telling him that Swamiji's work that kept him away best reflected the spirit of sannyāsa. He gave the vows to Narayan the following year, in 1944, and named him Sarvagatananda, meaning "the all-pervading bliss."

It was almost 10 years since Narayan—now Sarvagatananda —had arrived in Kankhal. A change was in the offing. The Order sent him to be an assistant to Swami

Ranganathananda, who had returned from the Order's center in Myanmar and had taken charge of the center in Karachi. The two swamis became close in Karachi and remained lifelong friends.

Once when several monks and devotees went for a swim at a beach in Karachi, it turned out that there was an undertow. One of the young devotees was being carried away. Sarvagatanandaji noticed this and, although he didn't know how to swim, he immediately rushed to rescue the young boy. When he reached the boy, in panic the boy caught hold of his neck from behind. The swami was going under and coming up and swallowing water, but every time he got his head above water, he shouted to the boy, "Hold on! Hold on!" They kept struggling until a wave came and threw them to the shore. The young devotee said later that he always remembered those words, "Hold on, hold on!" Years later, Sarvagatanandaji told his disciples: "In spiritual life there is a tremendous struggle with one's saṁskāras. But if you can keep your head above water, the time will come when a wave will throw you ashore and you will say, 'I'm glad I went through it. I'm glad I made it.'"

The Karachi center closed in 1948 due to the riots that erupted after the bloodied partition of India which created Pakistan. Sarvagatanandaji was then appointed head of the Order's branch in Visakhapatnam. In 1954 he was asked to proceed to the United States to assist Swami Akhilananda in managing the centers in Boston and Providence. When Swami Akhilananda's health declined, Sarvagatanandaji had to shoulder more responsibilities. With the older swami's passing in 1962, there were enormous hurdles and obstacles in officially taking charge of the two centers. Swami Sarvagatananda handled the delicate and difficult situation with fortitude and toughness, while also remaining steadfastly kind and forgiving.

For the next 40 years, the Vedanta centers in Boston and Providence thrived under Sarvagatanandaji's leadership. The workload was immense, shuttling back and forth between the two places 50-miles apart, spending half of the week in each place. With patience and loving care he nurtured the congregations in both the centers, building up cohesive spiritual communities. As the Hindu chaplain, he also gave a weekly class at MIT. The Boston center had a retreat place in Marshfield, on the way to Cape Cod. There the swami introduced the Krishna Festival and a camp for children, both of which were held annually during the summer. He also traveled to other Vedanta centers in US and Canada, and taught and guided spiritual seekers.

In 2001 he handed over charge of the Providence center to Swami Yogatmananda and, a year later in 2002, he handed over charge of the Boston center to Swami Tyagananda. He continued to guide devotees and disciples even after his formal retirement and in spite of his advanced age. When his health began to decline around 2007, he remained supremely calm and continued to bless everyone who came to meet him.

May 2, 2009, seemed like any other day. That night Sarvagatanandaji went to sleep at his usual time and in the early hours of the next morning, he entered *mahāsamādhi*, his face radiating peace and bliss.

He continues to live in the hearts of innumerable devotees and disciples, whose lives are forever changed by his love, wisdom and grace.

❄

ALSO BY SWAMI SARVAGATANANDA

"You Will Be a Paramahamsa"
Meditation as a Spiritual Culmination (2 volumes)
Vedanta for the Common Man
Sri Krishna Yoga

**More Books from the Vedanta Society, Boston**

Walking the Walk: A Karma Yoga Manual
Knowing the Knower: A Jnana Yoga Manual
Looking Deeply: Vivekacūḍāmaṇi of Śrī Śaṅkarācārya
A Drop of Nectar: Amṛtabindu Upaniṣad

Made in the USA
Monee, IL
10 July 2023

38584823R00252